Also by Douglas Hackney

The Next Name

Data Marts
Understanding and Implementing Successful Data Marts

How the World Works

How the World Works

601 Thoughts

on

Life, Work and Business

Douglas Hackney

Published by Amboy Media
Houston, Texas, U.S.A.

First Edition
First Printing 2008 / 12

Library of Congress Control Number: 2008909222

ISBN-13 978-0-9821719-1-2
ISBN-10 0-9821719-1-9

Unwanted Change Illustration reprinted with permission of
www.changingminds.org

Cover concept: Stephanie Hackney
Cover design: Douglas Hackney

Printed in the United States of America

For Amber

Table of Contents

Introduction

In the fall of 2006 I was speaking with my daughter, Amber, by telephone. I was building an expedition vehicle in Riverside, California and she was at home in the Minneapolis / St. Paul, Minnesota area.

We were discussing choices she was making about car maintenance, home repair, etc., the typical things a young woman would ask her father. I told her it was frustrating being so far away and unable to be there to provide those answers firsthand, and to provide the real hands-on support of doing the things a father does to physically, spiritually and psychologically help out his children.

Amber replied, "I need you to teach me those things. I need you to teach me how the world works."

Amber and I had been torn asunder by divorce when she was under 10 years old. Subsequent bitter custody and visitation battles, coupled with teenage rebellion, completed the goal of isolating us from each other. As she entered adulthood we'd both made the effort to bridge that gap and restore our close relationship of her early youth.

I saw her request as my opportunity to compensate for more than a decade of lost opportunities for fatherhood.

"OK," I replied, "I'll do that."

How I would do that I had no idea. It was a monumental task, even in the abstract, much less as a concrete task, a promise to your child.

I asked my son, Adam, about it. He encouraged me to take it on, to find a way to pass along all that I'd learned from my forebears and a lifetime of hard-won lessons.

I thought it might take a few weeks, maybe a month.

As it happened, over the next 24 months I kept a pen and a notebook with me. Every time I thought of something that encapsulated how the world works, I jotted it down. Every week or so I compiled the notes, and every month or so fleshed them out into the aphorisms contained herein.

Of course, no work of this type could ever hope to be complete. As I finish it, I still have notes that are not yet included and more still popping into my head every day. But at some point, if Amber and anyone else are ever to gain value from it, I must end the task, at least for now.

Furthermore, this collection of ideas is the fruit of my unique life. It reflects my small pool of experiences, so it may seem paltry, irrelevant or trivial to others who have walked a different path, learning different lessons.

In addition, this work is fundamentally limited by the quantity of my experiences. I am still young, only 51, so this work is inherently limited in the sample set of life it draws upon.

Nevertheless, it is my hope that this book will provide some answers to Amber's question, and show her, and others who read it, in a few small ways, how the world works.

Life

Life can often be challenging, and since it does not come with an owner's manual, bewildering.

However, there are some lessons, rules and general principles that can ease the day-to-day and overall challenges of life.

Specifically, it is very important to understand the following:

- Fear, and how it shapes your life and drives most of your behavior
- The fundamental characteristics of humans, especially how we are hard wired for drama
- Tribes, especially the rules for tribal membership
- Cultures and societies, especially the primacy of societal self-interest

Life Principles

1.   The Choice

There are only two choices in life: love and fear.

All else flows from which you choose.

2.   Look Where You Want To Go

When divers do a turn, rotation or flip, their eyes lead their body. They are always looking ahead, at their target, where they want to go. When race drivers, or even better, motorcycle racers, go through a corner, they are not looking at the corner, they are looking at the exit of the corner and the next section of track, where they want to go. When you are riding a motorcycle off-road along a cliff or a single-track trail on the edge of a chasm, you must look where you want to go. The body and the mind will always follow the eyes.

The opposite of this is looking at, and fixating on, what you want to avoid. If you stare at the rock you want to avoid, you will inevitably ride right into it. In motorcycling that's called "target fixation." In life it's called "bad luck." If you look at, or fixate on, what you want to avoid in life, you will inevitably create it, force it and/or run right into it.

Look where you want to go.

3.   What Will Grow

Whatever you put your life energy into is what will grow in your life. If you focus on worry, fear and negativity, then that is what will grow in your life. If you focus on growth, learning and love, then that is what will grow.

4.   The First Three Words of Wisdom

The first three words of wisdom are "I don't know." – Chinese folk wisdom.

This Chinese proverb encapsulates the Buddhist philosophy of being a lifelong novice. Only in a state of learning are you open. If you feel you know, then you are closed.

5.   Think, Say, Do

We are what we think. Thoughts lead to words. Words define, and result in, our actions.

What you think forms the framework of your existence. It gives you the references and the paradigms that you operate in on a day-to-day basis. Your thoughts give you the tools and coping skills to relate to and interact with your world.

This is why you are, at your most fundamental level, what you put into your head. If you put in wrong, incomplete or skewed information, day after day, week after week, you become formed by that, shaped by that and actually become that. It is essential to pay very close attention to what you put into your head.

This means you must be very selective with the people you are around, what you read, what you listen to and what you watch. Your thoughts define the framework, the reality of your existence.

What you think is what you'll say. What you say is what you'll do.

6. Take Responsibility

Nothing is more important than taking responsibility for yourself and your actions.

7. Walk the Fear Line

We are often seized by fear. Fear prevents us from making decisions, moving forward and advancing ourselves, our growth and our potential. The longer we avoid a fear, the larger it grows in our minds. Whether it is as trivial as balancing our checkbook or as major as starting down a new life path, the longer we put something off, the more it turns into a huge monster that we could never have hope of overcoming.

Two things are required to overcome this.

The first is to verbalize the fear. By verbalizing it, we literally give it form and dimension. We "put it on the table," where we can walk around it, prod it, poke it and most importantly, realize that it is not very big. Tiny, in fact, compared to how large we had made it in our minds.

The second is to walk down the line of fear. Step through each possible outcome down that line of fear. Answer each possible "what if" question until you run out of them. After you have thought through each of them, you will find that moving through the fear is not stepping off into an unknown abyss.

Instead, you are stepping down a path you have discussed, thought through and that you know.

Remember the first, most important lesson: There is only one choice in life, the choice between love and fear. Walking the fear line enables you to more often choose love. That leads to an unbounded life. The alternative is a life bounded by fear. A life bounded by fear is by definition small, limiting, confining and ultimately frustrating and anger inducing. An unbounded life enables unlimited growth and an unlimited range of potential outcomes.

8.   Spoonful of Arsenic

Carrying anger, hatred or resentment toward another person is like taking a spoonful of arsenic a day and waiting for the other person to get sick. Negative emotions breed an endless cycle of negativity. Their effects on you, especially long term, when nurtured, are incalculably bad.

9.   Your Garden

What do you grow in your garden? What do you nurture every day? What do you grow, what fruits do you reap?

If you carefully water, weed and fertilize hatred, resentment, jealousy and greed, your crops will poison you and everyone around you.

If you nurture positive things: growth, learning and love; your garden will yield a bountiful and healthy harvest.

10.   Pick a Lighthouse

Pick a lighthouse and row towards it.

If you constantly change directions and goals, you end up doing nothing but rowing around in circles. All you do is waste your life energy and your time.

If you establish a direction, a single goal, and move your life towards it, you will give your life a purpose, and make decision making extremely easy.

The only relevant question becomes, "Does this choice advance me towards my lighthouse, yes or no?" If not, then no. If so, then yes.

Concentrate your efforts. Focus on a goal. Become efficient.

Pick a lighthouse.

11.   The Universe's Positive Filter

The universe only recognizes positives. When establishing goals or requirements, you must only use positive statements. If you say "I will never date a smoker," the universe removes the "never" and you end up with "I will date a smoker."

12.   Winners Get Back Up

There will be times in your life when you are blindsided and knocked off of your feet by circumstances, unplanned events and the choices of other people.

It is easy to stay knocked down, wallowing in self-pity. It will feel very comfortable down there exchanging tales of woe with everyone else who suffered the same fate and is seeking comfort and reinforcement for their choice to stay there.

Everyone gets knocked down in life – again and again. The winners get back up. And, keep getting back up.

13.   Anger Is Easy

Being angry is easy. It's easy to adopt an angry, snarling attitude and watch others run for cover. It means you never have to face anything. It's easy. And it's lazy. It takes a lot of work to figure out why you are angry, to sort through all the underlying emotions, memories and insecurities. The path of anger is an inevitable spiral down. Choosing to be positive is a lot more work, but it inevitably leads up.

14.   Invest in Yourself

Before you spend a dime on things, or enhancing things, upgrading things or newer things, invest in yourself. Invest in your education, your ongoing learning and becoming a fulfilled and fulfilling human being.

15.   Your Table

Who sits at the dinner table of your mind? Who do you allow to pass judgment on you? Who sits at your mental table and reviews your actions, desires and goals?

It is extremely important to visit your mental dinner table and learn not only who is there, but why they are there. It is critical to dismiss people from your table who no longer belong there.

16.   Permission to Change

You must give yourself permission to change.

Friends, jobs, cities, interests and hobbies can all change. If you don't give yourself permission to change you end up trying to walk through life dragging multiple boat anchors. They don't do anything but slow you down and keep you from making progress. Just because they are familiar or once were important does not mean you must drag them behind you the rest of your life.

17.   Life Scripts

Many people get caught up in a life script and can never escape. They spend their entire existence playing out a role that they have defined, or others have defined for them.

Look at your life on a regular basis and ask why you are doing what you are doing. Is it because you are choosing to live that way, or is it because you have adopted a role that is pre-defined?

Even worse, are you simply playing a bit part in someone else's passion play?

18.   Celebrity vs. Credibility

Celebrity does not equal credibility. Or intelligence. Or capability. Or trustworthiness. Or integrity.

There are only a few professions that demand you perfect the skill of faking sincerity: politics, news reporting, acting and used car sales.

Be very aware of the source of what you put in your head. Celebrity does not equal credibility.

19.   The Scrap Pile

"Don't show off the scrap pile." – Clarence Hackney.

You will have failures in your life and in your efforts. You'll have false starts, bad ideas and versions that were later improved upon.

Don't show off the scrap pile. Show off the finished product.

Success breeds confidence and success breeds success. A successful finished product, project, skill, initiative or talent improves your self-confidence and the confidence and esteem others hold in you. Showing off the scrap pile undermines all of that.

20.   The Last Temptation

When you make a decision, a choice, especially to move in a new direction, life will almost always present one last temptation to remain in your old ways. Be wary of succumbing to its comforts and familiarity.

21.   If Aliens Land

If aliens land this afternoon, you will still need to go to work tomorrow. Keep life, and what may or may not happen, in perspective.

22.   99 Coins

In ancient times, a father needed to take a long journey that would last the full growing season.

He was to leave his two sons in charge of the family's large farm during his absence. He divided the growing lands in half, each of equal quality land. He gave each son a bag of 100 coins to fund the cost of seed, labor for cultivation, tending the crops and harvest. He wished them both well and departed.

On the first day, each of the sons lost one coin.

Both sons were distraught. They spent the entire day looking for the missing coin.

The next day, the first son went to the market town to buy seed and recruit laborers for the planting. The second son looked for the missing coin.

As the season progressed, the first son's laborers weeded the crops and chased away the crows. The second son dug holes in his fields looking for the missing coin.

At harvest time the first son reaped a bountiful crop. The second son, his clothes in shreds from searching through the thorns for the coin, simply sat and cried.

The father returned and asked his sons for the story of the season. The first son replied, "Father, we had a period of little rain, but with tender care and attention we were able to bring in a good crop. I have marketed our harvest and we now have 300 coins." The second son dropped to his knees and clutched his father's legs, sobbing. "Oh father, on the fist day, I lost a coin. I spent the entire season looking for it. I cannot find it. Please forgive me."

The father looked down and said, "Stand, my son. It is not the one coin, and its loss, that is important. It is what you do with the remaining 99."

We spend most of our lives obsessing over the one criticism, the one loss, the one flaw, the one mistake.

Focus not on the one loss, focus on the remaining 99.

23.   The Opposite of Love

The opposite of love is not hate.

Cultivating hatred or resentment of someone you used to love is not the end of love, it is the extension of love. Having ongoing arguments and disagreements with someone you think you used to love is not the end of love, it is extending and perpetuating the relationship.

The opposite of love is apathy.

24.   Changing Your Opinion

"The best way to become a better debater is to advocate for the position you actually oppose." – Lee Wochner.

The best debating exercise is one where the students must advocate the opposite position from that which they believe. If they adore mushrooms, then in the debate they must advocate the position for the eradication of mushrooms.

Along these lines, I didn't understand creationists, so I went and spent some time with them and listened to their point of view. I remain an avowed evolutionist, but I have a much better understanding of the positions of the creationists.

It's all about investigating and learning about other points of view. You learn little to nothing if you only listen to or read things from your own camp or tribe. You will learn much by reading and listening to those who you adamantly oppose or don't understand.

The fundamental question to keep asking is "When was the last time I changed my opinion about something meaningful?"

25. The Microscopic Truth

Try spending an hour telling the absolute, atomic level, microscopic truth. Do it just with yourself, in your own head. For one full hour, nothing but the absolute, total truth. No shading, no white lies, no distortions.

The experience will be extremely difficult, and very enlightening.

Then try to do it for half a day. Then a full day. Then a full week.

Being resolute about facing your world, and yourself, with only the absolute truth, down to the smallest unit of truth you can distill out of your existence, will be one of the most challenging things you will ever do, and probably one of the most rewarding.

Being completely, microscopically, truthful with yourself is a prerequisite for a full and complete life.

26. Leave it Better

Leave it better than you found it. Be it a place to live, a project or a community, leave it better than you found it. If you see a piece of litter, pick it up. If you see someone in need of help, help them out.

Putting yourself into the stream of making things better puts you into a mode of thinking and living that leads to a virtuous circle of growth and evolution.

27. Every Child Born

Every child born, at the moment of birth, is fully equipped to speak any language in the world.

That unlimited potential is extant in every one of us. We all have unlimited potential.

It is up to us, and no one else, to achieve it.

28. Cast Your Bread

"Cast your bread upon the waters." The call to benevolence is a fundamental rule of how the universe works. When you give, truly give of your heart, mind and soul, you will receive blessings well beyond measure.

29. The Mirror Limit

The only thing that limits you is what looks back at you in the mirror. The only thing that prevents you from growing, accomplishing and achieving anything, especially your full potential, is yourself.

The person you see in the mirror is the only limit to your outcomes. No one stands between any possibility for your life but you.

Believe.

Pursue.

Persevere.

Achieve.

30. Grandpa Level Work

When I did sloppy work my father would tell me, "You better hope your grandfather never sees that."

Grandpa had high standards for finished work. It might take a couple of attempts to get it just right, and suitable for public viewing, but when you left it, when you walked away, it better be done right. And, it better be done in such a way that the next person who came upon it to work with it, maintain it or change it would find it understandable, safe, well done and top quality.

The secret to this is that good work, in the end, is less work. Good work doesn't need to be re-done or fixed on a regular basis. Good work doesn't cause you embarrassment, or degrade your self-respect or the respect from others. Good work doesn't cost you time, money and productivity in waste, scrap and re-work. Good work, even if it takes longer to do the first time, is more efficient.

In your daily life, do good work. Do work that you would be proud to show to anyone, even Grandpa.

31. The Hard Work of Lying

Lying is very hard work.

Once you tell a lie, then you've got to remember it so that you always tell it the same way. You've got to remember who you told it to, and under what circumstances.

Maintaining a web of lies is full-time work. And who has time for that in today's world?

Being honest is easy. If you always tell the truth, you are not adding any additional burdens to your life. Life can be tough enough without adding an extra load of lies.

32. No Pockets

"There are no pockets on the burial shroud." – Kemal Ertem.

In a traditional Islamic burial, the body is cleansed and dressed in a plain, white burial shroud. The burial shroud has no pockets.

Our Muslim friend, Kemal Ertem, taught us this rule to illustrate that you can't take anything with you when you die. All the material things you spend your life accumulating turn to dust.

Remember this when you are thinking about what trade-offs you are willing to make in your life. Before you sacrifice your quality of life or your relationships so you can work more hours to buy more stuff, remember that there are no pockets on the burial shroud.

33. Face the World

"Face the world as it is, not as it was, or as you wish it to be." - Jack Welch.

Look clearly and objectively at the realities of your life. Stand up and face reality. If you don't acknowledge reality as it is, as it actually is, you will be nothing but continuously and endlessly frustrated as to why your life isn't changing and/or getting any better.

34. No Good Deed

"No good deed goes unpunished," is the old saying. You will notice in your life that this seems often true. Many times will you do a good deed only to later seemingly pay a price for it.

The reason for this is that the follow-on price you pay is just a simple test. The test is to see if you did the good deed for the right reasons.

If you did it to advance your social standing or make others feel better about you, then the price will seem outrageous and not worth paying. You will stop doing good deeds.

If you did the good deed from a true altruistic motive, then the price will be inconsequential. You will do more good deeds. And you will continue to reap the rewards.

35. Fools and Newcomers

"Only fools and newcomers predict the weather." – Coastal Oregon folk wisdom.

When you are new in a place, job, tribe or position, your first step is observation. The next is evaluation.

It will be some time, probably a long time, before you will be qualified to predict.

36. Stay Green

"If you're not green you are dying," is one of the oldest motivational speech catch phrases in existence. And, it's true.

To stay green you must consistently change and grow. You must continually adapt to changing environments and circumstances. If you are not showing green sprouts, you are dying.

37.   Interested = Interesting

If you want to be interesting, you must first be interested. You need to be interested in something, study it, understand it and be able to carry on a meaningful conversation about it.

If you want to be interesting to people beyond those who are interested in that particular topic, you need to be interested in a broad range of things. People get bored very quickly with you if you can only converse on one or two topics, regardless of their depth or your passion about them.

If you are not interested, no one will ever find you interesting.

38.   Love Yourself First

You will never be capable of loving anyone else, or capable of being loved by anyone else, if you first do not love yourself. You must love you. You must love what you are, who you are and what you want to become.

Until you come to peace with yourself, you will never be at peace with others.

39. The True Friend Test

There are plenty of people in your life you call friends who will tell you what you want to hear. A true friend will tell you what you need to hear.

40. Every Interaction Tells a Story

There is something of value in every conversation.

If you are open to it, and listen carefully, there is something worth taking away, something to learn, something to enrich your life and your existence in every interaction.

41. Repetition <> Truth

Repetition does not equal truth. You can tell yourself something over and over again, and it won't change reality. You and your friends can tell yourselves the same thing over and over again, and it won't change the facts.

Repetition, however, can shape perception, and become a self-fulfilling prophecy. This is especially true when applied to the media and mass culture.

42. Perception is Reality

In today's world, perception is reality. In your personal and business lives, this means that simply acting like you know what you are doing is 90 percent of success.

43. Hooker on Hooker

After years of inglorious defeats at the hands of General Robert E. Lee's Confederate Army of Northern Virginia, the Union Army of the Potomac, under its new leader, Joseph "Fighting Joe" Hooker, were poised to not only reverse that trend, but crush their opponent.

After a winter of refitting and reorganization that yielded a numerically vastly superior force much better outfitted and supplied, the Union forces were energized and ready for a battle of revenge and finality.

Hooker executed a masterful plan, slipping his forces across the river that separated the armies over the winter and placing Lee between 75,000 Union soldiers to the West, 40,000 to the South and 17,000 cavalry rampaging across his rear lines. Lee had less than half the forces facing him and was caught in a vice, facing near certain destruction and the end of the Confederacy.

On the morning of May 1, 1863, the Union officers and enlisted men were confident, if not already joyous. After years of inept leadership, death and defeat, they finally had a leader capable of forcing the battle, of brilliant tactics, in short, of leadership. Finally, after so many losses, today would be their day. They held an overwhelming numerical advantage, they had vastly superior amounts of supplies and reserves and they held commanding and favorable positions on high, clear ground. It was an open and bright path that lay before them, direct to Richmond, the Confederate capital, and a quick end to the war.

The day's skirmishes began, the scattered, running battles little more than the opening taps of a championship fight whose winner was all but predetermined.

But then, unbelievably, messengers arrived at the front lines from headquarters calling for retreat. The orders called for retreat from the Union's heretofore most advantageous positions, superior odds and a unique opportunity to end the war.

Hooker was turning his back on his best chance for victory. He was turning his back on all his preparations, all his training, all his brilliant tactics and all his leadership. He was afraid to commit to battle.

The Union forces retreated and General Lee, in the most celebrated example of tactical brilliance and military leadership of his career, decimated them in the battle of Chancellorsville.

On that May morning, the Civil war could have been over in weeks. Instead, the war raged on for another two years, with hundreds of thousands of unnecessary deaths as a result.

When asked about his sudden collapse of leadership, Hooker said "Hooker lost confidence in Hooker."

You will never know all the answers. You will never know for sure if every decision you make is correct. You will never know the outcome going into a new situation. But one thing you will always know is that if Hooker would have fully committed, cast his fears aside and had faith in himself, history would have been dramatically changed.

Have faith in yourself. Ignore your fears. Fully commit.

44. Planting Trees

"You don't plant trees for yourself, you plant trees for your grandchildren." – American folk wisdom.

When was the last time you did something selfless, something for someone other than yourself or your self interests? Planted any trees lately?

45.   You Must First Finish

"To finish first, you must first finish." – Traditional motorsports wisdom.

If you burn yourself out early in the race, you'll never make the finish line, much less win. This is applicable to athletic events, motorsports and life. The first and most important thing is to understand the duration and scope of the event, and then husband and expend your resources appropriately.

46.   Committing to a Line

In motorsports, when rounding an unknown corner you cannot commit to a line through that corner until you can see the exit. Once you see the exit from the corner you can select your apex, your braking point, your throttle point, your trailing throttle zone, your roll-on zone and your drive path outbound.

If you commit to a line before you see the exit then you're likely to be locked into a line that will force you into understeer (push) or oversteer. In either case, if you're in the mountains and someone is coming around the corner towards you, it's likely to be a really bad day.

The same is true of life. When the stakes are ultimate, you're on an unfamiliar road and you can't yet see the exit to the corner, you've got to keep a steady throttle until you see the exit. Then, you can pick a line and ride hard.

47. Arrows

How do you tell who the leaders are? By the arrows in their backs.

Leadership means taking a stand. It means driving change. It means motivating people. It means making the tough decisions that others avoid. It means demonstrating the differences between leading and following.

People who don't have what it takes to be a leader delight in attacking, denigrating and undermining leaders, and the attackers have lots of arrows in their quivers.

When you are a leader, you get used to the pinprick sensation of the arrows peppering your back.

48. A Good Dog

"Nothing ages faster than a good dog." – Lovidee Zane Strickland.

If you are very lucky you will have a good dog in your life. You will probably find, if you keep your eyes and mind open, you will have many good dogs in your life. They will be all the little and big things that brighten your day and bring you a measure of joy.

Treasure those good dogs, and celebrate every moment and every day you share with them. They pass through your life all too quickly.

49. Open Doors

Make sure you've got a new door open before you close one behind you.

Don't put yourself in a position where you have no open and available options for your life, as if you were in a long hallway where all the doors are locked. Make sure you've got some new and available options open before you close a life door behind you.

50. Luck

"Preparation + opportunity = luck." – Mike Ditka.

Life is a lot about putting yourself in a position to win.

You are never going to make the winning basket sitting in the stands eating a hot dog or riding the bench grousing about the coach. You've got to be on the court with the ball in your hands to be in a position to make the winning basket.

You've got to be well trained, in game shape and focused on the task. That's when you'll be prepared when the opportunity comes your way.

Preparation (being educated, trained, involved, engaged in your field of endeavor) + opportunity (the chance to execute and demonstrate your abilities in a payoff opportunity) = luck.

Winners make their own luck.

51. The Pursuit of Happiness

You will never find happiness in things. You'll never be happy because you finally buy that special thing. As soon as you do, it starts to deteriorate. And besides, next week there will be a bigger, better, faster, flashier, sexier, more desirable thing. Things do not bring happiness.

You will never find happiness in people. You'll never be happy because you finally date, bed or marry that special someone you desire so much. As soon as you get past the initial lust, bloom and glow, you'll discover that they are every bit as flawed as you are. And, all those cute little things that used to make you giggle now drive you crazy. If you leave them for someone new, you'll find they are just as flawed as the last one. People do not bring happiness.

You will never find happiness in experience. You'll never be happy because you finally climb that mountain or dive that sea. As soon as you do so, you'll need to climb the next mountain or dive the next sea. There will always be more and higher mountains, and deeper or broader seas. Experience does not bring happiness.

You will never find happiness in escape. You'll never be happy because you drank yourself into a stupor, did that one meter long line of cocaine or dropped all that acid. The next morning, if you live to see it, the sun will come up and you'll have the same life you did the day before. Escape does not bring happiness.

You will never find happiness in money. You'll never be happy because you make a million. Or two. Or three. There will just be another million to get, and another and another. The acquisition of money is never-ending, just another treadmill, just another addiction. The pressure to spend, manage and invest large amounts of money is intense and unyielding. Copious amounts of money do not bring happiness. Instead, it is guaranteed to bring new forms of stress and pressure. Check the outcomes for lottery winners. For almost every single one, their lives were destroyed and they ended up in misery. Money does not bring happiness.

Happiness can only be found within. Within you.

52. Hearts and Brains

"If you're not a liberal in your twenties, you don't have a heart. If you're not a conservative in your forties, you don't have a brain." – Winston Churchill.

Your world view and your corresponding political outlook are likely to change during your lifetime. Things like having a daughter and a mortgage are well known to bring on a conservative outlook.

Give yourself permission to change. Don't be bound to political philosophies by guilt, familiarity or blind loyalty.

53.   Good Attracts Good

Good people attract good people. The opposite is also true.

If you associate with good people, with good values and with integrity, your circle of friends, associates and your entire network will be populated with a vast majority of good people.

The opposite is also true. Choose good.

54.   The Dichotomy of Life

Life is, in many ways, one dichotomy after another.

You've probably noticed that some of these aphorisms are diametrically opposed to each other. Such is life.

Some similar situations require polar opposite approaches. Additionally, each of life's experiences, if you are open, brings both a Yin and a Yang component.

It is important to maintain the balance in the ongoing dichotomy of life.

55.   One Leg at a Time

People who are powerful, rich and famous are, basically, just like you.

They put their pants on one leg at a time, just like you do. They don't levitate into them.

Usually, the biggest difference between you and them is that they believed in themselves enough to pursue their dreams.

56.   Make No Little Plans

"Make no little plans; they have no magic to stir men's blood...Make big plans, aim high in hope and work." – Daniel Burnham.

In many ways, we create our own reality. We project our own future. Your life will follow your vision, your view and your dreams.

If you make big plans, if you aim high, your life will be big, and you will soar above those toiling below, trapped in their little plans, their little lives.

Make no little plans.

57. Signing the Front

There is a vast difference between signing the front of a paycheck and signing the back.

Unless and until you have signed the front of a paycheck, and lived through the challenges of making that payroll week after week, you have little to no room to criticize those who do.

58. The Right to Complain

Voting is the single most important duty of every citizen. It is what separates you from the oppressed, from those without a voice, from the abused and neglected masses.

And besides, if you don't vote, you don't have the right to complain about anything related to governance.

Vote. Every time.

59. Sharpen Your Tools

One of the greatest real-life adventure stories ever told was in the book *Once is Enough*, about the journey by Miles & Beryl Smeeton and their friend John Guzzwell. John interrupted his sailboat circumnavigation to join the Smeetons on their sailing passage from Australia to England in 1956.

In the middle of the night during a terrible storm, hundreds of miles southwest of South America in one of the remotest spots of the most feared ocean on earth, their 46-foot ketch Tzu Hang was pitch-poled (tumbled end over end) by a massive rogue wave.

Beryl, who was at the tiller, was thrown overboard. The masts were snapped off, the rigging was lost and huge portions of the deck were destroyed.

Miraculously, Miles and John were able to find and save Beryl. They dragged sails over the open portions of the deck and spent an entire day bailing out the water of the nearly swamped boat. They stabilized the ship in spite of their injuries, and then tried to get some rest.

Upon waking, Miles heard a strange, regular sound. He followed it back to John's quarters, where John had assembled his woodworking tools that had been scattered all over the boat. There John sat, carefully sharpening each of his tools. Miles was upset. He felt that he and John should be working feverishly to create a jury rig so they could sail to land. The sooner they got started the greater their slim chances of survival became. Instead, John sat and sharpened.

Once John was done, he carefully assessed the damage and the available materials he could scavenge from the floating wreck that was their boat.

Over the next few days, he created a jury rig, then another when the first proved inadequate. He modified the interior to maximize their available comfort. And he did it all with precision and economy of movement, with no energy lost to false starts, ragged cuts or injuries from dull tools.

When you are faced with crisis or emergency remember that panic helps no one, especially those in need. Stop and carefully assess the situation. Tally up your available assets. Take stock of your available methods, techniques, resources and tools.

Diving right into a crisis, in a blind fur ball of feverish activity, often yields little more than exhaustion. Instead, stop, assess – and sharpen your tools.

60.   The Insecurity Roots

Insecurity is at the root of most human behavior.

If you learn about the basics of human insecurity you will have the fundamentals required to interact with people for a lifetime.

61. Don't Take it Personally

One of the toughest lessons to learn in life is to not take things personally. When people treat you poorly, attack you, etc., it is almost always about them, their issues, their insecurities, etc.

If you can grow to the point of keeping this lesson in your mind, guiding your responses and avoiding getting caught up in tit-for-tat and escalating conflict, you can avoid a lot of human pain.

62. Never Take No

Never take "no" from someone who is *not* authorized to say "yes."

Keep working your way up the chain of command until you reach someone with the power to say "yes."

63.   A World of Nails

"If all you have is a hammer, every problem looks like a nail." – Anonymous.

It is extremely important to have multiple tools, multiple coping skills, multiple talents, multiple approaches, multiple philosophies, multiple historical views and multiple outlooks in your tool box.

You smash a lot of thumbs if all you have is a hammer.

64.   Valid Sample Sets

"I don't know anyone who voted for them. I don't see how the Republicans won the election." – New York City socialite and liberal democrat after a mid-20th century national election.

I used to work with some Masters and Ph.D. level statisticians. One of the most interesting things I learned from them was the concept of a statistically valid sample set. That means you must sample enough elements of any data set to have a statistically valid sample set before your results will be an accurate indicator of anything regarding that data set.

It's easy to take a few samples and think that you've identified a trend or the truth. But when you take more samples you realize that the first few were not average or normal and completely skewed your initial assumptions.

This is why it is so dangerous to base your opinion about anything on only a few sources of information, especially from only a few individuals. Make sure you are forming your opinion, your world view and your life based on statistically significant sample sets.

65. One Set of Facts

Everyone is entitled to their own opinion, so there are an infinite number of possible opinions about anything. But, there is only one set of facts.

66. Tonnage Rights

Sailboats have the right of way over any other type of water-going vessel.

Nonetheless, only a fool would sail his boat into the path of a huge container ship. The sailor may technically have the right of way, and the law on his side, but he's also likely to end up dead. In this case, the large ship has what are termed by sailors "tonnage rights."

Learn to discern the difference in life when you may technically have the right of way, but it's better to defer to tonnage rights.

67. No Rain, No Rainbows

If there's no rain, there are no rainbows.

Without some bad times, you would never be able to appreciate the good times.

68. Choices

Life is about making choices.

Every aspect of your life is determined by the choices you make. No matter what happens to you, your fate is determined not by what happened, but by how you choose to deal with it.

Every outcome of your life is determined not by fate or by arbitrary decisions of others. Instead, your outcomes are determined by your choices, big and small.

Life is about making choices. Make good ones.

69.   Chapters

The span of a lifetime is composed of chapters. It is important to recognize the chapters of your life, and to recognize the end of one chapter and the beginning of another.

Often, as when reading a good book, we don't want a particularly good chapter to come to an end. But, like the book, end it must. Better to end it well than cling to it, reading it over and over, and never letting life progress.

Celebrate your chapters, and recognize that each one has its own story, its own ups and downs, its own triumphs and its own rewards.

The book of your life is about the sequence, the sum total of the chapters and is not defined by any single one.

70.   The Paperback Life

Many people will read something in a magazine or a cheap paperback and treat it as holy writ descended directly from the heavens.

They know nothing about the qualification, background or status of the author, but if the article or book says they will be healthier, thinner, sexier, happier, more successful, etc. by eating kumquat seeds roasted in lime juice sprinkled with dead ants, or standing on their heads for 187 seconds twice daily or showering only when the moons of Jupiter are in alignment, they will spend the rest of their lives doing exactly that. And, they will tell everyone they know this secret of happiness and often be offended if others don't accept and adopt it as the undisputable, pure and direct truth as they have.

It doesn't take all that much to get an article published or get a book in print. The more writers and authors you meet you realize how little these people really know (and I'm including all the writers and authors I know, myself included). Don't believe much of what you read. Corroborate anything you might take seriously as a life direction by seeking confirmation in multiple sources that are fact-checked and authoritative.

Don't live a paperback life. Live an encyclopedia life.

71. The Post-Show Downs

In an early career I produced, directed and executed live events. Typically, there were months of very intense work leading up to the production, around the clock set-up of the venue, a rehearsal or two (if we were lucky), then the doors opened and the show commenced. After the show was over, it was common to go through a period of melancholy which we called the "post-show downs."

Life will have periods of intense activity, anticipation, stress and excitement. Know that it is not unusual for what follows to seem relatively empty, without the intensity, rewards and stark career-life-and-death realities of the "show." The post-show downs will pass. Give it time.

72. Depression

Depression is anger turned inward.

At some point in your life you will probably suffer some depression. When that happens, consider the factors that are perpetuating your feelings. If you are angry at the circumstances of your life but have no means or method for expressing them outwardly, you will express them inwardly, and that will trap you in a cycle of depression.

73. Social Lubrication

Manners are the universal lubricant of social interaction and existence. The more polite you are, the easier life becomes.

74. Others' Happiness

You are not responsible for the happiness of others.

You can be responsible for their well being, keeping them sheltered, fed, clothed and educated, but you are not responsible for their happiness. This includes everyone in your life.

You are responsible for your own actions and your own happiness. Others are responsible for their own happiness.

75. Honesty and Integrity

"His rugged honesty and sterling character will long be respected and remembered by his many friends." – Excerpt from the obituary of Elijah Hackney, 1834-1922, my great, great grandfather.

There could be no greater, or more meaningful, summary of anyone's time on this earth.

The way you leave a legacy, such as that of Elijah, is through honesty and integrity.

Be honest with yourself, and honesty will flow to others. Be true to yourself, and integrity will flow to others.

Make no small compromises in honesty and integrity, or you will begin a long slide down.

"His rugged honesty and sterling character will long be respected and remembered by his many friends" is a worthy life goal enabled by honesty and integrity.

76. 2:1

God gave us two ears and one mouth for a very good reason. If you listen twice as much as you speak, you will find that life is significantly improved for you and those around you.

That 2:1 ratio opens the way to learning from every interaction and, like some magic, enables and facilitates social grace.

Nobody likes a pompous, domineering conversationalist, and that is exactly what you'll be if you speak twice as much as you listen.

You have two ears and one mouth for a reason.

77. The Winter Project

Every winter grandpa Hackney would have a project. One year it was to rebuild the corn wagons, another year, to rebuild the motor on the M (McCormick International model M tractor). He always had a productive project for the winter time when the fields were frozen and the roads were bad.

In the spring, out came the finished winter project, freshly painted and functioning smoothly.

During the winter project grandpa learned new things about whatever he was working on, be it intricate woodworking or pouring babbitt bearings. Or, he simply refreshed old and familiar knowledge, such as electrical circuits and metal forging. He came out of every winter with more knowledge, refreshed knowledge and an expanded world.

Ensure that you always have a "winter project" in your life. Pick an area of study and read some books on that topic. Investigate an interest, develop a skill, learn a language, play an instrument, research, seek out – learn.

Expand your knowledge and improve your world.

78.   A Bigger Boat

There will always be a bigger boat. Or a faster car. Or a more fashionable dress. Or a more powerful computer. And on and on and on. You can never stay in a position of having the latest, greatest anything. As soon as you buy it, it is obsolete, yesterday's news. Visit some older homes on the market and look around at all the once high-end, latest-greatest furnishings and appliances and see how dated and antiquated they look.

Chasing self-esteem via material acquisition is a loser's game. As soon as you acquire anything material, it begins to deteriorate. It will eventually return to dust.

Happiness and self-esteem don't come from material goods. They come from within. Within you.

79.   The Critic

"It is not enough to criticize. You must also bring to the table suggestions and ideas to improve the situation. Nothing is emptier, more meaningless and more worthless than criticism without accompanying constructive ideas for improvement." - Paraphrased from Keith Hackney.

A good person, parent, leader or manager will welcome criticism, but only if it is accompanied by suggestions for improvement. If you are on the receiving end of criticism, welcome it if accompanied by genuine suggestions for improvement.

If you are offering criticism, remember it is empty and worthless without meaningful suggestions for improvement.

80.   The Cascade of Disaster

When people perish in the wilderness or on the water, it is almost always due to a cascade of disaster. A small decision is made, such as "I won't need that jacket, I'm only going for a short hike," or "We won't need spare batteries for the GPS, we're just going a few miles offshore," or "We don't need that water, the weight will just slow us down."

That small decision leads to another bad decision when things turn bad. One small error is piled onto another small error is piled onto a tiny bad decision is piled onto a minor miscalculation. Before long, things are in a total free-fall disaster. And people die.

You can have the same cascade of disaster in your life. Be aware that small decisions add up.

A few times a year take a walk or sit by some water and think, at the highest possible level, about the direction of your life. Are you going where you want to go or are you living the sum total of a series of small decisions? Are you in the midst of a cascade of disaster?

81. Revisionist History

History is, by its very nature, dead. That makes it hard to make headlines, build a career, gain fame and get on television if you are a historian. The challenge is that history has pretty much been written and nobody is very interested in hearing about it again.

What do you do if you are an aspiring historian who is looking to build a star-level personality cult? Enter revisionist history. The only way to make a splash in history, to get on the morning talk shows, or, to get a book onto the *New*

York Times best seller list, is to revise history, to re-invent history, to, in some cases, make up a new history.

As a starter, the revisionist historian needs to find, or create, something spectacular. Preferably, it will involve a cherished national belief, a national hero that can be tainted, crippled or destroyed, or, at a minimum, a new history that casts doubt on a foundation of religious belief.

The next time you hear about a spectacular revisionist history "discovery," keep in mind that it's all about advancing someone's career, attaining or retaining tenure and if possible, becoming a celebrity. It usually has nothing to do with history.

82. Failure is an Orphan

"Success has a thousand fathers. Failure is an orphan." – John Fitzgerald Kennedy.

You will never be lonely when you build a success. You will never be lonelier than when you fail.

Try regardless. Strive regardless. Endeavor regardless.

83.   Trips to the Toolbox

"You can judge the quality of a mechanic by how many trips they make to the toolbox for a given job." – Avery Innis.

Pay attention to the efficiency of those you employ for professional and technical services. How many trips to their toolbox do they make in the course of your job?

How efficient are you in your work? How many trips to your toolbox are you making for common tasks?

In both cases it is important to determine if you or your suppliers are suited to the task.

84.   The Boiling Frog

If you put a frog into a pot of boiling water, it will jump out and escape. If you put a frog into a pot of cool water and slowly bring it to a boil it will never notice the rising temperature and will be killed.

Humans are the same way. We don't notice slow, incremental change.

Look around your life and see what things about it are boiling water that you just slowly acclimated to. Would you be happy with who you are and the life you are living if the you of five years ago interviewed the you of today?

Don't be a boiling frog.

85. Byline Basics

You are what you put in your head.

Thus, nothing is more important than understanding the sources of what you put in your head. News organizations are headquartered in large urban areas and cater to large urban audiences. Consequently, they are skewed and biased to the agendas of large, urban populations.

This is especially true of newspapers. Before you read a story, check the byline. If it is from the *New York Times* or the *Los Angeles Times*, then you know that the reporter who wrote the story knows full well that if they want to keep paying their mortgage, they better be submitting material that will appeal to the agendas, politics, desires, aspirations, beliefs, angers and fears of a large urban population.

Over time, you will notice that certain news organizations consistently present/filter/skew the news in a certain way. You don't have to stop watching or reading material from them, you just need to develop your own filter to offset theirs.

86. Wasted Potential

There is no greater sin than wasted potential.

You were born with many talents and abilities. You have since acquired many more. What are you accomplishing with those talents and abilities?

87. Being Against

It is easy to be against: against the government, against the man, against the establishment, against religion, against corporations, against the war, against repression, against – as Marlon Brando's character Johnny Strabler said in the movie *The Wild One* – "Whaddya got?" Being against something is energizing. It's easy to join the rally, join the march and become one of the "Against" tribe.

Being against doesn't require much thought, just nod along with the leaders who've done all the thinking for you. They'll give you all the reasons, all the rationalizations and all the purposes you will ever need to be against whatever they've determined you need to be against. It will all be a noble cause, a David vs. Goliath struggle to save the world, and you, and everyone who is against, will be heroes.

Being against is easy.

Being for is hard. Being for something requires sustainable will. It requires independent thought, and even more challenging, independent action.

Think about what you are for and what you are against. Think about which of those issues you made an independent decision about, on your own, and which decisions you made by simply jumping on a popular bandwagon in which someone else provided all the ideas and rationalizations.

88.   Body Language

Buy a book or two on body language and read them.

Understanding body language and other physiological clues or "tells" for behavior, such as why people yawn, is a critical component of successful communication skills. Some studies have shown that communication is 55% body language, 38% tonality and only 7% the words we use.

I have made critical, life-course-altering decisions based on people's body language, including financial investments, business contracts and personal relationships.

It is extremely important to understand body language and its role in communication.

(Communication components percentages source: study reported in *BusinessWeek* 14 February 2007)

89. He Who Hesitates is Lost

Whether it's entering a freeway, making a career choice or disciplining a child, he who hesitates is lost.

Be decisive. Call the ball. Make the pass. Decide. Move on.

90. That Which Doesn't Kill Us

"That which doesn't kill us can only serve to make us stronger." – Genghis Khan.

There are many tests and travails in life. Every one has a potential lesson to teach.

You can spend your life bemoaning its pitfalls and travesties, or you can learn from its struggles and strife, using the lessons learned to make you a stronger person.

91.   Tell it All, Tell it Early

The number one rule of corporate public relations damage control is, "Tell it all, tell it early."

The same goes for your personal life. No lie or untruth will ever remain. "The truth will always come out," as the saying goes. The truth will always be discovered or revealed, and when it does come out, you will only look worse for having suppressed or sublimated it. Be honest with yourself and with others.

When you are responsible for something, tell it all and tell it early.

92.   The Need to Know

At some point in your life you will be exposed to information or have access to information which you have no need to know. It may be as simple as a friend's bank balance or as important as national security information.

In either case, you have no need to know that information. You then will be forced to make a very important choice, and one that will be extremely difficult. The temptation to look or listen, and learn information that we have no real need to know, is huge. It is very difficult to resist. It will be a true test of your character and maturity.

Choose wisely.

93. Sleep On It

My grandfather, Clarence Hackney, taught me to sleep on a problem that I couldn't solve. Almost always I'd have a solution by the morning.

The same goes for any big challenge or unsolved issue that comes your way. Sleep on it.

94. The Most Boring World

The most boring world possible would be one in which everyone thought and acted exactly like you.

95. The Moving Box

Someday you will move your household. During that move, in the fur ball of activity and the chaos of unloading, you will have a box in your hands. You won't know exactly what to do with it, so you will set it down.

A few years later you will move again. That box will still be sitting exactly where you put it down the day of your previous move.

You will also make life decisions in the midst of frenzied activity. They will be quick decisions, spur of the moment decisions or not thoroughly considered decisions. Years later, you will still be living a life based on those quick, shallow decisions.

Is that spot in the hallway the best place for the moving box? Or, after five times walking past it did the box blend into the background of your life?

Are those quick decisions still the best decisions for your life? Or, after a few days, weeks or months, were they merely the decisions you made, so they must, therefore, be the correct decisions?

Live a life based on thoughtful, well-considered decisions; not a life constrained and defined by moving box decisions.

96. Learning to Juggle

I once knew a guy named Tim Williams. I learned to juggle from Tim Williams. He was one of my best friends at the time.

Tim and I were in Peoria, Illinois, working on a project for Caterpillar. While we were in town we worked hard, swapped life stories, laughed a lot, dreamed about what we'd do when we won the Lotto, smoked Questa Ray cigars and he taught me to juggle - all great bonding activities for a couple of young guys.

Tim and I remained very good friends right up to the day I learned he was accused of conspiring with one of my clients and two key employees to take the technology I invented and divert a huge amount of my company's money with the goal, successfully reached, of destroying my business.

Being betrayed by clients happens once in a while and being betrayed by employees in the media production business is nearly an everyday affair, so those aspects were at least familiar parts of the business landscape. Having people conspire to steal your money, your client and prospect data and your technology were also not unknown events. As nefarious as those acts were, I was just another victim, probably just one of quite a few in Chicago that month.

But, Tim, someone I thought was one of my best friends, being accused of betraying me, was a very tough experience. That one took me a long time to work through.

I had two choices: a) I could cultivate, nurture and revisit a burning hatred for Tim every remaining day of my life, or b) I could get over it and move on.

At some point in your life you will be betrayed by those you trust the most. It is up to you to decide how you will manage that experience. Clinging to anger and hatred only makes you angry and hateful.

I once knew a guy named Tim Williams. He was bright, positive, had a great sense of humor and tremendous love for his son.

I learned to juggle from Tim Williams. The secret is: there is only one ball in the air at a time.

97. Four Years From Now

Given good fortune, you will wake up four years from tomorrow.

On that day, what will be different in your life?

Will you have a larger set of potential life outcomes, or the same, or even more limited ones, after those four years have passed?

Will you have expanded your range of marketable job skills? Or, will you be out there trying to sell the same set of marketable skills you have now, but against kids who are four years younger than you, and who are willing to work for less money than you since they don't have four years of additional commitments and responsibilities?

Will you have significantly changed your range of potential futures? Or will you be facing the same basic set of futures you are now?

Given good fortune, you will wake up four years from tomorrow.

What will look back at you from the mirror?

98.   A Single Step

"A journey of a thousand miles begins with a single step." – Confucius.

Take that step.

99.   Time Management

When my brother, Jeff, was in his 30s he was living a very busy, active life. He invested time and energy into his marriage and his family, he worked hard and conscientiously at his job, he was involved in his community and church, he was a scout leader and he coached his son's sports teams. He lived a schedule that barely gave him time to breathe, but, during all of that, he found the time and energy to earn a college degree.

When asked how he managed to find the time his reply was simple, "I stopped watching television."

The average American watches over four hours of television a day. What else could you be doing with that time?

100. Learning to Play the Piano

Fifteen years ago, my friend, Neil Raden, was watching his daughter take a piano lesson. Neil off-handedly said to her teacher, John Garvey, "You know, John, I always wanted to play the piano."

"No you haven't," was John's instantaneous response.

Neil was a little put off by his peremptory and sort of rude response and said, "Yes, I have."

"No you haven't. If you wanted to, you would have."

Neil replied, "OK, I see where you're going with that. What I mean is, I always really wanted to, I just never got around to it."

"Nonsense!" the teacher retorted. "Let me tell you about someone who always wanted to play the piano." Mr. Garvey was getting warmed up now. "I have a student now, he is 19 years old. He came to the U.S. from a rural village in China six months ago. He has a repertoire of over 100 pieces that he plays flawlessly."

When he was four, a traveling band of musicians passed through his village, and he was so taken with the piano that he memorized the arrangement and the sound of each key. When they left, he drew the keyboard on a piece of scrap wood and *practiced on the wood, hearing the sounds only in his head*, for almost 15 years.

Villagers eventually found a phonograph and some old scratchy records, and he learned the pieces by ear. When he got to the U.S., he actually touched a real piano for the first time."

"Neil," he said, "*He* always wanted to play the piano."

Do you like talking about the idea of things you want to accomplish in life, such as playing the piano, or do you really want to accomplish them?

101. No Babies Will Die

When I produced live events I had a client who was deathly terrified to witness any event we produced for her. As soon as we rolled the walk-in music she would begin to panic. If she left the room she risked her career, as her bosses expected and demanded she be there. If she stayed she would suffer a complete nervous breakdown. Every show, she was a basket case, dog paddling in a sea of stress, not often keeping her mouth above the water.

One day, at a show we produced for her in Atlanta, just before we opened the doors for the audience to enter the room, my sound engineer leaned over to her and said, "No matter what happens in the next few hours here, no babies will die."

She looked at him, shocked, and then her face slowly relaxed into a big smile. She never suffered during an event again.

Keep things in perspective. Do not let relatively small things overwhelm you. Always view your life through the lens of the big picture.

102. The Search for Truth

"The search for truth is more precious than its possession." - Albert Einstein.

What is important is the search for truth, the striving for truth. If you set out on a path of a lifelong pursuit of truth you will never be disappointed. If you try to declare what you currently know as the defining, never-ending, unalterable truth, you will not only be inaccurate, but immediately frustrated as the world continues to change around you and your never-changing truth.

Seek the discovery of truth, not the possession of truth.

103. Soul at Peace

Find out where your soul is at peace and go there regularly.

That place will change throughout your lifetime. It may be one place when you are young, a different place when you are a young adult, a different place when you have children and a different place when your children become adults.

Find out where your soul is at peace and go there regularly. It is a key to a happy and healthy life.

104. Own Your Story

In business and in life it is critical to own the story. That means you must own your own story, about who and what you are, about what you are doing, about your choices and about the consequences of your decisions.

If you let someone else own your story by defining or telling your story, you will never be able to get it back. You must not allow other people or organizations to define you, characterize you, describe you, slot you into a category or label you.

Always own your story.

105. Good Advice

Good advice is very rarely what you *want* to hear. It is always what you *need* to hear.

106. The Hierarchy of Needs

In 1943 Abraham Maslow published the concept of the hierarchy of needs.

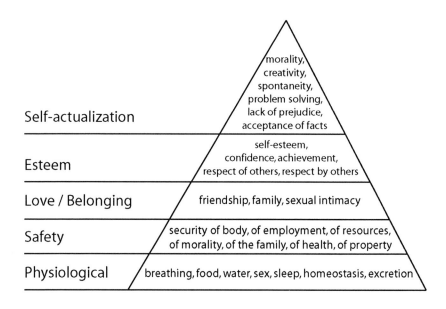

Note where you spend most of your time. You will probably be spending most of your waking hours providing for things on the bottom two levels. If you have any time and energy left, you will be pursuing things on the third level.

Note that what is truly rewarding and meaningful in life lies between the third and top levels.

How much time and energy are you investing in pursuing the top two levels?

107. Forced Passages

There is a rule in sailing: Never force a passage to make a schedule.

What that means is you never set out to cross an ocean or sail to a new destination just because you think you need to be there at a certain time or date. To stay alive sailing, you must let the prevailing conditions, not an arbitrary schedule, determine when you depart and when you arrive.

A friend of ours, John Kretschmer, wrote the book *At the Mercy of the Sea*. It is a true story about three sailors killed in a hurricane. The main character is a man named Carl.

Carl and the other two sailors were all forcing a passage on a schedule. They all got killed.

Let the prevailing conditions determine your passages.

Never force a passage in your life.

108. Put Yourself in a Position to Win

You cannot drive in the winning run if you are sitting in the stands.

You cannot drive in the winning run if you are sitting on the bench.

You cannot drive in the winning run if you have not invested the time and energy to learn the required skills to bat.

You cannot drive in the winning run if you have not repeatedly practiced hitting a breaking ball or a hard slider.

You cannot drive in the winning run if you are not standing at the plate with the winning run on base.

You cannot drive in the winning run if you do not believe in yourself and your abilities.

Winning is not about thinking about winning or dreaming about winning. Winning does not fall out of the sky and hit you on the head. Winning requires a long term commitment to ensuring that you are in a position to win.

Put yourself, your family and your children in a position to win.

109. One Chapter Ahead

If you are one chapter ahead in the book, you are a teacher. If you finish the book before anyone else you are an expert.

110. Our Own Time

While in the Himalayas with the Buddhists, we were taught that, as humans, we make our own time.

This means that we create artificial time and overlay our life with that framework. We create artificial deadlines and responsibilities related to arbitrary time. With every one of those deadlines and responsibilities comes stress. We create our own time. Thus, we create our own stress.

Look at your life. How much of it is driven by artificial time? How much of your stress is created because of the artificial deadlines and responsibilities you have imposed on your own life?

111. Fear

You will spend most of your life living in fear. If you can escape it, you will truly live for the first time.

112. The Coping Strategies of Fear

People who live in fear build a matrix, a framework, of insecurities to obscure and protect their fear.

To interface with the outside world they build coping strategies to bridge between others' fears and their own.

Negative human behaviors are those coping strategies, from gossip to passive aggression to violence.

113. The Power of Position

Pay attention to where you are positioned in a conversation or interaction. If you've got the sun or lights over your shoulder and the bright light is shining in the other person's eyes, it puts them at a disadvantage. If you are on a higher physical position looking down at them, even the tiniest distance in elevation puts them at a disadvantage. If you are interacting over a barrier, be it a wall, a desk or any structure or obstacle, it puts them at a disadvantage.

Observe how conversational and interactional position are used in society, such as a judge's bench. Be aware of where you are in that position relationship. If you are at a disadvantage, seek to neutralize it. If you are at an advantage, be aware of it, and unless you need the advantage, seek to neutralize it to enable a balanced interaction.

114. The Slowest Student

A teacher can only go as fast as the slowest student. If you are teaching and a single student is markedly slower than the rest of the group, you need to make a choice regarding leaving that student behind or employing additional resources, such as tutoring or a teaching assistant, to keep them up with the class.

115. Table Manners

Know proper table manners and teach them to your children. This is a life skill that is essential and irreplaceable. You have no way to know where life is going to take you and when you'll be there. Be prepared.

116. Forward

The way forward, moving forward, is just that, forward. It is not backwards or sideways.

117. The Busy Person

"If you want something done, give the task to a busy person." – American folk wisdom.

To the busy person it will be just another task to be completed among all of the others. The busy person has efficient processes in place for executing tasks. The busy person knows the resources available and required for executing tasks. A busy person is efficient and effective.

A person who isn't doing much will be overwhelmed by any task. The task will take on huge proportions because they don't have any other tasks at hand to provide a context. They will not have the coping skills to handle a new or unfamiliar task, or the means to adapt to it. They will not know of the full set of available resources, and they will have very little experience utilizing the resources they have available.

A busy person is a valuable resource. A non-busy person is a burden. Be that busy person.

118. Grandpa's Ax

There was no greater treasure in the toolbox than grandpa's ax. The handle had been broken and replaced. The head had worn out and been replaced. But, there in the toolbox, was grandpa's ax.

How many grandpa's axes do you have in your life? Separate the sentimentality of your life from the reality of your life. Know the difference between the two.

119. C Words

Life consists primarily of three C words: choices, consequences and chapters.

You will make choices in your life. Those choices will lead to consequences. The choices will often define the beginning and the ends of the chapters of your life.

Make choices consciously. Be aware of the consequences of your choices. Be aware of the chapters of your life and know that each will come to an end.

120. Drinking from the Faucet

When drinking directly from a faucet you hold your hand open, like a cup, under the stream of water. The water flows into your hand, fills it continuously, and you can drink as much as you like from it. No matter how much you drink, the faucet keeps your open hand full.

If you try to grasp at the water, clutch it, hold it, the water will squirt out of your fist and you will have none.

This is the same for everything you desire in your life, be it money, love, success, happiness, etc. If you try to clutch it, hold it or possess it, you will lose it all. If you hold your life open and let what you desire flow through you, you will have all you need.

Clutch, grasp and hold in life and you will have nothing. Stay open in life and all you need will be yours.

121. One Degree of Difference

A compass has 360 degrees. The course of an airplane or a boat is expressed as one of those degrees, for example, a heading of 182 degrees. One degree out of 360 doesn't sound like much, for instance, only the difference between 258 and 259 degrees.

Over a short time, and thus a short distance, one degree won't make much of a difference in direction or in destination. But over a long time, and consequently a long distance, it will make a huge difference in direction and, most importantly, destination. .

For instance, if you stand on the beach in San Diego, California, and hold your arm out you can point towards Hawaii on a heading of about 258 degrees (true, on a great circle route). If you sailed a boat on that heading for 2,530 miles / 4,071 kilometers you would make landfall in a paradise of beautiful beaches and lush tropics.

If you move your arm only one degree and sail that new course of 259 degrees you won't end up in Hawaii. You'd miss the islands and sail an additional 4,738 miles / 7,625 kilometers before you tore off the bottom of your boat on Australia's Great Barrier Reef.

Just one tiny degree of difference, the choice of a heading of 258 versus 259, is the difference between making landfall in paradise and being shipwrecked and eaten by great white sharks on the world's longest reef.

Tiny changes in course, only a single degree or less, when extended over long periods of time, add up to large distances and make a huge difference in where you arrive.

This is true not only in aviation and sailing, but in life.

Tiny changes in the course of your life, when extrapolated over time, add up to life-altering differences in destination. These tiny course changes are most important with young people, especially adolescents and teenagers.

The difference between taking one class or another, being involved in one extracurricular activity or another and most importantly, being associated with one peer group or another, can easily shift the course of a life a degree or two, or twenty.

Tiny little decisions, miniscule alterations in course, one degree or less, when stretched out over a few years or a decade, will completely change a lifetime's destination.

Be aware of the effects of small changes to the course of your life. Be steady at the wheel and be very, very careful in your navigation, especially when you are young.

122. The Memory Stream

When someone experiences something significant in their lives, either a traumatic or exciting event, a first-time experience or something that induces adrenaline, they will have an overwhelming need to relate the experience, over and over and over.

The story will be a long stream of memory, and they will take the trip down the stream again and again. During the retelling, aspects of the experience that would be minor details or insignificant to someone with extensive relevant experience, will be accorded great import and drama. The outpouring of the memory stream is an important part of processing the experience for many people.

It is very important to be a good and patient listener in these circumstances. Let them tell the story, over and over and over. Be patient.

After all, you probably did the same thing the first time you experienced something similar.

123. Projecting Our Future

In the most fundamental way, we project our own future.

Our fears and insecurities limit us to seeking out futures that are comfortable and un-challenging.

Our dreams are just that, dreams. They provide an escape, a comfortable fantasyland, but we lack the courage to pursue them. We make choices that keep us from facing anything threatening.

We determine our future, we project it like a movie, and it is usually little more than an endless loop of our fears.

The only escape from that endless loop is to break out of the safety of the known and seek a life filled with new experiences, new challenges and places other than the safe and comfortable.

124. Meteorites

Life does contain random chance. Despite all your planning, despite all your diligence, despite all your hard work, for no good reason, like a meteorite falling from the sky and hitting you on the head, random chance events happen. And they will happen to you.

This doesn't mean you are cursed, or that the gods are out to get you. What it means is that random chance is part of life.

You then have a choice. You can spend the rest of your life bemoaning how you got hit on the head by a meteorite and never get past it, or you can pick it up, put it on the mantle as a conversation piece and move on.

125. Comfortable Growth

Growth, by definition, is not comfortable. Growth is challenging, stressful and, sometimes, scary as hell. It is also the most rewarding thing you will ever do with your life.

Commit to a lifetime of growth.

126. Life is Good

The next time you don't think your life is good, take a long, careful look around you. It usually only takes about five minutes to find someone who has it worse than you do.

127. Write More Books

Arthur Schlesinger, Jr., one of America's leading historians and social commentators of the 20ᵗʰ century, was asked near the end of his life for his greatest regret. He replied, "I wish I would have written more books."

This, coming from a man who authored 29 books, some recognized as milestones, was a striking comment. He elaborated that he had written hundreds of thousands of words for periodical publications on current issues of the day. He regretted that he invested so much energy into topics that were, in the grand scope of his lifetime, relatively meaningless. He felt if he had instead invested his energies into producing more books, works of meaning, impact and longevity, he would have contributed more to the world and felt more fulfilled.

How much energy do you expend on topical activities that do not matter that much in the larger scheme of things? How much of your life and efforts are invested in worthy projects that will stand the test of time and, when viewed from the perspective of the end of your life, be worthy of that precious time and energy?

Be very careful about getting caught up in the foam and froth of current events. It is easy to wake up at the end of your life with nothing but a hangover. Invest your time and energy wisely. Write more books.

128. The I Words

Life has a huge challenge around two "I" words. The challenge is to stay *in*formed without *in*doctrination.

Due to the nature of human behavior, especially tribalism, the underlying goal of almost every source of information is indoctrination into a certain point of view.

Be determined and dogged in your pursuit of information and staying informed.

Be very wary of, and resist at all costs, becoming indoctrinated as a result.

129. One Wish

If you had one wish that could be fulfilled, and an endless supply of additional wishes is not an option, what would that wish be?

This is not a question to answer in a second or a minute or an hour. Ponder this question for a week or two or three.

If you had one wish that could be fulfilled what would that wish be?

The answer will reveal much about you.

130. The Butler Test

One of my toughest and best clients was Tim Butler at GE Medical Systems. Being a technologist at the time, I was constantly trying to convince him to provide budgets so I could build something with the latest, greatest technology.

When I came to his office and proposed that week's grand scheme to revolutionize the business with a bleeding-edge technology, Tim would lean back in his chair and say, "So, Doug, if we build this thing, what will be different for the business on Tuesday morning a year from now?"

It was very rare that I could pass that test, the Butler Test.

I later adopted the Butler Test and taught it to my students and clients as the first litmus test for any proposed project of any type.

When you consider any purchase, any investment of time or energy, any project or any change, put it through the Butler Test. Ask yourself, "What will be different on Tuesday morning a year from now in my life or business?" Will those differences be meaningful? Will those differences be measurable?

Ensure you are investing your money, your time and your energy, only on things that will bring about meaningful, measureable change.

131. Congratulations! You're a Four

We are measured in every way from physical attributes and performance to our personal, professional and business characteristics our entire lives.

Every life and every business must have performance metrics, the measures of its existence. You must measure your performance and characteristics in order to gauge progress against your internal goals. But none of those measures mean a thing unless you know how you rate in the context of your peers, and the world as a whole, outside your immediate existence.

Metrics are critical for understanding what we are, but they are meaningless without context. If someone rates you or your business as a four, what does that really mean? If it is on a scale of four, fantastic; a scale of ten, there's lots of room for improvement; a scale of one hundred, and you've got real problems.

Set goals and measure your performance against those goals, but ensure that you always analyze your metrics in context.

132. Ideas are Easy

In a past career, I had the best job in the world. I got paid to stand up in front of an empty white board and fill it with my ideas for solutions to complex, challenging problems.

I had the ability to quickly perceive the core issues of the challenges, knew the possible technological solutions, had pragmatic techniques to overcome the cultural and political hurdles and could synthesize all of it together, on the spot, and communicate it via an interesting, spontaneous presentation.

When I was done I had a white board filled with my ideas. Usually, the clients were happy to finally find a range of viable solutions to their problem set. They were left smiling and I got to ride off into the sunset with them singing my praises.

That was great for me - all I had to do was come up with the ideas. But ideas are easy. The hard work, the infinitely more challenging work, was implementing and sustaining the ideas I left behind.

Never forget that just like children, conceiving and giving birth to an idea is the easy part. Building, implementing and sustaining that idea is the real work.

133. **Remain Curious**

If you can do only one thing with your life, remain curious. The insatiable desire to learn and grow will serve you well.

134. Teaching People

"You teach people how to treat you." – Dr. Phil McGraw.

By what we allow other people to do to and for us, we teach them how to treat us. Once we teach them that lesson it becomes an unwritten, unspoken contract. If we later try to change the rules of what we will allow them to do to and for us, we are in breach of that contract and conflict usually results.

You must be consistent over time in the lessons you teach others about how to treat you. If you demand your boundaries are respected from the beginning, they will be. If you don't at first and require it later, it is unlikely they will be by the people you have previously taught that lesson. If you want new rules, then you will probably need to seek out new people and new relationships.

Be aware that every interaction with the people in your life is a small or large lesson in how they can treat you. It is critically important to be aware of this with children.

135. Intrinsic vs. Extrinsic Rewards

There are two reward systems in life. Intrinsic rewards come from within, the rewards you give yourself. Extrinsic rewards come from the outside world, what others give you.

Of the two, intrinsic rewards are the only sustainable type.

Extrinsic rewards such as status, money, love, loyalty, adulation, membership, etc., are all variable and dependent on the actions and behaviors of others.

Be sure that the rewards that determine your choices, influence your actions, drive your behavior and form your life are intrinsic.

136. A Life Well Lived

Lead an interesting and fulfilling life. That is a life well lived.

137. The Moose on the Table

Every human group, from families to companies to countries, has a moose in the room.

Everyone knows the moose is there, but everyone walks around it, everyone avoids it and everyone is careful never to talk about it. The moose is huge, it is smelly, it consumes a massive amount of resources and leaves an incredible mess, but no one addresses the issue of the moose.

Standing up, facing reality and being honest with yourself, your family, your tribe, your community and your nation requires you put the moose on the table.

Once the moose is on the table, everyone must acknowledge its existence. Everyone must address the problems caused by having the moose. Everyone must participate in overcoming the challenges of the moose.

Stop ignoring the moose. Put the moose on the table.

138. Reef Before You Need To

The power that drives a sailboat is derived from its sails. The more sail area you have aloft, the more power you can generate. Sailboats are made to carry as much sail area as required to drive the boat in low wind conditions.

It is important to keep the amount of sail area exposed to the wind correctly proportioned to the strength of the winds. This means that if you are in high winds, you must reduce the amount of sail area you are exposing to the wind or you can damage the boat, its passengers or its contents.

The act of reducing the amount of sail area is termed reefing. The rule of long distance, ocean-crossing sailing is, "Reef before you need to."

If you wait until the winds are strong it can be extremely challenging to reef your sails. The boat will be under strain, you will be under stress and the seas will likely be deteriorating.

It is much better to reef before the winds become strong, to reef when you can easily reduce the amount of sail area to match the prevailing and expected winds.

The same is true with life. Use all of your power and energy when the prevailing conditions are suitable. Throttle back, reduce sail - reef, before conditions turn ugly and your life gets away from you.

139. Decision Sample Sets

In statistical analysis you must have a statistically significant sample set in order to derive correlations. In other words, if you want to draw conclusions, you must have enough evidence to consider for your conclusions to be valid.

Most people make decisions without a valid sample set. They will hear something from a friend, or read something on the Internet, or learn of a celebrity blessing, or the paid recommendation of a commercial endorsement. Based on a sample set of one or two they will make a life or business decision with outcome-determining consequences.

When you think about it, that's a pretty silly way to live your life or run your business.

Would you take a drug if it was tested on only two or three people? Wouldn't you want to take a drug that had been tested on enough different people, a statistically significant sample set, for it to be truly known to be safe and effective?

When you set out to make a decision for your life or your business, make sure you are basing that decision on a large number of inputs, on sufficient evidence or on a statistically significant sample set to ensure your choice to be both valid and well considered.

140. Ask

The worst they can say is no.

How many times in your life have you needed help, a mentor or assistance and you have suffered without it simply because you were afraid to ask?

Just ask. The worst they can say is no.

141. Perspective

An interoffice softball game was held between the company's marketing and support staff. The support staff whipped the marketing department soundly.

To show just how the marketing department earns their keep, they posted this memo on the bulletin board after the game:

"The Marketing Department is pleased to announce that for the Softball Season, we came in 2nd place, having lost but one game all year.

The Support Department, however, had a rather dismal season, as they won only one game."

It's not what happens in life, it's how you perceive it, how you think about it and how you present that perspective to others.

142. Good Attracts Good

Good attracts good, negative attracts negative. If you nurture and project a positive outlook on life, you will attract others who do the same. If you nurture and project a negative outlook on life, the same is true.

Each of these are multipliers. As you attract more good people into your life, more good things happen. The bad things that happen will be so few in comparison they will be small bumps in the road of life.

Conversely, if you are negative, as you attract more negative people into your life more negative things will happen. If any good things do come along, you will be so cynical about them you will be incapable of appreciating them or using them as building blocks to create a more positive life.

Create, nurture and propagate a positive life. The returns and rewards are limitless.

143. The Therapy Tool

"A therapist is a paid friend." – Don Ivener.

Therapy is a valuable life tool, if used as such. If you need it, use it, achieve your goal and then put it back in the tool box. It is as easy to become addicted or dependent on therapy as it is on any chemical.

144. The Rescuers

The ranks of the helping professions, such as therapists, marriage counselors, etc., are filled with rescuers. These people picture themselves as knights in shining armor, usually saving damsels in distress. Generally, they view clients as one of two types: evil villains or pristinely innocent victims. Consequently, a rescuer is incapable of providing services of any value.

If they cast you as a victim, they will tell you everything you want to hear, which will not help you at all. If they cast you as a villain, they will do little but castigate you, which will not help you at all.

If you are seeking therapy or counseling, interview a few and weed out the rescuers. They will not help you. They will leave you worse off than when you started.

145. The Key Delta

The most important delta to measure in your life is the difference between your potential and your outcome. There is no greater sin than wasted potential.

Ask yourself often, "Does my outcome equal or exceed my potential?"

146. A Fact-Based Life

Most people live an anecdotal-based life. If they hear a friend assert something, they will believe it. If they hear a celebrity assert something, they will believe it. If they read it on the Internet they will believe it.

Unfortunately, very, very little of what people hear or read anecdotally is actually true.

Strive to live a fact-based life. Research things and find second and third sources to confirm assertions before taking them as fact.

Make your life decisions as fact-based decisions.

147. Statistics

"There are lies, damn lies and statistics." – Samuel Langhorne Clemens as Mark Twain.

Anyone with any talent and imagination can take a dataset and make it tell any story they want. Be very, very wary of adopting points of view based on data or statistical analysis that you do not directly investigate yourself. This is especially true when related to media reports, which are almost always based on distorted subsets or out-of-context data analysis.

148. Betrayal

If you live long enough, you will probably be betrayed by one or more people you love and trust more than anyone else in your life.

If you are in business long enough you will definitely be betrayed by spouses, children, partners, key employees, bookkeepers, major clients and suppliers.

There is no escaping betrayal in life and it never gets any easier. What is important is not that the betrayal happens - that is inevitable - but how you handle it.

Don't let the betrayal of others twist and distort you into a bitter, resentful person. Grieve the loss of trust, process your anger and then move on.

149. Ready for Change

You know you are ready for change when you get tired of listening to your own complaints.

150. Prerequisites for Change

The first steps of change are recognition and acknowledgement. You must first recognize and acknowledge there is need for change. Without this, change is impossible.

This rule applies to individuals and any size group of humans, from two to billions.

151. The Curse of Beauty

Beauty is usually viewed as a blessing, but it often is a curse.

Beautiful people spend their entire lives having doors opened for them, literally and figuratively. Things come easily, including adulation and tribal integration. This lifetime of ease and assistance, of the road constantly rising to meet their feet, becomes a problem when a beautiful person is faced with a real challenge.

They have never needed to develop any problem-solving skills because their problems have always been solved by those desiring to share in the glow of their beauty. Consequently, if they are on their own, alone with a challenge, they are usually incapable of overcoming it.

Of course, beauty will eventually fade, eroding beyond the scope of modern chemistry and surgical techniques. At that point the beautiful person is faced with a lifetime of loneliness and incompetence. They are no longer surrounded by admirers, and so there is no one else around to handle the formerly beautiful person's challenges.

Beauty is not always a blessing. It is often a curse.

152. Learn How to Land

The first step of learning to hang glide is to learn how to land. Keep this in mind when you set out to learn new skills and seek new adventures. Always ensure you know how to get safely back down to the ground.

153. 40,000 Feet

On a regular basis, step back away from your life and re-examine what you are doing and why. Get up to a high altitude where you can see all of your life's landscape and the curvature of your life's earth. From that perspective ask all the basic questions. Why am I doing this? Where am I going? What is my goal? Have conditions changed?

It is only by regularly reviewing your life and its course from maximum altitude that you can you spot an obstacle that requires a change in course or a new, long range opportunity. If you don't step back on a regular basis, you will continually run head-long into the icebergs of life and miss out on new opportunities because you are too far off course.

154. Toes up vs. Toes Down

"Any morning I wake up and can put my feet on the floor is a good morning." – Lois Strickland.

Life is good. It is much better than the alternative. Be thankful for every day and live it to its fullest extent possible. If you are lucky enough to get old, every day will become very precious to you.

Don't waste days while you are young, or you will likely live to regret it.

155. Two Wolves

One evening an old Cherokee told his grandson about a battle that goes on inside people.

He said, "My son, the battle is between two wolves inside us all.

"One is Evil. It is anger, envy, jealousy, sorrow, regret, greed, arrogance, self-pity, guilt, resentment, inferiority, lies, false pride, superiority and ego.

"The other is Good. It is joy, peace, love, hope, serenity, humility, kindness, benevolence, empathy, generosity, truth, compassion and faith."

The grandson thought about it for a minute and then asked his grandfather, "Which wolf wins?"

The old Cherokee replied simply, "The one you feed."

156. Teaching Wisdom

"Knowledge can be communicated, but not wisdom. One can find it, live it, be fortified by it, do wonders through it, but one cannot communicate and teach it." – Sidhartha, Hermann Hesse.

Wisdom is the summary of accumulated experience. In a very practical sense, it is largely a waste of time to seek to directly learn wisdom or to teach it.

Those who spend their lives seeking to directly learn wisdom, especially in a compressed, "Cliff's Notes" form, are destined for disappointment.

Those who purport to teach wisdom, especially in a brief, high-speed format, are almost always charlatans.

Wisdom is best learned by observation and best taught by example.

157. Parked Cars

"Dogs don't chase parked cars." – Western American folk wisdom.

If you make a difference in life, if you advocate change, if you drive innovation, then you will attract barking dogs. It is part of the package of life.

Be a moving car.

158. Punch

A martial arts student wanted to be a better puncher. He wasn't good at it. He wanted to be as good a puncher as his teacher. He was sure there was a training technique, an exercise, maybe even a diet that could make him a better puncher.

He approached his teacher and asked, "What can I do to become a better puncher?"

The master looked at him impassively. Seconds passed. Finally the sensei said, "Punch. Throw 10,000 punches a day," then turned and walked away.

The young student stood dumbfounded, and then slowly a thin smile formed on his face.

From that day forward, every day, without fail, he punched - 10,000 times a day.

Subsequently, that student, our friend, Glen Heggstad, became a multi-discipline black belt and martial arts champion.

If you want to become better, or the best, at something, then do it.

Focus your energies on it. Commit to it. Persevere. You will achieve your goals only by doing.

159. Sunday at Starbucks

Walk into a Starbucks anywhere in America on a Sunday morning. While you are standing in line take a look around and count the zombies.

The Starbucks Sunday Zombies are the mindless drones, brows knitted, studying every word in the Sunday *New York Times* editorial section. They are incapable of having any opinion different from what they read there. In fact, if they didn't read it every Sunday, they wouldn't know what to think for the following week.

Don't be a Starbucks Sunday Zombie. Be your own person. Have your own thoughts. Research your own facts. Build your own opinions.

160. Marketable Skills

Employment opportunities are determined by your range of marketable skills.

If you have a high school diploma, you have a very limited range of marketable skills. The marketable skills you have are not highly compensated and never will be.

If you have a college degree you have one to two orders of magnitude more marketable skills. This range of marketable skills is more highly compensated and always will be.

If you have a master's degree, you have another one to two orders of magnitude more marketable skills. Again, these skills are much more highly compensated and always will be.

If you achieve a doctorate, you have at least another one to two orders of magnitude more marketable skills. If you pick the right field of endeavor, you can write your own ticket.

Your range of options, your opportunity set of potential life outcomes, increases dramatically with every step up in your education.

Don't pass up the opportunity for advancing yourself academically and then rail against the unfairness of the world. The world compensates in direct proportion to marketable skills.

Enable yourself and your future with a viable range of marketable skills.

161. Advance the Plot

The first thing you learn in film making is that in a successful film every scene advances the plot.

If you have a scene that you love as a director - the shot was perfect, the lighting was perfect, the sound was perfect, the timing was perfect, the acting was perfect, everything was perfect - except the scene does not advance the plot of the film, then it must be cut and, in the vernacular of the classic film making days, end up on the cutting room floor.

You must ensure that every scene of your life advances your plot. Are you investing energy into things that are not advancing you toward your goal? If so, then you must cut them.

Every scene of your life must advance the plot.

162. Billy Taylor's Chin

My Junior High school wrestling coach was Billy Taylor. He was a compact, wiry guy from the East Coast with an exotic accent for my small Iowa town.

Billy Taylor's secret to wrestling success was to find your opponent's weak spot and establish a leverage point, a point of control, at that very spot.

His favorite technique was getting your opponent down on his back and nailing your chin on their sternum. Merely placing your chin there wasn't enough; Billy Taylor wanted your entire body weight on your chin, relentlessly grinding, with nothing but your toes on the ground and your chin on that chest.

He would demonstrate the technique's effectiveness by having the smallest guys on the mat use it on the biggest guys. Amazingly, it worked. The small guy, just by drilling his chin into his opponent's sternum, could effectively control and near-fall or pin guys much larger.

I never forgot Billy Taylor, with his Eastern twang and bow-legged walk, or his lesson about controlling others through their weaknesses.

We all have our weak points, our points of vulnerability, our Achilles' heel. Most of our weak points aren't physical, they are emotional and psychological.

People with highly developed controlling skills, control freaks, can discern weaknesses in milliseconds and exploit them to bend others to their will.

Through the course of your life you will be around many control freaks and others who will endeavor to control you.

Through the course of your life, you will also be in situations when you need to leverage others.

Do you know your weak points?

Do you know how others leverage your weak points to control you?

Do you know how to leverage the weak points in others to achieve your goals?

163. Becoming a Man

"The day you bury your father is the day you must become a man." – Traditional Mexican folk wisdom, via Jimmy Sones.

You can spend your entire life avoiding maturity. There are plenty of people and businesses that will be more than willing to help you do it. You'll have plenty of friends along the way as long as your money holds out.

But eventually, if you outlive your parents, you will be forced to face maturity, and face reality.

164. A Captain's Boat

When coming aboard a captain's boat, it is imperative to always find something complimentary to say about it.

This is a good practice in life as well. Always find something complimentary to say about others and their endeavors.

165. Wants vs. Needs

The most important step for achieving adulthood and obtaining financial independence is to understand the difference between wants and needs. Many never do.

Do you *want* it or do you *need* it?

166. 21 Days

It takes about three weeks of repetitions before something new becomes a habit.

That means if you want to change something in your life, you need to repeat that change, that new behavior, for at least 21 days for it to take hold.

167. Being Self Limiting

Most people live a self-limited life. They like to blame others for their outcomes, but most people create the boundaries within which they live their lives.

The most common fears that keep us within strict limits are:

- Fear of leaving your tribe
- Fear of making mistakes as you learn something new
- Fear of starting at the bottom of something new versus being above the bottom in your current position

The only way your life will ever change is if you knock down the barriers that you have created between yourself and what lies in the world of unlimited potential outcomes.

168. Large Tasks

Large tasks are often overwhelming. Taken as a whole they can simply crush your spirit with their enormity.

If people concentrate on the entire task, nothing ever gets done. The Panama Canal, the Empire State Building, even your local highway would have never been completed if the builders only thought about the entire scope of the finished project.

The key is to break big projects down into smaller and smaller units of work until they are small enough to be manageable and accomplishable.

If you are considering a project, any project, whether it is obtaining a college education or painting your bedroom, and it seems overwhelming, break it down into smaller and smaller incremental units of work until you know you can accomplish the first one, then the next one and then the next one.

Before you know it, you will be done.

169. Salary = Spending

Immutable law of life: The more you make, the more you will spend.

You will escape this law only by making financial independence your top financial goal.

170. Kill Your TV

Television lowers your IQ.

It is almost all lowest-common-denominator, mindless cultural indoctrination content. It is nothing more than the opiate of the masses.

No amount of Discovery, History or National Geographic channel viewing will ever make up for the brain cells you kill by watching the commercials inherent there or the other content you view.

Save your life and those of your children. Kill your TV.

171. The Unhappy Life

"If you don't like your life, change it." - Jeff Hackney.

One day when I was relating my tale of woe to my brother, Jeff, he cut me off and said, "If you don't like your life, change it."

At the time I thought he was being entirely unfair in not listening to my complaining for the 28th time. After all, I thought I'd developed a highly enhanced version with even more nuanced reasons why none of it was my responsibility.

But, after a while, I carefully considered what he'd said and realized he was right.

It was probably the best advice I have ever received.

I didn't like my life. So I changed it.

Are you unhappy with your life? Then change it.

172. Being Yourself

"Do not wish to be anything but what you are, and try to be that perfectly." — St. Francis de Sales.

It is extremely easy to spend your life wishing you were someone else or something else. Racked by inferiority or driven by aspiration, you can wake up on your deathbed never having spent a day simply being content with who you are.

Be yourself, be all of yourself - be it the best you can be.

173. Endurance

The First Voyage, The National Antarctic Expedition, 1901-1902

As with most of the early British expeditions, food was in short supply; the personnel on long treks were usually underfed by any measure and were essentially starving. Scott, Wilson and Shackleton reached their "furthest south" point of 82°17'S on December 31, 1902. They were 857 km (463 nautical miles) from the Pole. Shackleton developed scurvy on the return trip.

The Second Voyage, British Antarctic Expedition, 1907-1909

"I cannot think of failure yet. I must look at the matter sensibly and consider the lives of those who are with me...man can only do his best..." - Sir Ernest Henry Shackleton

The end of their southern journey began at 4 AM on January 9, 1909. They left the sledge, tent and food at the camp and took only the Union Jack, a brass cylinder containing stamps and documents to mark their farthest south point, camera, glasses and a compass. Their farthest south point was reached at 9 AM: 88°23'S, longitude 162°--just 97 miles from the South Pole.

At 1 AM on March 4, all were safe on board the Nimrod; they had walked, in Antarctic conditions, 1,700 miles.

The Third Voyage, Imperial Trans-Antarctic Expedition, 1914-1916

"I called to the other men that the sky was clearing, and then a moment later I realized that what I had seen was not a rift in the clouds but the white crest of an enormous wave. During twenty-six years experience of the ocean, in all its moods, I had not encountered a wave so gigantic. It was a mighty upheaval of the ocean, a thing quite apart from the big white-capped seas that had been our tireless enemies for many days. I shouted 'For God's sake, hold on! It's got us.' Then came a moment of suspense that seemed drawn out into hours. White surged the foam of the breaking sea around us. We felt our boat lifted and flung forward like a cork in breaking surf. We were in a seething chaos of tortured water; but somehow the boat lived through it, half full of water, sagging to the dead weight and shuddering under the blow. We bailed with the energy of men fighting for life, flinging the water over the sides with every receptacle that came to our hands, and after ten minutes of uncertainty, we felt the boat renew her life beneath us."

- Sir Ernest Henry Shackleton

Ernest Shackleton was born in Ireland to a family with no nautical heritage. He found his way to college, which he abandoned for the sea. He had no nautical training or experience, yet he worked his way up to commander on Britain's finest shipping line, which he left to become an Antarctic explorer. He had no training or experience as an Antarctic explorer, yet he became one of the most noted of all explorers from the Heroic Age of Antarctic Exploration.

On 5 December, 1914, Shackleton's ship, the Endurance, and its crew of 28 shoved off from Grytviken, South Georgia to Antarctica with the audacious goal of an overland crossing of the entire southern continent, from the Weddell Sea, south of the Atlantic, to the Ross Sea, south of the Pacific, by way of the pole.

By 17 January, 1915, the Endurance was trapped by the pack ice, to which it finally succumbed and sank on 21 November, 1915. After fruitless attempts at overland travel, the crew camped on the ice for months. On 9 April, 1916, the crew was forced into their salvaged life boats and set upon the sea as the ice broke up beneath them. After seven days with little food and water in the open boats the crew made landfall at Elephant Island, as bleak and remote a spot of land that exists on the planet.

Immediately realizing that rescue was improbable without seeking help, Shackleton prepared to sail an open whale boat, the 23 foot long James Caird, 800 miles across the most treacherous seas in the world, the 50° to 60° south latitudes of the Southern Ocean, back to South Georgia.

In the age of sail the rule of the sea was "Below 40 degrees, there is no law, but below 50 degrees, there is no God." Shackleton's course ran from the southern boundary of the Drake Passage at 61°S to his destination at 54°S. There would be no God on this passage.

The Drake Passage averages gale force (40 – 45 MPH / 64 – 72 KPH) winds over 200 days a year. Wave heights are typically 20 feet / 6 meters, with much higher waves common during the endless, relentless storms that sweep unblocked and unhindered by any land mass around the planet in that region. There would be no God on this passage.

Knowing what they faced, Shackleton refused to ship provisions for more than 30 days. He believed, rightly so, that if they hadn't reached their destination by then, the tiny open boat would surely be lost. There would be no God on this passage.

The diminutive boat shoved off from the shore of Elephant Island on 24 April, 1916. The men ashore, left to their diet of penguin meat and nothing else, had little hope they would ever see their leader again as they watched the small boat disappear over the gray horizon.

In one of the greatest feats of seamanship, and undoubtedly the greatest feat of celestial navigation in modern history, Shackleton, navigator Frank Worsley and three others made the 800-mile passage to South Georgia in 14 days with only four bouncing, sliding, jarring, seconds-long sextant shots along the way to establish their position and course.

They sighted South Georgia late in the day, but knowing their chances of making successful landfall on a strange, uncharted coastline in the dark were nil, they stood off the coast to wait for daybreak. That night, a storm of hurricane force raked the channel. The storm was so fierce it sunk a 500-ton steamer en route from Buenos Aires to South Georgia with loss of all hands. Shackleton and the four crew fought the storm for nine hours, barely managing to keep the plucky James Cairn off the rocks. Finally, day broke and they made their way ashore. At last they set foot on solid ground.

But, their challenges were not over. They landed on the coast opposite the whaling station, the only manned outpost on the island. Their choices were to sail around the island, and risk being blown out to sea by the prevailing winds to certain death, or walk over the towering peaks that formed the spine of the island, something heretofore never accomplished.

And, that they did. With no proper clothing, no mountaineering equipment and no provisions, Shackleton, Worsley and decorated explorer Thomas Crean trekked, climbed, clawed and crawled across the mountains and glaciers of South Georgia Island. They made the journey in 36 hours of non-stop travel, a feat no modern mountain-climbing team has ever found easy to duplicate.

Finally, on 20 May, 1916, they staggered into the whaling camp at Stromness, to civilization, to food, to drink and, most blessedly, to heat.

After rescuing the men who were left with the James Caird all that remained was for Shackleton to sail back to Elephant Island and rescue his crew.

He immediately rallied a local sailing ship, the English owned Southern Sky, for the journey. They sailed on 23 May, 1916, but were turned back by ice 100 miles from the stranded men.

They tried again on 10 June, 1916, aboard the Uruguayan government owned survey ship Instituto de Pesca No. 1, which came within sight of Elephant Island before pack ice turned it back.

Undaunted, Shackleton traveled to Punta Arenas, Chile, and set out on 12 July, 1916, aboard the schooner Emma, chartered by the British Association. He got to within 100 miles of Elephant Island before storms and ice forced them to return.

Unwilling to give up hope for his crew, Shackleton persevered. He returned to Chile where Chilean authorities loaned the Yelcho, a small steamer, which set sail on 25 August, 1916, with Shackleton, Worsley and Crean for Elephant Island.

After 22 months of temperatures typically ranging down to -20 F / -29 C, -50 F / -46 C and lower, subsisting primarily on seal and penguin meat, living in a smoke filled hovel with nothing but seal blubber for heat, about lunchtime on 30 August, 1916, a cry arose among the shipwrecked crew of the Endurance, "Ship-O!"

Ernest Shackleton, self-made college student, self-taught mariner, self-taught Antarctic explorer, wanted nothing more than to visit the South Pole. On his second voyage to Antarctica he was within 97 miles of his goal but turned back to save the lives of his fellow explorers.

On his third voyage he was again thwarted in his quest for the pole, then endured unimaginable hardships to personally survive, ensure the survival of his crew, cross the deadliest stretch of ocean in the world in a tiny boat, cross an arctic, glacier-filled mountain range and face down repeated failures before finally rescuing his stranded crew.

Through it all, Shackleton, one of the greatest leaders of men the world has ever known, lost not a single man.

Through it all, Shackleton's crew never waivered or lost hope. They endured.

Through it all, Shackleton never waivered, never lost hope, never stopped striving. He endured.

When you are faced with challenges, daunting challenges, terrifying challenges, insurmountable challenges, remember Shackleton.

Endure.

174. Art

Art initiates thought.

A work of art that does nothing but initiate reaction, that is designed to provoke, does not meet this test. It is simply juvenile.

Art causes you to think, and by thinking, to broaden your mind, your being and your life.

175. The Biggest Fear

"There is nothing with which every man is so afraid as getting to know how enormously much he is capable of doing and becoming." – Søren Kierkegaard.

Nothing is more intimidating than knowing that you are capable of doing and accomplishing anything you set out to do. But, being intimidated does not change that fact. How much of your life is controlled by your fears of what you are capable of accomplishing but are too afraid to try?

176. The Sea

The sea is. It just is.

It will be peaceful, it will rage, it will simply be what it is, where it is, when it is.

It will do all of these things whether you or any other humans are on or under its surface.

The sea will pay you no mind. It will simply be.

177. Bad Wine

Life is too short to drink bad wine.

Bad wine is a compromise not worth making.

How many other things in your life are compromises not worth making?

178. The Money Deal Rule

Never, ever enter into a transaction or agreement regarding money or things of value with friends or family.

Break this rule at your own peril and with the knowledge that you are committing yourself to a course that almost certainly brings pain, suffering and failure.

179. Bad Writing

In the movies, no amount of special effects, ensemble acting or star power can overcome bad writing.

The same goes for your life. If you lay out a fundamentally flawed story for yourself, nothing you do will ever overcome that.

180. Robbing the Banks

Legend has it that one day in the height of the American gangster era, legendary criminal John Dillinger was walking down the sidewalk when he was approached by a young newsboy. Looking up into the stone cold killer's eyes the boy asked, "Why do you rob the banks, Mr. Dillinger?"

Dillinger looked down with eyes as lifeless and hard as ebony and replied, "Because that's where the money is, kid."

Although a flawed legend, the question was actually asked by a reporter of bank robber Willie Sutton, it is a perfect insight into a critical business and life principle. If you want money, you go where the money is.

If you want to achieve something in business or life, you must go directly where that goal lies to find it.

181. Always Abandoned

Any creative project is always abandoned, never completed.

Deadlines, new assignments, changing priorities, new interests, fresh means of creative expression or simple boredom determine that any creative project is never completed, always abandoned.

For a creative person, there will always be a little bit more, a further improvement or some additional content they would add to a project, if only they had more time and energy to invest in it or were not being pulled away onto the next endeavor.

It is important to learn to release a past creative work and allow yourself to move on to the next challenge without being haunted by feelings of incompletion.

Instead, strive to continually raise the level of creative completion for each of your projects. If you consistently raise your level of creative completion in your work your sense of satisfaction and fulfillment will rise with each project. That will enable you to step away from your projects feeling fulfilled instead of frustrated.

182. Going Through the Day

You can go through your day happy or unhappy, but either way, you are going through the day.

Happy is a lot less stress, less work and a lot more fun.

183. The Magic Number

"Financial independence is achieved by reaching your magic number." – Dave Waugh.

The magic number is the total of your investments when they produce sufficient annual after-tax income to support your desired lifestyle.

The magic number is easy to calculate and very possible to achieve. By having a specific number to work toward, financial independence becomes an achievable goal, a defined target.

If you don't have a magic number, you will spend your life chasing amorphous visions that you think represent freedom and wealth, meanwhile never achieving either.

Calculate your magic number and go achieve it.

184. Seven Words

A good billboard has seven words or less. The modern world moves very quickly, like cars on a freeway. People have less and less time to invest in anything, including you.

Learn how to express your thoughts and ideas succinctly. Express your fundamental concepts like a billboard, in seven words or less.

185. Hummingbirds

You will attract more hummingbirds to a feeder with honey water than with vinegar.

The same is true of life.

If you display a positive attitude and outlook you will attract many more positive, enjoyable people and experiences to your life than if you boil with negativity, disdain and bitterness.

Fill your feeder with sweetness.

186. Saving the Good China

Most people spend their life saving the good china. They never use it, even for special occasions, because there might be an even more special occasion in the future.

What, exactly, are you saving the good china of your life for? Get out the special things and use them, enjoy them and celebrate them.

This day, every day, is the special occasion you've been waiting for.

187. Anger Motivation

Anger is often used as a motivational tool. You can amplify your energy by channeling your anger into your activities.

However, anger motivation is not sustainable. It is caustic and will erode you from within, leaving you a hollow, bitter shell.

Understand where your motivation comes from and ensure that it is not from anger.

188. Living on the Edge

Living on the edge, financially, legally, emotionally or physically is extremely addicting – more so than any drug.

And, as always, addicts cluster, they seek each other out and form mutually reinforcing communities of addiction. It is very, very challenging to break out of the cycle of addiction once embedded in a group of like addicts.

Do you enjoy the rush of living on the edge? Are you addicted? Is it distorting your life, altering your decision-making criteria? Is it affecting your work, your relationships?

Know your addictions well.

189. Right Here, Right Now

When you travel, each place, destination, neighborhood, city and country you visit offers different things. One may feature beautiful landscapes, another energetic cities, another excellent cuisine, another interesting people, another amazing adventures and another exotic cultures.

If you arrive in a destination that features an energetic and dynamic urban experience and spend all of your time pining for a previous area's peaceful river, you will miss the available experience.

It is critical to be open to, to recognize, be aware of and take advantage of what your current situation offers you. If it is long hikes in the mountains, so be it. If it is noisy, chaotic markets, so be it. If it is long conversations over strong coffee, so be it. Look around you, appreciate where you are and what it has to offer and experience that. Right here, right now.

The same goes for your life. Each chapter of your life has different things to offer. If you spend all of your time longing for a past chapter or anticipating a future one, you completely miss what your current chapter can give. Live your life right here, right now.

190. Turning Off the Servers

I once had a high technology business, and like all technology businesses, the heart of the operation was the bank of servers (specially architected computers).

The servers ran the computer programs that enabled the business's operations, e.g., financial, email, database, file storage and other systems. The servers were housed in a special room, with dedicated power, heating and cooling systems. We didn't have to do much with them unless there was a problem. Otherwise, they just hummed along, the heartbeat of the business.

Eventually that business was destroyed by the people I trusted the most. The process and experience were painful beyond description, and very emotionally wrenching. Finally, the day came when the business completely and finally shut down. The defining moment was when I walked into the server room and shut down the servers. One by one, I turned off the core functions of the business, and when the last server power light blinked out, the business I started, 12 years before on my kitchen table, was dead.

Shutting off those servers was one of the most painful, difficult and gut-wrenching things I'd ever done. But I had to do it, I needed to be the one. It was very important that I personally face the symbolic and physical end of the business. If I had simply told my technician to turn them off, I would never have fully processed all the thoughts and feelings associated with the end of that chapter of my life.

There will be times when you will have your own servers that need to be turned off in your life. You won't want to be the one to turn them off. The thought of it will chill you to the bone and you will doubt you have the emotional strength for the task. But it is critical that you, personally, do the job.

Your servers will take many forms, e.g., jobs, relationships and neighborhoods, but they will all be equally challenging. Don't delegate the task. Turn off your own servers.

191. Architecture

Architecture elevates the quality of life.

Compare a city or neighborhood with creative, dynamic, inspiring architecture to one without it and imagine living and working there every day.

A visually stimulating environment facilitates thought and creativity.

192. A Culture of Excellence

If you want to experience or achieve excellence in your life then you must cultivate and demand a culture of excellence. This means you must surround yourself, personally and professionally, with excellent people, systems, environments and experiences.

You will never experience or achieve excellence while mired in mediocrity.

193. The Blow

"The blow that does not land is the same as a blow that was never thrown." – Martial arts principle related by Bob Gramling.

The origin of this maxim is martial arts but it also applies to emotional, verbal and psychological conflict. If you sidestep a blow, it is as if it was never thrown.

In fact, the only energy expended is by the attacker. The more they throw punches that do not land, the more they exhaust themselves, while you stay strong and uninjured.

All you need to learn is how to sidestep and ignore the blows.

194. Look Them in the Eye

I have a friend who has a body language / personality quirk: he cannot look you in the eyes when he speaks to you. When you engage him in conversation he constantly averts his gaze. When you talk with him you end up feeling very uncomfortable.

The unfortunate result of his lack of eye contact is that you can never really, fully, believe him. Even if you know what he is saying is true, his lack of eye contact sends a subliminal message that if he isn't willing to look you in the eyes, then there is something untrustworthy about his message.

When you speak to people, look them directly in the eyes. It cements the bond between you and delivers your message with no caveats.

Most people have a dominant eye. That is the eye that will stay locked on you at close range. Within the first minute of conversation, identify the dominant eye, and stay locked on that target.

Look them in the eye. It will make a big difference in your ability to effectively communicate.

195. The Money Shot

In professional photography you take thousands of shots, sometimes thousands per week. Almost all of those shots never get used. Only the very rare image is used, and only the rarest of the rare is truly valuable. That is the money shot, the shot that you know will be selected by the editors, the one you know will produce revenue, the one that could change your career and your life.

To succeed as a shooter, when you see an opportunity for a money shot coming, you must have the training, skills, abilities, resources and timing to capture it.

In your life you will have thousands, millions, billions of experiences. A very, very select few will be money shots. Be ready for them.

196. Risk. Reward.

"I have too deeply enjoyed the voyage not to recommend to any [person] to *take all chances*... he will meet with no difficulties or dangers (excepting in rare cases) nearly so bad as he before hand imagined... the effect ought to be, to teach him good humored patience, unselfishness, the habit of acting for himself, and of making the best of everything... at the same time he will discover how many truly good-natured people there are... ready to offer him the most disinterested assistance." – Charles Darwin. The last entry in his diary of the five year research and charting circumnavigation voyage on H.M.S. Beagle.

Charles Darwin was a disinterested, failed medical student on the verge of seeking refuge in his last career option, the clergy, when he was offered the position as naturalist on the research voyage of the H.M.S. Beagle in 1831.

He was 22 years old and at a critical juncture of his life. If he took the voyage he would return at age 27 with no further career prospects and terminally, fatally behind his peers for any opportunities. Taking the voyage could literally mean the end of his professional life before it even began. Taking the voyage was the biggest possible risk.

There is no meaningful, positive or lasting reward in life without risk. If you never take a risk, you will never know reward.

Take all chances. Take a risk.

Only then will you know reward.

197. Life Will Find a Way

No matter how harsh the environment - bare, windblown rock; dry desert; frozen landscape; boiling lava vent at the bottom of the ocean - you will always find life.

Life will always find a way. Always.

198. Occam's Razor

Colloquially, the rule is, "All things being equal, the simplest solution is the best." Even more colloquially, the rule is, "Keep it simple, stupid (KISS)."

The term razor refers to shaving away all the unnecessary components, theories, ideas and alternatives to arrive at the simplest possible solution.

Avoid needless complications. Keep it simple.

Background: The principle is often expressed in Latin as the lex parsimoniae ("law of parsimony" or "law of succinctness"): "entia non sunt multiplicanda praeter necessitatem", or "Entities should not be multiplied beyond necessity."

The principle is attributed to the 14th-century English logician and Franciscan friar William of Ockham. The principle states that the explanation of any phenomenon should make as few assumptions as possible, eliminating those that make no difference in the observable predictions of the explanatory hypothesis or theory. In his Summa Totius Logicae, i. 12, Ockham cites the principle of economy, "Frustra fit per plura quod potest fieri per pauciora." [It is folly to do with many what can be done with few.]

199. Love is Out There

Love is out there, everywhere. It's everywhere around you. It's in everything and everyone in your world.

All you need to do is learn to sense it, learn to see it, learn to identify it and learn how to tap into it.

200. If It's Worth Doing

"If it's worth doing, it's worth doing well." – American folk wisdom.

When doing anything you will make a fundamental choice: a) do it right, or b) do it sloppy, slipshod, slapdash or in other words, do as little as you can get away with.

If you choose the latter, your life will be filled with misfortune and negative consequences, for everything you do will not be done well. But even worse, it will not be done as well as you could have done it. You will not be living up to your potential, which is the premier mortal sin. You will always have that nagging worry or rhythmic fear of what your life could have been if only you had tried your best.

If you choose the former, your life will be filled with contentment because you will always know that, no matter what, you gave it your best shot; you always gave your best effort.

201. The Cup of Tea

Ask an experienced, ocean veteran sailor what they do when they've got a problem with their boat and they will probably reply, "Have a cup of tea and think it over."

When you've got a problem or challenge, unless it's an existential emergency, sit down and think about it before trying to solve it. Have a cup of tea or a cup of coffee, put your feet up and think through the situation. What are your available resources? What is your timeline? What are your alternatives for addressing the challenge(s)?

If your boat of life is sinking, you must immediately plug the leak, but short of that, before diving in and flailing about, take some time to think about the situation you are in and how to best overcome your challenge(s).

202. Saving the Town

"You can't save the whole town." – Gary DuBois.

After hurricane Katrina, we were in Mississippi doing relief work, working from first light to last light, cutting fallen trees out of people's homes and property. I was working feverishly and growing short tempered with any perceived delay in our progress through the devastated neighborhoods.

One afternoon I was near exhaustion when our friend who was working with us, Gary DuBois, told me, "Doug, you can't save the whole town." And he was right.

There were millions of trees down in tens of thousands of homes across the state. Where we were working, in the Gulfport area, there were countless thousands. My chain saw and I could not save the whole town.

Be aware of your resources and abilities in whatever situation you are in. Choose a realistic goal and pace yourself accordingly.

203. The List

When you are feeling overwhelmed, write down the list of the challenges, tasks and responsibilities that are troubling you. Get things out of your head and onto paper and they will instantly become less intimidating, less overwhelming, less stressful and less powerful.

204. Step Up into the Life Raft

In the book and movie, *The Perfect Storm*, a sailboat was caught in the storm. Its crew, certain they will die, put out a radio Mayday call for rescue. A U.S. Coast Guard rescue team was dispatched into the teeth of the howling winds. After a heroic rescue, in which all lives were at high risk, the sailboat crew was saved.

A few days later the sailboat was found, in good condition, completely seaworthy.

The sailboat crew, like most humans under stress, panicked much too early.

They were in an unfamiliar situation, frightened and under duress. They decided that nearly drowning in the stormy seas and being plucked from the towering waves by a bucking, rocking Coast Guard helicopter with a cable that could catch in the boat's rigging and cause a crash that killed everyone, was preferable to riding out the storm in a perfectly safe sailboat.

The crew bailed out long before it was warranted, and in the process, nearly killed the Coast Guard rescue team as well as themselves.

They violated one of the primary rules of sailing: step up into the life raft. In other words, you never abandon a perfectly good sailboat. You don't step *down* into the life raft off the sailboat's rail. You wait until the boat sinks out from under you. Then, you step *up* into the life raft.

At some points in your life you will be in unfamiliar, scary, very challenging situations. You may be terrified of the unknown that awaits you, you may be under extreme duress and you will probably be suffering extreme stress. It is essential in those situations to remain steady on your course. Do not panic. Do not call Mayday. Ride out the storm.

Do not abandon your boat until it sinks out from under you. Then, step *up* into the life raft.

205. A Single Living Thing

When we were traveling in the Himalayas we learned that strict Buddhists believe in life so strongly they strive to live in a way that will not kill a single living thing. We found this very interesting and tried to adopt that philosophy during our travels there.

The next time you are on a walk or a hike through the countryside, try stepping over the bugs instead of squashing them.

When you are home, try shooing a fly out the door instead of swatting it.

The more you try it, the more you will come to understand how difficult that challenge, to live a life that will not kill a single living thing, is to weave into your everyday life.

But, if you try it, you will learn much from the process.

206. Adulthood

You know you are an adult when you wash your hands even when no one else is watching.

Adulthood is about taking responsibility for yourself, your choices and the resulting consequences.

207. Close to the Goal

The closer to the goal you get, the tougher the challenges become. The continuously escalating level of challenges can be very daunting and the process frustrating.

But, if you persevere and achieve your goal by overcoming the challenges, regardless of their level of difficulty, you will accomplish a goal that is uniquely yours. That unique reward is something no one will ever be able to take from you – self-confidence.

208. Dangerous Tasks

When facing a dangerous task, stop and think through, to the end, what you are about to do.

Think about each step of the process. Visualize in your head exactly what you are going to do and how you are going to do it.

Think through all your options if something goes wrong. Know exactly what you will do for each eventuality.

Focus your attention solely on the task.

Then, and only then, proceed with the task.

209. The Marketing Building

During my career I had the opportunity to work with some of the world's largest companies. While engaged on projects I often worked with or interacted with their marketing departments.

These departments employed the best educated, most thoroughly trained and well-seasoned marketing professionals in the world. To build their marketing programs, the marketing departments utilized the most advanced computer models, the most extensive human behavior research, the most comprehensive market testing and the most encompassing focus groups available.

The marketing departments employed hundreds to thousands of employees and usually had not a floor, or a wing, but an entire building. In fact, they usually had multiple buildings in various locations around the world.

They were, in effect, a marketing army whose sole mission was to create in every consumer the perception of need for their product or service.

You, as an individual, are helpless in the face of their sophisticated onslaught. They know your behavior, they know your motivations and they know, intimately, how to push your buttons. You will never, ever be able to resist their temptations.

There is only one defense: turn off your television.

210. 100 Hour Pilots

The most dangerous pilot is not a rookie. Rookies are very careful about following procedure and, if anything, are usually overly cautious.

The most dangerous pilot is not a grizzled veteran. While a veteran may know which procedures can be marginalized and when it is possible to do so, they only became grizzled veterans by applying that knowledge with discretion.

The most dangerous pilots are those with about 100 flight hours. At that point they've passed through the stage of rookie terror and now feel very confident that they know what they are doing. Pilots with about 100 flight hours top the charts of fatal pilot errors.

The same is true in life. The most dangerous time is when you begin to feel very confident that you know what you are doing.

211. A Day Without Work

Try to go through a day without a conversation relating to your work or anyone else's work. Then, try to go through a day without a conversation about your children or your religion or whatever your favorite, dominant topics are. Next try to go through a week without talking about those things in conversation.

Broaden your interests and your knowledge until it is a normal part of your life to converse with others about meaningful things, things other than the topics that typically dominate conversation.

212. My Favorite Baseball Game

One summer afternoon, sometime in the mid-80s, we were sitting around the kitchen table at my friend Floyd's place. It was the 2nd story of a typical Chicago brick three flat in Wrigleyville. The back door was open, the flies were buzzing around the screen door and the rattling, clattering, dull roar of the L trains paced the afternoon as they rumbled by along the elevated tracks that ran down the alley. It was hot and the wind was absolutely still. The curtains hung listlessly, and our attempts to conjure up a breeze by opening every window in the place were fruitless. It was a classic August afternoon in Chicago – "cooler near the lake."

We spent the day chatting about work, people we knew, all the stories of the day and the stories from our past. Attenuated by the heat and humidity, the tone was quiet, punctuated by soft laughter as we shared a common memory. During a lull, we suddenly heard a distinctive sound, a sound that could only come at that time, in that place, in that season. It was a sound that was distinctively American, distinctively Chicago, distinctively north side and distinctively of that era and no other. It was the sound of "A one, a two…" followed by 30,000 people singing "Take Me Out to the Ballgame," led – if you could ever use that term in reference to his singing – by Harry Caray.

We sat transfixed, as the lyrics echoed through the neighborhood. We didn't utter a sound until the last note had faded away, melting into a passing L train.

It is one of my favorite all time baseball memories, and of the dozens of Cub games I attended, that game remains my favorite, even though I wasn't even there.

Sometimes, if you are open to them, the best experiences aren't direct experiences at all.

213. Show Up For Your Life

When Michael J. Fox achieved fame and stardom he lost himself in the typical celebrity swamp of wealth, fame, adulation, alcohol and intoxicants. His life spiraled down until he hit rock bottom.

When he asked what he should do a trusted advisor responded simply, "Show up for your life."

Many of us, even the non-superstar celebrities, slide through our lives just going through the motions. We do what we need to do to survive, and otherwise just float down the river of life, bouncing off of rocks and tumbling over rapids as we encounter them.

Like Michael J. Fox, we are not really involved in our lives, we are passive, just letting it happen.

But, to really live your life, to fully experience what life is all about and what it has to offer, we must show up for our life. We must be a pro-active participant in our life.

Don't just let your life happen.

Show up for your life.

214. Better Than This

While in the Middle East we visited a beautiful small island along the eastern Mediterranean. The views were exquisite, the weather was perfect and the food incredible. As we sat staring out at the scene, our friend, Kemal Ertem, turned to us and said, "Better than this, an apricot in Damascus." It was the traditional Turkish and Middle Eastern way to say, "It doesn't get any better than this."

A few weeks later we visited Damascus and wandered through the local market. Along the way we tasted some apricots. Sure enough, they were the best apricots we had ever tasted, anywhere in the world.

Life has much to offer, including moments, places, people and experiences that are truly the best the world, and this life, have to offer.

Never settle for a life that does not include those moments, places, people and experiences. While you are alive, taste and experience the best the world and this life have to offer.

Strive to discover and savor the moments, places, people and experiences that deserve the phrase, "Better than this, an apricot in Damascus."

215. Time

Time is an artificial construct introduced into the world by merchants and bureaucrats to make their lives more convenient and the lives of the masses easier to regulate. Before the rise of the merchant class, time, as we know it, did not exist.

In agrarian societies, people rose with the sun, worked while it was light and went to sleep when it was dark. The merchants and traders lived by the same rhythm.

Surplus food production enabled the expansion of a newly dominant merchant and governing class. When technology produced a somewhat reliable clock, the merchants and governing classes imposed it, overlaid it, on the sun-regulated life of humans.

Artificial light, first by torch, later by lantern and finally by electricity, now extends the day from before sunrise to long after sunset. Indeed, in many places and in many societies, the natural day is completely irrelevant.

Interestingly, patterns of disease incidence and states of adverse health correlate to these historical developments and to areas of strongly non-natural day cycles.

Time, and being ruled by the clock - the need to be somewhere and doing something at a specific time - have introduced sustained and endless levels of high anxiety and stress into human existence.

Try de-coupling your life from the clock. Try rising with the sun and resting with the dark for a few weeks and see how you feel.

Never forget that time is artificial.

216. Spending Your Life

Go down to the bank and get a roll of 100 pennies. Put them in a bowl on your counter. Whenever you want, take out a penny and spend it on something or just throw it away.

In a few days or weeks, the bowl will be empty.

Now imagine that bowl is your life and the pennies were how you spent it.

If you had it to do over again, would you spend your life differently?

217. The Blues

At some point in your life you will have the blues. You will be low, down and depressed. You will feel like there is no reason to carry on, and little to live for.

During those times it is very important to remember that this, too, is a chapter in your life. It is important to remember that there are things to learn from this chapter, things to take away, things to make part of yourself.

But, most importantly, you must remember that, given perseverance and fortitude, this time will pass.

When you have the blues, keep yourself active and physically exercise – for most people it is as, or more, effective than pharmaceutical treatment. When you are feeling low, give yourself permission to change, give yourself permission to release old interests or passions and move on. When you are feeling depressed, turn away from the past and look to the future, seeking new paths, new discoveries and new purposes.

At some point in your life, you will have the blues. Don't become a permanent member of the blues tribe. It is a very seductive and self-reinforcing tribe, and very difficult to separate yourself from once integrated.

Give it some time. The blues will pass.

218. Keep Pushing

There will be times in your life when not much, if anything, is going right. It will seem that everything you touch turns to dust. It will seem that everything you try to accomplish is thwarted. It will seem that even the simplest goals become complex, challenging and difficult.

In those times, keep your head down, your shoulder to the wheel and keep pushing forward. Push on through and eventually those times will turn.

219. Problem vs. Inconvenience

"This steak is well done!" Charlie yelled across the restaurant.

Everyone at the table stopped talking and looked at him.

"Waiter, get over here! I told you medium! M-e-d-i-u-m," Charlie spelled out, speaking the letters loudly as the waiter scurried over and took the plate, offering apologies.

"I don't want your apologies! I want my steak!" Charlie yelled back, the entire restaurant now paused in near silence.

The old man in the sales force leaned into the table and said evenly, "Charlie, your problem is you don't know the difference between a problem and an inconvenience."

Charlie turned toward him, his faced still flushed from his outburst.

"Oh yeah? Is that so? Well, I'm telling you that a well-done steak is a problem!" Charlie retorted, rising to the challenge.

Charlie was less than half the senior salesman's age. Charlie was a new guy, and didn't even know the old man's name, much less anything about him.

The old man reached down and unbuttoned his shirt sleeve. None of the other salespeople had ever seen as much as a thread out of place on the always impeccably dressed old man, much less a button undone. They all stared, silent, not knowing what would happen next between the most experienced salesman in the company's history and the brash but high-performing young upstart.

The old man never unlocked his eyes from Charlie's as he rolled up his sleeve. He stood up in his chair, leaned across the table and stuck his forearm in Charlie's face. The tattooed numbers were less than six inches from Charlie's nose.

The old man said forcefully, "Your steak is an inconvenience." He pointed to his Nazi death camp identification number and said coldly, "This is a problem."

Never lose sight of the difference between an inconvenience in life and a genuine problem.

220. The Haitian Taxi Driver

It was a dark, clear night as I climbed into the taxi at Miami International airport. I gave the driver the address and we headed for the coast.

As we rode along we chatted about current events, then I asked him about his background.

He grew up in Haiti, the poorest country in the Caribbean and one of the poorest in the world, and taught himself tailoring. He worked his way up to owning a small tailor shop, but could see that for his small family and young child, life opportunities would always lie elsewhere - across the water.

He saved up enough money to buy his passage on a ship. Along the way, he and the rest of the passengers nearly died of thirst and were eventually abandoned at sea by the crew. The ship broke up, but he made it to the beach; most did not.

He arrived dripping wet, with not a dime in his pockets after being robbed by the ship's crew. He was a black man, who spoke not a single word of English, standing on a beach in Florida. His prospects were dim, but he had belief in himself and a purpose: his family back in Haiti.

He found menial work and studied English at night by a single bulb in his squalid sleeping quarters. He slowly saved money and brought his wife and child over. His wife found menial work the first day ashore. They both worked two jobs, then three, as their children multiplied and grew. They did whatever it took, on their own, to build a future and a family.

In the end, their three children all went to college. All three earned college bachelor degrees and two were, at that very moment, working on masters degrees.

In all that time, through all their struggles, the family had never once asked for or received a single penny from any government or non-government program. They earned it all, every penny, every step along the way.

As we pulled up to my hotel, I complimented the driver on his beautifully tailored vest and shirt.

"Oh, I still do some tailoring in my spare time," he replied, smiling.

The next time you think about how your life is tough or hear someone complaining that the government or charities should do more for them, give them more, make life easier for them, remember the Haitian taxi driver. And, remember his three children.

221. The Starfish

Two friends were walking along the beach the morning after a big storm.

As they walked along one occasionally stopped to pick up and toss back into the ocean one of the hundreds of starfish surrounding them that had been washed up by the storm.

"What are doing that for?" asked his friend. "There must be thousands of them. Throwing them back is a waste of time."

"Not to this one," his friend replied as he tossed another starfish back into the surf.

Anything you can do to make the world a better place, no matter how small and seemingly insignificant, is the right thing to do.

222. Righteous Indignation

Righteous indignation is never righteous, it is just indignation. It is almost always pompous, sanctimonious and arrogant.

If you find yourself caught up in righteous indignation, stop and take a very close look at what you are saying and how you are saying it.

223. Either Way, It's OK

One day I was sitting at the dinner table coughing and my wife expressed concern about my health.

"Look," I replied, "either this thing will kill me or it won't. Either way, it's OK."

I wasn't trying to give her a flip answer, I was trying to be truthful.

At some point you need to face your own mortality. If you spend your entire life running from your fear of death, then you will experience only a tiny fraction of what life has to offer.

To fully experience and enjoy life, you must come to terms with your own death. It will happen. It is inevitable.

The day you come to terms with the end of your life is, in many ways, your first day of life.

224. Why Me?

There will be times in your life when bad things happen. There will be times in your life when you are faced with what you think are insurmountable challenges.

Those are the times you will most likely ask, "Why me?"

At those times, instead, ask, "Why not me?"

225. The Lee Shore

In sailing, the land that lies downwind of you, in the path of the wind, is your lee shore. The space between you and the lee shore is your leeway. If you don't allow enough leeway, and something bad happens, you can get blown onto the rocks of the lee shore.

Life also has lee shores. It is very, very important to maintain sufficient leeway when you are passing through a stage of life when the prevailing winds are blowing you towards a dangerous reef and rock-studded lee shore.

Do not allow others to sell you on the upsides of the thrills and adrenaline inherent in sailing the boat of your life closely along a lee shore. Like rats, they will jump ship to save themselves, while you will not have that choice.

Maintain sufficient leeway in life.

226. Winning

Winning in life has very little to do with chance and almost everything to do with how much you expect to win, how much you envision yourself winning.

If you find yourself consistently losing, closely examine how you perceive yourself and what type of future you envision for yourself.

Create and project a model, a vision of yourself as a winner.

Winning will follow.

227. Visiting Santa Clause

When children are young they can be very excited about going to visit Santa Clause. They will talk about it for days or weeks, nearly bursting with anticipation. While standing in line they chatter endlessly about seeing Santa, sitting on his lap and telling him their entire wish list for Christmas. Their eyes glitter with delight as they get to the front of the line, and their smiles broaden as they realize their time will be soon.

But, when they reach the front of the line and see the big man dressed in red motioning them forward, the children often burst into tears and scream in abject terror at the thought of this giant, bearded stranger holding them.

For the children, the concept of Santa Clause is one thing and the reality is quite another.

This is true of many things in life. Whether it is a new relationship, a new job, a new location or a radical change of lifestyle; the dream, the concept is one thing, and the reality of the choice is quite another. Be certain you are making life decisions based on the reality of a choice, not the concept of a choice.

228. Patrol Your Boundaries

It is critical to establish and patrol your life's boundaries. A boundary that is marked but not patrolled, not enforced, becomes laughable. It becomes a negative rather than a positive.

Boundaries can be functional, such as enforcing a no-smoking ban in your home, or emotional, such as not allowing others to manipulate you in specific ways.

In whatever form, it is essential to clearly mark your boundaries and rigorously enforce them.

If you don't, others will simply force you to live by their boundaries, not your own.

229. Tests

You will face many tests in life. Some you will pass and some you will fail.

As long as you maintain perspective about them and don't let them destroy your self-image, you will learn more from those you fail. They will lead to your greatest improvements, most significant self-growth and to your life's most meaningful experiences.

230. Play to Your Strengths

You can spend your life wasting energy by taking on challenges to which you are not well suited. If you are vertically challenged, it doesn't make a lot of sense to get frustrated because you are not starting on the basketball team.

Identify your strengths and match your challenges to them.

231. Sculpture

Additive sculpture, such as creating a sculpture by adding bits of clay to form the shape, is readily understandable.

But subtractive sculpture, such as chiseling away a block of marble to reveal David, is more challenging to comprehend.

It all comes down to removing what doesn't belong.

All of us have a potential Michelangelo's David with our lives. All we have to do is remove what doesn't belong.

What in your life doesn't belong?

232. Avoiding Mr. Meis

In my high school, the most feared class was Mr. Meis's English. He was a strict hard liner from the old school of instruction. He graded ruthlessly and everyone, bar none, worked hard to pass, much less to earn a good grade.

He taught English grammar via sentence construction and architecture, with a strict method of illustrating the components of sentences. You could fail a test just by slightly misaligning a clause dangling below the subject.

Mr. Meis was rigid, and granted no quarter to athletes, beauties or brainiacs. He was an equal opportunity killer of GPA. Everyone, regardless of tribe, dreaded his class, which was unavoidable in order to graduate.

Unavoidable to all, that is, except me.

Being rather clever in my high school years, I devised a way, through detailed and persistent study of the graduation requirements, to earn enough required credits in enough required areas of study to qualify for graduation without taking a single class from Mr. John Meis. I thought I was quite the brilliant one, never having to sweat out a single quiz or test in Meis's northeast corner classroom. Little did I know.

Figuring out a way to avoid the brutally hard work of a John Meis English class was the stupidest thing I've ever done in my entire life. John Meis instilled in every single one of his students deeply-seated knowledge of the structure of the English language. He required, and thus created, discipline and dogged perseverance in his students. He set high standards and, as a consequence, his students learned that they indeed had the ability to work hard and climb those heights. Not only did they earn their grades, and intimately learn the English language, even more importantly, they earned a true measure of confidence and accomplishment.

What did I learn? I learned nothing. What did I earn? I earned nothing. I came away with a lifetime deficit in the grammar and structure of the English language that I have worn like a millstone every day since. I have worked 10 times as hard to learn 10 percent of what John Meis would have taught me had I been just a little less clever.

Be very careful about finding ways to avoid the challenging parts of life. Your short term gain can easily turn into a lifetime of deficit.

233. Once in Your Life

At least one time in your life

- Win, and be part of a winning team
- Lose, and be part of a losing team
- Earn an award
- Be the best there is at something
- Be lonely, in complete solitude
- Be surrounded by loving friends and family

- Do a project to full completion, with absolutely no compromises; make it as good as it can possibly be
- Change your mind about something meaningful
- Love another person 150 percent
- Go on an adventure
- Travel overseas
- Learn about yourself
- Teach yourself a new skill and a new subject
- Be scared
- Be content
- Create something new

And always, throughout your entire life, remain curious.

234. Always One Person

The automobile, the light bulb, the X-Ray, the telephone, the airplane, whatever innovation or invention you can name, they all started with one person. Everything, from the first arrowhead to the latest scientific breakthrough, all began with one person's curiosity, innovation and perseverance.

Everything begins with one person.

You can be that person.

Relationships

235. Opportunities and Relationships

Almost every opportunity in life is related to a human relationship. This is why the relationships you form, the context of those relationships, the venues of those relationships and the nature of those relationships can largely determine your fate.

236. Twenty Minutes

"It takes about 20 minutes to get married. There's no need to be in a hurry." - Earl Watson, Sr.

Take your time when you are thinking about marriage. The actual ceremony is pretty quick, but the implications and the commitment last a lifetime.

237. What I Don't Like About You

What we find most irritating about other people are often things we don't like about ourselves.

238. A Little Bit More

"If I only love them a little bit more things will be OK," is the classic quote from a spouse of an alcoholic, an adult child of alcoholics (ACOA), or an addictive personality (drugs, gambling, etc.). The spouse falls into the trap of believing they have some ability to influence, help or cure the problem just by being more understanding, more supportive or more loving.

Unfortunately, loving the alcoholic, ACOA or addict a little bit more does not help, it only makes things worse. It encourages them to continue their ways, it facilitates their behavior and it deepens the eventual and inevitable pain when it all comes to an end.

There is no way anything can change for a spouse in this situation other than the person with the problem acknowledging and addressing it. No amount of love from you will change that fact.

239. The Story

When relationships break up each person develops their version of events which becomes "The Story." For a long-term relationship, the story will usually endure for two or three years.

If the person is mature and psychologically healthy, they will eventually change the story to more accurately reflect reality. This happens when they begin articulating the mutual roles in the breakup, in other words, they recognize each person's part of the breakup and take responsibility and ownership for their own contributions.

If a person never reaches the point of maturity or psychological health, they will carry "The Story" to their grave.

240. Extending Relationships

When relationships end it is common for one or both of the parties to generate ongoing conflicts.

People who initiate, maintain and cultivate ongoing conflict with past friends, lovers and spouses do so to extend the relationship. They are not ready to let the relationship end. They extend the relationship via conflict.

It is not about the conflict, real or imagined. It is about extending the relationship in the only way they have left. Regardless of what the combatant says about how they feel, look closely at their actions and you will see that they are not ready to say goodbye.

Only when they heal, recover, grow or mature enough will the conflict, and the relationship, end.

241. Three Years

It takes people about three years to fully recover from the end of a meaningful relationship. Don't expect to recreate or form a mature, healthy, long-term relationship before this period of grieving, healing and recovery has completed.

242. Net Negative People

You will always have a wide variety of people in your life. Each of those people will bring some positives and negative attributes. Each will have strengths and weaknesses.

It is very important to make an objective evaluation of the people in your life, in your relationships, in your social circle and especially your work environment. Then, use that objective evaluation to understand when their positives and negatives add up to a negative number.

Someone may be a lot of fun at social events, but be completely irresponsible financially. Someone may be a huge help working on your car, but be a raging alcoholic. An employee may be extremely valuable for a particular function, but be a boiling pot of negativity and conflict. Each of these people is a net negative, the sum of their positive and negative attributes results in a negative value.

You must, without exception, remove net negative people from your life. You must do this regardless of the short-term pain, inconveniences or consequences, because if you don't, the long-term consequences are always very negative for you.

243. People and Their Baggage

Everyone comes with baggage. Some come with a matched set. Some come with a full cartload.

Be sure you know what you're getting into. Dealing with a bag or two in a relationship is one thing, managing an entire baggage warehouse is quite another.

244. Finding Relationships

If you are interested in finding someone for a relationship, then do what you enjoy doing. When you meet someone along the way, you will already have that in common.

Be yourself, and those who you meet while doing so will know what and who you are, and vice versa.

245. Enduring Relationships

People change over time. As a direct result, relationships change over time. The relationship you have today will not exist tomorrow because in those 24 hours, you will both change.

The true test of a relationship is weathering those changes, not the initial attraction, things you have in common or shared experiences. The only enduring relationships are adaptive, flexible relationships.

246. Marrying the Parents

When considering marrying someone, pay very close attention to their parents.

Parents are, in normal circumstances, the largest and most important influence on a person's life. Your potential spouse is imprinted and indoctrinated in the methods and coping mechanisms their parents taught them for communication, problem solving and other life skills. Your beloved is steeped in a particular life view and world perspective, even if they are currently rebelling against it with all of their might.

People, to a large extent, turn into their parents. If you can't stand the parent, then you probably won't think much of your spouse in a few decades, if not a few years.

247. One Set for Another

If you are unhappy in a relationship and think you will solve all the problems by swapping one person for another, you need to keep in mind that all you will be doing is trading one set of issues for another.

All people have issues, problems and challenges. If you leave one person for another person, you are merely leaving one set of issues, problems and challenges and taking on another set.

248. The Three Most Important Words

The three most important words in a relationship are not "I love you," they are "I am sorry."

It is easy to profess love for another in a casual, offhand manner or a meaningful, heartfelt way.

It is much more difficult to take responsibility for your actions and express genuine remorse.

When you make a mistake in a relationship, be it a big mistake or small, say the three most important words, "I am sorry."

249. People Don't Change

By the time people become adults, they are, for better or worse, who they are.

Once people become adults they are very unlikely to change in any fundamental way. They may make a few alterations around the periphery, or temporarily alter some behavior to buy short-term peace in a relationship, but they very, very rarely make changes in the fundamental aspects of their character, values or personality.

If you are basing a relationship decision on an assumption or a hope that your potential partner will, or even may, change, you should rethink things.

In general, people, especially adults, don't change.

Children

250. The Second Toughest Job

Parenting is the second toughest job you will ever take on. The toughest is marriage.

If you want to be a successful parent, then focus first on being a successful spouse. Keep your marriage strong, vital, growing and evolving, and you'll more than quadruple your chances to be an effective parent.

251. A New Tractor

When I was about eight I went to my grandparent's farm with my mother. My grandparents were both at work and my mother was busy all day canning garden tomatoes.

I was bored and wanted to drive the lawn mower around. I convinced my mother that I knew how to move the big tractor out of the way so I could get the lawn mower out. Unfortunately, the big tractor had a different shift pattern than the little tractor I'd been trained to drive on, so instead of selecting reverse, I selected first, dumped the clutch and proceeded to drive the big tractor through the machine shed door.

That was bad, but what was worse was my mother making me call my grandfather to tell him what I'd done.

After confirming with my mother that I was not hurt and hearing my story, sputtered out between sobs, he said, "We can always buy a new tractor, but we can't buy a new grandson."

Remember that story every time you discipline one of your kids.

252. The United Front

Children can be the most manipulative, conniving, conspiratorial, sly and wily creatures you will ever know. Their most effective tool for achieving their goals is to divide and conquer the forces of parenting via the age old, "But mom/dad said I could" tactic.

No child can be effectively raised by divided parents. Regardless of the circumstances, you must present a united front to your children. The day you allow a child to drive a wedge between you as parents is the day you lose that child.

253. Girls and Fathers

Girls who have an interrupted, flawed, incomplete, dysfunctional, distorted, non-existent or otherwise abnormal relationship with their fathers will have psychological, behavioral, substance abuse and/or other issues as teenagers and adults.

Until they address their issues they will repeat a cycle of sabotaged, distorted, unhealthy, abusive and/or dysfunctional male, and often female, relationships.

In more than 50 years, I have never known an exception to this rule.

254. Follow Through

When I was a child I was one of many cousins. If any of the cousins was being a problem at home, becoming a problem child, there was a universal solution: a visit to the farm.

Off you'd go for a one- or two-week visit to the Hackney farm out at Amboy. While at the farm, you'd be respectful and you'd do what you were told because you knew, without a shadow of a doubt, that if there was a threatened consequence to one of your actions, that consequence was as certain as tomorrow's sunrise. As a result, you'd come back home a different child.

The key to child behavior is consequences for behavior. If you threaten a consequence, you must follow through and implement that consequence. The day you threaten a consequence and don't follow through to implement it is the day you lose that child.

255. It's All About Example

Parenting is not an abstraction. It is not high theory applied in a vacuum to a select group with a corresponding control group. Parenting does not take place in the arena of debate or intellectual discourse. Parenting does not take place by making a list of rules or a list of aphorisms and mailing them in.

In parenting, you can pontificate all you want, shout all you want, demand all you want, force all you want, espouse all you want, quote all you want, cite all you want and even beat all you want, but in the end, parenting is almost all about example.

256. Unconditional Love

Some parents feature unconditional love as the most important attribute of being a successful parent and the only parameter worth evaluating when considering the quality of a parent.

Featuring "unconditional love" as a primary, defining aspect of parenting is like an apple farmer featuring "I plant my seeds in the ground" as a primary, defining aspect of apple farming. Of course you have unconditional love for your child and of course you plant your apple seeds in the ground. It's part and parcel of the situation, it's a fundamental aspect of the relationship and it's only the first step of the job.

The first real question is: Does the farmer have the discipline, strength and character required to eliminate the weeds? For some parents the weeds are celebrated. "Look at those weeds, they are so underappreciated. They have such vigor and such improvisational skills. They have some beautiful flowers. People are so wrong to hate weeds. Look, my children are surrounded by weeds, they provide companionship and friendship to my child. My child lives in such a unique garden, unlike all the others."

Weeds choke out plants and children. Weeds require constant vigilance and a lot of work to eliminate. If any crops or children survive the weeds they will be stunted and distorted. Meanwhile, the weeds will have moved on. Do you have the discipline, strength and character to hoe the weeds out of your child's garden?

The next real question is: Does the farmer have the discipline, strength and character required to prune his young apple trees? Can he walk down the row and take a saw to his young trees? Can he cut off some of the growth so that the young sapling will grow into a strong productive tree with a long and healthy life? Many parents cannot stand for this. Every piece of their child, every manifestation of their behavior, is to be celebrated and coddled.

To build a strong apple tree or a strong child you must have the fortitude to take the saw to the young trees. You must identify the naturally strong elements of the tree and eliminate the shoots that will do nothing but suck up the nutrients required to form a strong, resilient, productive and robust adult tree.

Un-pruned trees are squat, gnarled, tangled rats' nests of malformed, stunted branches - no single or limited group of branches ever receive the required nutrients and water to grow and prosper. By letting every sprout suck the life juice out of the tree, the tree as a whole fails. If the farmer wants the sapling to grow into a strong adult tree, he must prune the sapling. Do you have the discipline, strength and character to prune your child's unnecessary sprouts?

The last real question is: Does the farmer have the discipline, strength and character required to stake, restrict and form his young apple trees? Some trees do not naturally grow straight and tall. Some, blown by strong winds or misshapen by circumstance, will bend and curl.

Can the farmer drive stakes in the ground and tie ropes to the young trees to pull them back into shape? Does the farmer have the strength and discipline to maintain those restrictive stakes and ropes, adjusting them regularly to maintain their hold, long enough for them to give those young trees a chance at a full and healthy life?

Many parents say, "No, those ropes are so restrictive, so painful to the young trees, so medieval, so choking. We will let the young trees grow however they will grow and we will celebrate them. There will be no discipline, no corrective action in our orchards."

Uncorrected, undisciplined apple trees grow into curved and stunted trees. They will never fully grow into adult trees, nor be capable of producing a full crop. Do you have the discipline, strength and character to limit and restrain your child and pull that child back into shape?

Raising apple trees isn't about planting seeds in the ground. That's the first, most fundamental part of the process, just like a parent's unconditional love for their child. Mature, psychologically healthy parents move past that stage in the first few months of parenting. Parents who are not psychologically healthy hide behind the catch phrase of "unconditional love" to hide their own inabilities or unwillingness to parent like an adult. They use the mantra "unconditional love" to hide their own lack of discipline, strength and character.

Compare two farms. The first has row upon row of healthy, productive apple trees, grown to their full potential, free of disease, producing bountiful crops of big, juicy fruit. The second is a weed-choked plot where a few scraggly, distorted, grotesque apple trees barely rise above the weeds; on each ugly tree a handful of worm-eaten, rotten apples dangle.

Both farmers planted their apple seeds in the ground. Which do you think finished the job?

257. Timing Children

Immutable law of the universe: A psychologically healthy parent always wants their child to have a better life than they did.

Think about that in the context of why you want to have children. What are your goals in having kids? Ask that question again. What, specifically, are your goals in having kids? Sit down and talk that one out a few times. Write some things down. Why do you want to have kids? Is it for you? What's in it for the child?

Think about that also in the context of when you want to have kids. If you have a child when you are just getting started in life it will be incredibly difficult to have a good life for your child, your family and yourself. It will be extremely hard to get yourself into a position where you can provide for that child and the children that may follow.

If you have a child early, what prospects does that child have for a life? Will it ever live in a home you hold a mortgage on or own? Will it always live in apartments or rental houses? What will that child wear in comparison to the other kids at school? What quality of school will that child attend? What are its prospects for special programs, summer camps, field trips, extracurricular activities? Those things may not seem important now, but they are very important later on, especially for the child that is bearing the brunt of being on the outside looking in.

Life is not all about materialism or money. In fact, the most important parts of life have nothing to do with those factors. But, the flip side of that coin is a kid who grows up "without" will, at a minimum, have a hard time relating to kids who grow up "with."

Project yourself forward 23 years. If you have a child a year from now, that would be when that child would be graduating college, ready to head out onto a life path fully equipped with all the prerequisites that society and the workplace demand. If you have a child a year from now, how would a conversation 23 years from now with that child sound? Would they be four years into working dead-end, no future jobs?

Can you, with honesty and integrity, project a future where you could give that child a decent childhood in decent neighborhoods in decent schools with a decent shot at going to college and having a better life than you did?

A psychologically healthy parent always wants their child to have a better life than they did.

258. A Responsible Child

A child that grows up with responsibility will be ready for it when they are grown. A child that has no responsibilities will be incapable of managing their life, or any aspect of it, when they reach the age of responsibility. Give your children the gift of responsibility.

259. The Knobs and Levers

As much as you'd like to, you cannot reach inside your children's heads and turn the knobs and pull the levers to make their decisions for them. No matter how clearly you can see how their life choices are leading to negative outcomes, you cannot make their choices for them.

This is especially painful for parents as their children become young adults, and particularly so when the parent knows with clarity the future that their children's choices are guaranteeing.

260. College = College

If you want your children to go to college, go yourself. A parent with a college education is the top correlation factor in first year college students.

College graduates set up an expectation of a college education throughout their children's lives. It's not an option or an afterthought, it just is what is going to happen.

Make a lifetime difference in your own life and the lives of your children. Get a degree.

261. The Lucas Light of Reality

In the post WWII era, British automobiles, especially the sports cars, were brought back in droves by returning American servicemen. They remained popular for decades, although they were all plagued by their extremely unreliable electrical components manufactured by the British firm Lucas.

The running joke was that a British car's Lucas headlight switch had three positions: dim, flicker and off.

When people become young adults, the light of life reality either comes on or it doesn't. They may spend the entire decade of their 20s, and sometimes their 30s, wandering around doing little of meaning or merit before the light of reality pops on and they suddenly realize they are 10 or 20 years behind their peers. Those people have a Lucas Light of Reality with three settings: dim, flicker and off.

Ensure that your children understand the importance of life and, most critically, the infinite value of time. Work hard to get their light of reality on fully by the end of their teenage years.

262. Bubble Children

The greatest challenge America faces is the crop of bubble children being raised by helicopter parents who hover over their children intent on removing all instances of risk from their existence.

The absence of unsupervised, free-form outdoor play is turning America's children into obese automatons devoid of the risk taking, problem solving and high energy characteristics that previous generations leveraged to build the luxurious society that now coddles them.

Their dodge-ball-less, everyone-passes, consequence-free childhoods do nothing for anyone except their parents, who seek to insulate themselves from peer group criticism should they have the audacity for their children to walk or ride their bikes to school.

What future awaits when these children become adults and their parents are no longer there to protect them from all possible negative consequences?

What awaits America is a generation of adults who have never tasted failure, never suffered rejection and never dealt with consequences.

How will they deal with the real world when they are so ill-equipped for it?

263. Children = Stress

According to multiple surveys and studies, the highest stress, least happy time in a relationship is when there are young children.

This is important to remember when you feel your marriage or your life is going to hell as your little children scream, cry and wail.

Endure. The children grow and the stress and strain lessen. The relationship can survive, but only if you are both committed to that survival.

264. Looking for Fathers

People who are abandoned by, or separated from, their fathers in their youth usually spend the rest of their lives looking in vain for one.

265. Affording Kids

If you wait until you can afford to have children, you will never have children.

266. The Twins Game

One of the most formative experiences of my childhood happened at a Minnesota Twins baseball game. I was a young boy and my father took me to a major league game at the old Metropolitan Stadium. We were sitting high up in the bleachers and the vendors were working the aisles shouting their wares, "Cold Beer!" "Hot Dogs! Get your Hot Dogs!" "Popcorn, Peanuts!" etc.

My father asked me if I wanted a drink and I replied, "Yes." Little did I know how fateful that response would be.

He handed me a dollar and pointed to a vendor climbing the stairs below us holding a soft drink aloft shouting for customers. "Go ahead," he said, "get yourself one."

The blood drained from my face. I was terrified. I didn't know how to do this. I had never conducted a retail transaction in a public place like that, especially one surrounded by several thousand shouting baseball fans.

The vendor drew nearer. I remained frozen in panic, my hand clutching the dollar, shaking.

"Go on! Get yourself a soda!" my father commanded.

Torn between fear of my father's retribution and the overwhelming unknown, I chose the only response available to me – I began to cry.

My father ripped the dollar from my grasp, raised his arm and yelled, "Pepsi!"

The vendor stopped at the end of the row and passed the cup down. My father's dollar was passed down the row in the other direction. In seconds the transaction was complete.

"Here, take it," my father said, disgust dripping through his words.

I put the cold soda down and clutched it between my feet, my falling tears adding to the condensation dribbling down its sides. I had failed. Again.

Many decades later I asked my father if he had any recollection of that day, of that transaction, one of the most traumatic moments of my life. He had none. For him it was just another day, another baseball game, another day in the bleachers.

This is a very common occurrence. Moments and experiences that are life-defining for children are just one of many thousands, many millions of moments for a parent. It is rare for the same moment to be highly significant and lifetime-memorable for both parent and child.

If you have the opportunity to be a parent, always remember that what is just another day, just another moment, just another life experience for you may be one of the most significant for your child. That moment could be their Twins Game.

267. Under the Sycamore Tree

I spent many weeks during the summer at my grandparents' farm. Typically, my grandfather and I would work on a project in the morning and break for lunch around mid-day when my grandmother called us in.

After the usual huge spread of homemade foods, we would retire outside and sit leaned up against the sycamore tree that grew in the yard. As we sat in the shade, our legs extended on the cool grass, my grandfather always had a story to tell.

It was always entertaining and always contained a moral or lesson relevant to a young boy's life, even if I didn't realize it at the time.

When you have children or grandchildren, try to create a special place and time that you share with them. Try to have your own version of our post-lunch sessions under the sycamore tree.

268. Parenthood

It is impossible to explain what it means to have children to anyone who is not a parent. "But we have a cat," they explain. "We've had our nephew, little Timmy, over a lot of times, so we know what it's about," they are quick to offer up. "We have a full grown dog, and let me tell you, she's a lot of work, what with twice-daily walks, grooming, boarding - it just never ends," they say earnestly, desperately trying to earn their way into the mysterious guild of parenthood.

But, that can never be. Until you have children, you can never really understand. Until you try to raise a child, day after day, year after year, you can never understand the joys and frustrations, the sleepless nights, the heart-busting pride, the first steps, the first words, the first recitals, the first little league hit, the first date, the first driver's license, the endless stream of daily firsts that define "parenthood."

So, think long and hard about who you will rely on in your parenting. You wouldn't turn to a family counselor who was unmarried and had no children. You wouldn't count on a spouse who was only good for conception, development and delivery.

When it comes down to the day-to-day reality of parenting, you need more than theories on conception and the ideal child, more than diaper salespeople, more than obstetricians, more than chums who are quick with advice, but short on experience.

There is no reward comparable to a well-rounded, capable, truthful, mature young adult you have raised from a child. A young adult that is a credit to their age group and a contributing member of society is the full measure of parenting success.

Parenting can be one of life's most rewarding experiences, but only if you finish the job. You must sustain the child over time to be successful.

Humans

269. The Drama Delta

Humans are hard wired for high drama. Our bodies and minds are built for a time when "Tigers ate the kids!" was a typical conversation. That life was full of high drama, real life drama, life and death drama and we are put together, literally hard wired, for that world.

In contrast, our modern life is easy, boring, in fact. We flip on the light switch and we get light. We turn the tap and we get safe, clean drinking water. We open the fridge and pull out fresh food, regardless of the season.

When compared to the life of a hunter/gatherer, which we are physiologically and psychologically structured for, our modern life has every single thing humans have strived for since we crawled out of the swamps or descended from the trees, except one very important thing: drama.

To make up for this lack of real life drama, we create false drama to satiate this very real need. Sports, movies, television, neighborhood gossip and local, national and international politics all fill this important gap. If there is no drama in our lives, we will create some.

It is very important to recognize what in your life and in the world around you is artificially created, false drama. It is also very important to recognize your need for drama and be very careful how you fill that need.

270. Human Politics

Any group of humans numbering larger than one has politics. Learning how human politics works and how to navigate your way through the rapids of that raging river is a large part of surviving and thriving in life and the workplace. This is especially true in tribes and large-scale corporations.

271. Stridency vs. Credibility

People who are strident are generally not credible. They have adopted a loud, boisterous and intimidating front to avoid detailed investigation and examination of what they advocate.

In general, the more strident someone is, the more insecure and less credible they are.

272. The Last Solution

Humans, when faced with a new challenge, will always attempt to apply past methods and approaches. Only after repeated attempts to force-fit a past solution on the new problem, followed by repeated failure, will humans develop new solution sets for new challenges.

This is a very powerful attribute of human behavior. It is extremely important to be aware of this in your own life and in those around you.

It is particularly common in child rearing, with its endless sets of new challenges, and in work settings, especially with project teams.

Can you recognize new challenges versus old ones?

Do you realize when you are wasting time trying to apply inappropriate old solutions to new challenges?

273. Humans Cluster

Humans cluster. They come in waves. Ask anyone who has ever worked retail. The store or counter will be empty for half an hour, then packed for 10 minutes, then empty for another half hour. Watch a gas station and you'll see the same thing is true.

There is something unifying about human groups and some undercurrent that drives common temporal human group behavior.

274. The Cheating Rule

A person who cheats on their spouse will always, eventually, cheat on you. There is no exception to this rule.

If you learn someone you are dealing with is a cheater, end the relationship, regardless of personal or business impact. They will always, eventually, cheat you too.

275. Be More Like Me

For most people, they would say the definition of a better friend, a better person, a better neighbor, a better community, a better world would be if everyone was just more like me.

In fact, the world would be a very, very boring place if everyone was just like you. Or me.

276. Unwanted Change

You will, without doubt, experience unwanted change in your lifetime. Shock, denial, anger, testing and acceptance are the five classic stages of human response to unwanted change. It is very helpful to know about these stages and how they commonly manifest themselves in you and in others, before you experience a deeply unwanted change. If the unwanted change involves death, the stages are usually expressed in "the grief cycle," illustrated below.

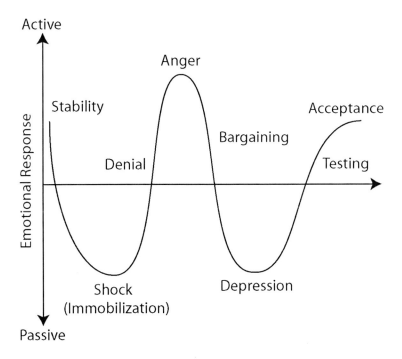

The stages, in general, are:

- Shock stage: Initial, immobilizing paralysis at hearing the bad news

- Denial stage: Trying to avoid the inevitable

- Anger stage: Frustrated outpouring of bottled-up emotion

- Bargaining stage: Seeking in vain for a way out

- Depression stage: Final realization of the inevitable

- Testing stage: Seeking realistic solutions

- Acceptance stage: Finally finding the way forward

Note that people can get caught in a loop and cycle within or between stages for a long time, for instance within a single stage, e.g., denial, or between multiple stages, e.g., bargaining and depression.

Recognize these stages within yourself during small instances of unwanted change, a flat tire for example. Knowing how you react, and being able to recognize the stages, will be a big help when a meaningful example of unwanted change occurs in your life.

277. The SME Secret

A SME is a Subject Matter Expert. They are critical to automating business processes. You need to identify a SME and extract their knowledge in order to automate what it is they do or know. Interviewing a SME for this purpose can take hours or days. It can take multiple interviews to learn all there is to know from a SME about their subject. I've personally spent over 40 hours learning from a SME in order to automate their little corner of the world.

In their own way, every single person you meet is a SME. Everyone is an expert in something. The key to being a good listener, a good friend and to be good at social interaction, is to become efficient at identifying what every person is an expert at, and ask them about it. People like nothing more than talking about themselves and their interests, and especially talking about something they know something about, or at least believe they know something about.

The more efficient you become in identifying and conversing about each person's area of expertise, the better conversationalist you will become.

Everyone is a SME about something. Find out what that is.

278. The Taxonomy of Friends

You will have scores to hundreds to thousands of people you call friends in your life. In today's world, where the word "friend" has been significantly devalued to include just about everyone you meet, the number of "friends" a person has is very large.

Using a stricter definition of friend, an acquaintance becomes a friend via trust. Only through building mutual trust does a person become a friend in your life.

There are six types of friends: situational, commonality, opportunistic, transcendental, life and true.

Situational

A situational friend is based on sharing time and place. This is the most common form of friend and is where most acquaintances make the transition via trust to become a friend. Examples of shared time and space include work, neighborhood, school and resource (child care, mechanic, doctor, etc.). Situational relationships come and go throughout life as your life circumstances change, e.g. change neighborhoods, change schools, change jobs, etc.

Commonality

A commonality friend is based on common interests or activities. Shared enthusiasm for a sports team, a type of music, recreational activity or other interest is a common platform for this type of friend. This type of friendship is based on the common interest, so if one or both of your interests change, then the friendship usually ends unless it can transform into another type of friendship.

Opportunistic

An opportunistic friendship is based on one or both of you using the relationship to advance a personal agenda.

Opportunistic friendships are by their very nature transient. When the agenda is advanced, the relative positional aspects of the relationship change, and one or both of you are less likely to be able to further advance the agenda. Thus, there is no further rationale for the relationship and, consequently, the relationship ends.

Opportunistic relationships can be symbiotic, where both of you are advancing your agendas, or parasitic, where one of you is using the relationship to advance your agenda. Parasitic opportunistic relationships are more common than symbiotic.

Transcendental

Transcendental friendships are forged in the crucible of unusual or exceptional shared experience, often dynamic, highly stressful and/or transformational experiences. Examples include shared emergency experiences, such as a fire, tornado or other calamity; extreme work environments involving shared dislike of oppressive managers or clients; or, a highly emotional group experience such as a religious event.

Transcendental friendships are by their very nature situational with a strong temporal component. They are also usually disproportional in their level of bonding compared to the length of time of the transcendental experience, in other words, exceptionally "deep" friendships are formed in a very short time period with the perceived depth of the relationship uncorrelated to the depth of knowledge of the other person.

Transcendental friendships often last only for the duration of the shared experience, or shortly thereafter. After a return to "real life," the transcendental friendship often fades away or is abandoned outright.

Life

Life friends are marked by their ability to pick right up wherever you left off the last time you saw them, be it two weeks, two years or two decades. The shared trust is immediately active, as is the fundamental basis of the friendship.

Life friends are the incubators of long-term memories, recollections, reminiscences, etc., which are usually revisited regularly within the context of the relationship.

Life friends may or may not be true friends.

True

> Every type of friend will tell you what you *want* to hear. A true friend, uniquely, will tell you what you *need* to hear.

There is no right or wrong categories of friends, but it can be painfully wrong to be unaware of them. It is important to understand the taxonomy of friends and to have awareness of how your current relationships fit into it. There is great human pain when you think you are in one type of friendship, only to find out it really is another. For instance, if you think you have a true fiend, but they are really an opportunistic parasitic friend, you are headed for pain.

Keep the taxonomy of friends in mind as you move through life. Your friendships will often shift from one category to another as your circumstances change. This is OK.

You will have many hundreds to thousands of friends during your lifetime, but will likely only have a handful of true friends. Treasure them.

(True friend definition inspired by Dennis Stajic; all other parts of the taxonomy developed by Douglas & Stephanie Hackney while driving across New Mexico in 2006)

279. The Only Color is Black

When I owned and managed a computer graphics company in Chicago I hired a lot of kids fresh out of art school. Every one of them wore all black clothes. For them, black was the only color.

They all, to a person, were fiercely individualistic, fiercely anti-establishment, fiercely unconventional and every day fiercely displaying their absolute and incontrovertible uniqueness - by wearing exactly the same color as every one of their peers.

The same is true of other fiercely individualistic, anti-whatever groups such as Harley Davidson motorcycle riders. They are all fiercely individualistic, and every one of them has nearly identical loud exhaust pipes and nearly identical clothing.

In both cases, those who are seeking to be different are seeking something else even more. They are seeking a tribe of others who are "rebelling" in the same way that they can bond with and find common identity with.

True individuals, people who are truly unique, with authentic new ideas and fresh thinking are exceedingly rare. You won't find them wearing all black or with loud pipes.

280. The Last Word

Pay attention to day-to-day life and its conversations. Watch what happens with simple interactions such as with a store clerk. Who has the last word? Who is compelled to have the last word, even if it is "thanks" or "bye?"

Having the last word is a classic power issue indicator. Having the last word imprints the experience with the speaker's ownership. It wraps the experience in their wrapper. It brands it.

People who usually, or always, must have the last word almost always have major control issues.

281. The Greed Factor

Greed is a basic human characteristic. It must be accounted for at every level of human social interaction and structure.

At a personal level, you must be aware that greed courses through the veins of every person you know. If you want to see it exhibited in its most ugly manifestation try giving some things away to your friends.

At the largest scale, it forms and drives social structures. The main reason the ultimate egalitarian form of governance, communism, has failed miserably in application is that it makes no structural allowance for greed. The reason capitalism has done so well is that it inherently provides an outlet for greed.

Be aware of greed and its dangers in yourself, in those around you and in society as a whole.

282. Passion

I had a client in Denver who employed the most zealous front desk guard I've ever encountered in the private sector. He was legendary for being a stickler about everything, even the tiniest detail. He required the proper forms, with the proper number of copies, exactly filled out, with every signature and stamp, for any activity that crossed his domain.

One day I was in a conference room chatting with the client and his staff prior to a meeting. His staff was grousing about the guard and how difficult he made their day-to-day working lives with his pedantic insistence on exact process and procedure. My client, a vice president in the company, observed that he wished he could find more people like the guard. His staff was stunned into silence.

"Do you want everyone to be such a pain-in-the-butt stickler for detail?" one brave staffer asked.

"No," the VP replied, "I just wish more people had his level of passion."

That was a very revealing insight, and one that I took to heart. When I checked out at the security desk at the end of the day, I looked at the guard in a totally different light. Instead of being frustrated by his insistence on my staying within the box on the sign out sheet, I appreciated how seriously he took his role and how passionate he was about what could be a very mundane job. Since then I've tried to apply that lesson to others I've met along the way.

Appreciate and honor people who exhibit passion in their work. It is a rare commodity.

283. Emotional Investment

Con artists are called con artists because they inspire *con*fidence. The confidence is inspired by getting the victim to create an emotional investment in the con artist. The emotional investment can outweigh logic.

Even after con artists are arrested, tried, convicted and sent to prison there are often victims who swear by them and work to obtain their release. The victims have such a large emotional investment in the relationship that they cannot pull back to see what has been done to them: they've been conned.

The technique of emotional investment is played by every single successful salesperson in the world. It starts by forcing you to say something. It can be as simple as their asking you, "How are you today?" They stroke your ego with compliments such as, "That's a beautiful outfit," or, "You're obviously a smart shopper." Every single time they can entice you to participate in the exchange they deepen your emotional investment. Soon, you are caught in the tar ball of your own emotional investment. You cannot back out and they've got you.

Emotional investment is the primary driver in Buyer's Blindness. Once people have made the purchase, they are loathe to admit their own stupidity or lack of judgment and will rationalize it to their dying day.

284. Buyer's Blindness

How many times have you asked someone who bought a new car how they liked it and had them reply, "I really shouldn't have bought this car. It costs more than I can afford. It doesn't match my needs. I could have found a better value." I would wager never.

Once people make a purchase, especially a high-dollar purchase, they are wedded to the choice. If they express displeasure with the choice they are showcasing their own stupidity or lack of judgment.

In a society that is all about materialism and consumption, making a poor purchase decision is entirely unacceptable, so they will develop blind spots to any negatives about their purchase and its negative qualities.

Be aware of buyer's blindness in yourself. Be honest with yourself about your strengths and weaknesses in this area, especially with high-dollar purchases.

285. The Most Powerful Reinforcement

There are three types of behavior reinforcement: positive, negative and irregular. B. F. Skinner, who defined behavior modification, found through his experiments that the most powerful reinforcement is irregular. In his experiments rats worked to exhaustion pushing on a bar that irregularly delivered a food pellet.

How many aspects of your life deliver irregular reinforcement? How many destructive or negative relationships do you cling to because they occasionally deliver a reward?

Learn to recognize the reinforcements, the rewards, in your life. Be very wary of those that deliver irregular rewards, as they are the most powerful, and the most likely to lead to bad decisions seeking them and negative consequences as a result.

286. The Food Pellet

Every human behavior has a reward, a food pellet.

Somewhere in each individual and group action there is a reward. Take a look at your life, at your actions, at your choices, and identify what the food pellet is for each. What is the reward for your choices? What is the reward for your actions? What is the reward for your behavior?

Understanding your own rewards will help you understand yourself. It will also help you to understand others when you look at their choices, actions and behaviors.

Every human choice, action or behavior has a reward. From the individual to nation states, it is true on every level. When you see an action, choice or behavior and you seek to understand it, always start with the question, "What is the food pellet? What is the reward?"

287. Cognitive Dissonance

When people's actions don't match their values, they will change their values rather than change the momentum, the inertia, of the actions. This is termed cognitive dissonance.

How often would your choices meet this definition? How about the choices of those around you?

Be wary of the slippery slope of cognitive dissonance. It is very easy to wake up in the bottom of the chasm wondering how you got down there in the mud when all you started with was one small compromise in your values.

288. Basic Fears

Most humans live their lives bounded by fear. The way they interact with the world is determined and shaped by their fears. Four major types of fear determine most people's behaviors, actions, choices and consequently, their lives:

- Abandonment - the fear of being left alone or behind by other people, especially in relationships, and/or by family and friends
- Rejection - the fear of not measuring up, being found lacking and being cast out by a person or group
- Tribelessness - the fear of being without a social group, without a kindred tribe to provide support, protection and reinforcement
- Failure - the fear of trying and failing, of falling short of requirements, of not meeting performance standards

If you can understand how these four major fears work in people's lives, how these four fears determine and drive behavior, you will be able to navigate a much smoother passage through life.

289. Foot Soldiers

In human groups - organizations, causes, political parties, religions, etc., - true believers usually only exist at the bottom levels. The people at the top levels have risen there because they learned how to manipulate and leverage the foot soldiers at the bottom levels.

The top-level players are adept at motivating the foot soldiers, the true believers, and rallying them to action. The leaders identify an enemy that must be overcome and send the foot soldiers forth to accomplish the goal.

In most cases, the leaders are sharing drinks with the very enemy they sallied forth the true believers to destroy.

Are you a true believer? Are you a foot soldier for someone else's gain? If you are part of any group, any organization, be aware of where you are relative to the leaders and the foot soldiers.

290. Being Late

People who are consistently late are not just scatterbrained or forgetful. They are consistently late because they use it as a tool for control.

People who are consistently late communicate two very clear messages:

- My time is more valuable than yours
- Because you all had to wait on me I am controlling you and your actions

Are you consistently late? What is your internal reward for that behavior? What unresolved issue do you have within you that generates that need to control others?

291. You Can't Coach Speed

My father-in-law, Jim Stant, coached high school girls' basketball for over 25 years. One year he was hired to build a girls' basketball program from the ground up at a new school. When I talked with him after tryouts he was exuberant.

"I've got a girl, she's 5'10" and she's faster than lightning. I've got a junior who's so fast I can't read her number when she flies down the court. I've got two freshmen who are nothing but blurs," he enthused.

"Jim," I asked, "can any of these kids pass, dribble or shoot?"

"Doug, I can teach them all of that," he replied, "but you can't coach speed."

There are certain intrinsic talents and abilities that humans have that cannot be taught, coached or indoctrinated. Some people have inherent talents that set them apart in measurable ways from their peers.

As an individual it is important to identify the things about yourself that fall in that category. What are the inherent talents and strengths that set you apart?

As a leader, coach, teacher or manager, it is critical to recognize the unique talents in your team members. You must understand what is teachable and what is not. Identify those with unique skills, talents and abilities and leverage them.

Remember that you can teach someone how to pass, dribble and shoot, but you can't coach speed.

292. Inheriting the Wealth

It is extremely rare for accumulated wealth to outlast the surviving spouse. It is even rarer for accumulated wealth to outlast the next generation, the children. It is incredibly rare for accumulated wealth to outlast the succeeding generation, the grandchildren.

An infinitesimally small percentage of family businesses are successfully passed down to further generations. Even if the founder can successfully navigate the taxes designed to kill the business upon their death, the surviving spouse and/or children almost always wreck the business soon after they gain control.

In both cases, the passing of wealth and the passing of a business, the core issue is usually the fact that those on the receiving end have no appreciation of, or experience with, the incredibly hard work it takes to build wealth or a business.

293. Zeros on the Table

Having money may or may not change people, but the *prospect* of having money absolutely, without question, changes people.

The higher the stakes, the more people will compromise their ethics and their integrity. As more zeros are placed on the table, as the opportunity for profit and wealth in a given opportunity gets larger, the less the parties involved are likely to remain honest and ethical.

The more zeros on the table, as in the decimal place moving to the right and the larger the number, the more people change.

This can be a painful experience if the people involved are people you know, are friends with, respect or trust.

When presented with a situation where the prospect of money is involved, everything you think you know about people will continue to become less and less relevant to their actions, the more zeros there are on the table.

Remember that, with most people, integrity is inversely proportional to potential profit. Remember that, with most people, the more zeros on the table, the less honesty and integrity likely in the outcome.

People who consistently compromise their integrity rarely have ongoing opportunities to participate in major deals with lots of zeros.

The only way to consistently participate in high-profit opportunities, with lots of zeros, is to maintain your integrity.

294. If Enough People Care

"Anything is possible if enough people care." – Lou Holtz.

If nobody cares, nothing will happen. If you can create a sense of caring, of investment, in enough people, anything is possible.

This rule applies to all sizes of human organization from one to the entire planet's population. It is essential to understand this rule when attempting to effect any change involving humans.

295. Locks

"Locks keep honest people out." – Clarence Hackney.

If you want to keep something safe from honest people, put a lock on it.

If you want to keep something safe from dishonest people, your only chance is to make it look a little harder to get your stuff than the next guy's stuff.

Dishonest people will not be stopped by any amount of locks or security. They will always find a way, even if you recreate Fort Knox.

The only successful strategy for dishonest people is to secure your things a little bit more than your neighbors secure theirs.

296. The Last Generation

Wars and rumors of wars were everywhere. Plagues ravaged the land. Refugees crowded the streets. The faithful were declared heretics, imprisoned, tortured or killed. Surely the time was nigh.

All were convinced that the end of the world was imminent. Masses left their homes and communities to await the second coming, standing vigil for the imminent end of mankind, the end of the world.

The time was the late 1500s. The place was northern Europe.

Most adults of that time and place were convinced the end of the world was days, weeks or at most, a few months away.

Every generation before then and since then has shared the same belief, that they are the last generation.

That recurring belief speaks to a fundamental human trait. Humans usually believe that their era, their generation, is the most important one to ever live.

Correspondingly, they believe that if something as important as the end of the world is going to come along, it will come along while their generation is alive.

Do you think yours is the last generation?

Is that based on evidence, belief or generational hubris?

297. Can't Do People

"Those who say it cannot be done should not criticize those who are doing it."
– Chinese proverb.

Avoid, at all costs, "Can't Do" people. They are, by nature, defeatists. They are, by nature, pessimistic and cynical. They are, by nature, convicted to a life sentence of disappointment.

Seek people who *Can* Do, who believe anything is possible. With them, anything is.

298. Your Story

The key to understanding modern human conversation and communication is comprehending that no one is all that interested in your story.

People in modern, developed societies are, as a group, overwhelmingly self-focused. They are really only interested in one topic: themselves. They may endure a few minutes of talk about you, but usually they are just waiting to get back to the topic that really matters: themselves. They may feign interest or enjoyment about something you have learned or experienced, but their response will invariably reference how your learning or experience relates to what really matters: themselves.

This phenomenon is an outgrowth of an aspect of human psychology related to new experiences or challenges. Humans will always attempt to relate the known to the unknown. They will attempt to apply a known paradigm to a new, unknown situation. They will attempt to apply a known solution to a new, unknown challenge.

Similarly, when told of a new, unknown insight or experience, humans will attempt to relate it to their known framework of experience and knowledge. If you tell an acquaintance that you learned a life-changing insight from monks who wore orange robes, the acquaintance is more likely to respond with something related to their experiences with the color orange or knowledge of monks than to the insight that was the subject of your story.

When you are communicating with people from developed societies, especially modern America, always remember that they are likely to be fundamentally disinterested in your story. The combination of modern self-absorption and basic human characteristics makes your story mostly irrelevant. If you want to have a conversation with someone your best bet is to talk about what matters most to them: themselves.

299. Humans Need Heroes

Humans have an inherent need for heroes. Heroes inspire, heroes provide an example of triumph over life's challenges and heroes prove that it is possible to achieve the goal. Heroes provide role models for people to aspire to.

By demonstrating positive characteristics, heroes can generate positive behavior and outcomes in the lives of masses of people.

Not every hero wears a cape and flies through the air. Not every hero catches a ball. Not every hero is a celebrity. Not every hero is a performer. Not every hero is famous. Some heroes are everyday people just doing their jobs: paramedics, firemen, policemen, doctors or the guy climbing the pole in the thunderstorm to turn the lights back on.

No matter what you do, you could be someone's hero, anytime, anywhere.

You never know when you could be someone's hero. You just need to live your life like you already are.

300. Beware Zealotry

Zealotry is inversely proportional to rationality.

Zealous people have checked their critical thinking at the door. They have lost the ability to reason where it concerns their cause.

Beware zealous people and zealotry in general.

301. The Five-Minute Rule

In a trustworthy interview, therapy or counseling session, almost all the valuable information is offered in the last five minutes.

302. Humans Hate Change

Humans hate change. They will do anything to avoid it until it is absolutely the last possible option before disaster or death.

Never put yourself, your family, your team or your business in a position where your success is dependent on human change. Chief among these scenarios is success dependent on cultural or process change.

303. Committees

Committees are the anti-leadership component of the universe.

No original or creative idea has ever come from one. No example of leadership or courage has ever come from one.

A camel truly is a horse designed by a committee.

Committees are exercises in finding the lowest common denominator. Committees are a group exercise in risk avoidance.

Avoid committees.

304. The Rarest Critic

The rarest critic is one that produces critiques that concern something other than the glorification of the critic.

305. Racing Rocks

Once there was man. Then man discovered a round rock will roll down a hill. Then there were two men. They immediately started racing rocks down the hill. Nothing has changed since.

306. Big Numbers

Humans have a hard time comprehending big numbers.

I am a believer in science. Consequently, I never understood people who believe the world is only a few thousand years old. To help me understand their views, I spent some time with them and listened to them explain their version of events.

In the end, it was clear to me they, like most humans, just could not get their minds around the concept of very big numbers, as in millions of years and billions of years. They needed a creation story that used numbers within their abilities to conceptualize, understand and believe.

Humans are good at small to medium numbers. Anything up to a hundred can be easily conceived. Once you get into the thousands, it gets harder, but since you can go to places and physically see 40 or 50,000 people in a stadium, it is possible.

Millions is a very big number and gets into the area where humans are forced to simply believe in the number, as there is no way the human mind can mentally conceive of that many objects / things / people / etc. Intellectually, we can understand and converse about millions of people, but we cannot actually conceptualize it.

Once we pass into and past billions, it is simply hopeless. The numbers become blurs of lots of zeros or double and triple-digit scientific notation. It all becomes faith.

When you are communicating with humans about very large numbers, always remember that they cannot easy conceptualize anything beyond a few thousand. Anything bigger than about 50,000 is simply all about faith.

307. The Language of Laughter

All humans laugh in the same language. It's just another example of how humans everywhere are more alike than different.

308. Strategy vs. Logistics

Amateurs discuss strategy, professionals discuss logistics.

When you see a talking head pontificating, use this test. They will almost always be talking about strategy.

309. The Same, But Different

The easiest choice, the seductive choice, is one that is the same, but different. It is the same enough that all of your existing references, coping skills, frameworks, paradigms, etc., are still relevant. It is different enough to convince you that you are making a change.

A choice that is the same, but different, is not different at all. It is merely seductive.

310. No Normal

There is no normal. It's all a matter of where you are on a relative scale, especially for families.

311. The Height of Power

With humans, height or stature implies capability. Consequently, tall people, regardless of ability, tend to ascend to power. Also, as a consequence, short people often have Napoleon complexes.

Learn how to spot the tall incompetents and the vengeful vertically challenged.

312. Learning Styles

There are three main learning styles: visual, auditory and kinesthetic.

Know which type you are so you can learn efficiently.

When you teach, teach the same lesson all three ways to ensure all your students have an opportunity to learn effectively.

313. Tightfisted People

"Tightfisted people are as mean with friendship as they are with cash – suspicious, unbelieving and incurious." - Paul Theroux.

When I grew up in the Midwest, I had a friend who would never use his windshield washer during winter. Instead, he would drive around with his head out the window, unable to see through his opaque windshield, until he found some clean snow. Then he'd jump out and use the snow to clean his windshield. His goal was to never, ever pay for a bottle of windshield washer fluid. He was tightfisted in that way about everything.

I had another friend who would go into hotels and work his way back through the service corridors until he found the employee cafeteria, where meals were often subsidized and therefore very cheap. He did this everywhere he went. He was tightfisted in that way about everything.

Both of those guys ended up losing every penny they had. Every tightfisted person I've ever known suffered the same fate.

It works the same way with friendship. There's no use being tightfisted about friendship, as you are not working from a limited supply. The more friendly you are, the more friendship you will have to give.

314. Cigarette Punctuation

The second saddest sight in the world is a young woman smoking.

The only sadder sight is an older women, usually pickled, punctuating her sentences with a cigarette.

315. Simple Solutions

Humans are very oriented to seeking simple solutions to complex problems.

In former times it was the sacred stick or the sacred slug held aloft by a priest voicing the simple solution. Today, it is the sacred celebrity, the slick politician or the advertisement, all offering the same thing: simple solutions to complex problems.

There are no simple solutions to complex problems.

Avoid, at all costs, becoming another sheep following anyone who promises one.

316. Core Motivation

While traveling in Chile we had a difficult time buying map software for our GPS. We worked our way all the way up the chain of command at the local distributor for the software but had no success. Finally, we went to a local retailer and talked to a salesperson who was delighted to sell it to us.

The moral of the story is: In order to accomplish your goal, target people's core motivation.

The managers who thwarted our efforts were compensated for defending fiefdoms and perpetuating the bureaucracy. The salesperson was compensated for retail sales.

If you are in need of a product or service, find someone who is motivated and compensated for what you need.

317. Stuck People

Many, if not most, adults are stuck. They are stuck in an unresolved life issue arising from some incident or situation of their lives. Some are stuck in early childhood, many in teenage years and many more in early adulthood.

In terms of computer programming, they spend their lives in an endless "Go To" loop, which means they progress through a series of steps then loop back to an earlier point in the series. In colloquial terms, they reach a decision point where they could advance their lives, grow to a new level and experience what life truly offers, only to choose the same old destructive path of least resistance again and again. They loop right back to the same old starting point, the same old traumas and the same old unresolved issues.

Through the course of your life you will encounter and interact with many people who are stuck. Learn how to spot them and their recurring issues. Avoid, at all costs, long-term relationships with people who are stuck in damaging or destructive places.

You may be stuck too. If so, do the work to discover why you are stuck and climb out of that hole. Get unstuck and thereby enable yourself to fully live life, to experience everything life has to offer.

318. Marking Territory

A good way to spot a domineering, controlling person is to watch them mark territory. Just like a dog, people mark their territory in various ways.

It may be physical marking. They will walk in and move things to suit themselves or serve their compulsions. In some way, subtle or strong, they will shape the physical environment to their own ends.

More often, it is psychological marking. They will establish their dominance and superiority via verbal means, body language or emotional manipulation.

Controlling, dominance-oriented people will also mark their territory by controlling time. They will be consistently late and use manipulative behavior such as always using the restroom prior to meals so everyone waits on them. Regardless of the method, they will mark their territory over everyone else's time.

You will often need to relate to or interact with controlling, domineering people. Be aware that they are blind to boundaries, so they will trample over yours.

Know how to spot controlling, domineering people and their behaviors, and develop coping strategies to protect yourself and your priorities.

319. The Cause

At some point in their lives most people adopt a cause and make it the central point of their lives. It gives their life meaning and purpose where it otherwise would have none. And, for some, the cause provides a ready rationale for making it easy to bulldoze others.

People who are wrapped up in a cause lose their ability to be objective about anything related to the cause. Even worse, they often look at the world through a filter that forces every single thing in life to be either for or against the cause.

Beware people who are cause-centric.

320. The Unhappiness Food Pellet

Every human behavior, bar none, is based on a reward system. Just like an animal will perform for a food pellet, a human will continue a behavior as long as they are being rewarded for it. This includes both positive and negative behavior.

If you are unhappy or you are doing things that consistently result in unhappiness, you need to identify how you are being rewarded for the behavior, intrinsically or extrinsically. You need to identify the food pellet you are receiving that motivates you to continue the behavior.

321. The Curse of Success

Nothing kills motivation like success.

Nothing makes a person or an organization less motivated to change, to improve, to be better, than success.

322. Is It Being Eaten?

Within the first hour of our game drive in Botswana's Okavango Delta we saw a herd of impalas.

"Stop, stop the truck!" we all shrieked as one in response.

For the next three minutes all external sound was drowned out by the cacophony of autofocus beeps and camera shutters. When we were finally exhausted, out of memory or our camera batteries were dead, our patient driver started the truck and we rumbled on through one of the greatest concentrations of free-roaming wildlife on the planet.

On the next afternoon a voice was raised, "Look, there's an impala."

"Is it being eaten?" was the laconic reply.

Within one day we had changed from passionate lovers of all things impala to jaded veterans of the real-life food chain.

The moral of this story is that humans are extremely adaptable to changing circumstances and new sensory inputs. If you put a human in a setting of stunning natural beauty, usually within a week the majesty will fade to background status.

Consequently, be very wary of making life decisions based on things and factors that may initially seem very important, but are destined to quickly become just another part of the background of your life.

323. Disproportionate Response

When people display disproportionate response to normal inputs, such as emotional outbursts or verbal abuse in response to innocuous situations, stimulations or conversation, it is important to understand the cause of the behavior.

They may be doing it out of true passion, which can be understandable and acceptable. It may be a control tactic, e.g., "the best defense is a good offense," which is a sign of significant control and insecurity issues.

It may also be emotionally fueled, which is usually a sign of displacement. Displacement means they inject emotions and feelings into the situation that are displaced from the original source of their anger and frustration. They are unable to exhibit or display those feelings of anger and frustration in their original, relevant context due to temporal (time), location, circumstance, role or societal / cultural norm constraints.

When people consistently display disproportionate responses due to control or displacement issues, especially in work or public settings, they are best avoided.

If you maintain a relationship with such a person you will inevitably become direct or collateral damage due to their issues.

324. Brilliant <> Smart

Brilliant does not equal smart. I have a friend who is the most brilliant person I have ever known in my life, and I have known and worked with hundreds of C.E.O.s, C.F.O.s, C.O.O.s, C.T.O.s, Ph.D.s, M.D.s, M.B.A.s, Commanders, Captains, Colonels and Generals.

My friend is incredibly brilliant. He knows and understands things in depth that I can barely begin to comprehend in the most general terms. His powers of analysis and recall are astounding. His experience with advanced projects rivals anyone's.

My friend is indisputably brilliant, but he has made some of the stupidest personal and business decisions I have ever seen. Fortunately, he is aware of this and takes it in good humor as part of the balance of his life.

No matter how brilliant you think you are, or you actually are, never forget that you are capable of making some very stupid mistakes. Maintain perspective on yourself, your talents, your capabilities and your shortcomings. Brilliant does not equal smart.

325. The Seeds of Doubt

No one will ever know who killed President John F. Kennedy. The reason is not that the truth is not known or cannot be known. The reason is that the people who don't want the truth known did the best possible thing to prevent the truth from being known: they sowed the seeds of doubt early and often.

There are so many conflicting theories and allegations about who killed JFK that even if today you discovered the absolute, indisputable truth about what happened, it would be completely impossible for you to convince the majority of the public of that fact.

That is the power of widespread doubt. No matter how much you know about what is actually the truth, it doesn't matter. There is so much widespread doubt that it is impossible to convince people of the truth.

If you observe a person, team, tribe, organization or country sowing the seeds of doubt, you know one thing for certain: they desire to obscure the truth.

326. The Star of the Movie

Every person is the star of their own movie. Inside their heads, they are playing the leading role in a story never before told. Each person is the hero of their own story and everyone else in their lives, indeed everyone else alive, plays a secondary role.

Always remember that everyone you know, or will ever know, considers themselves destined for a "Best Actor / Actress in a Leading Role" Oscar award.

And, always remember that for everyone else, you are playing a secondary role in their movie and can be written out of the story at any time.

327. Strengths and Weaknesses

Every single human, every human group and every human nation is a combination of strengths and weaknesses.

Avoid generalizations and painting with a broad brush. Maintain awareness, and attribution, of both positive and negative aspects of people and groups.

328. The Barnyard

In the barnyard, as in life, all animals are equal. But in reality, as in the barnyard, as in life, some animals are more equal than others.

Regardless of political rhetoric, there will always be those with easier access to power, influence and control.

Don't allow yourself to be deceived as to the nature of human social reality. And, don't allow yourself to be consumed by the unfairness of it all. It is the way of humans and of human tribes.

329. The Nobility of the Poor

I've been poor. I've been very, very poor. There is no inherent nobility of the poor. It is people who are poor, who belong to and embrace the tribe of the poor, who hold up and champion the badge of honor of the nobility of the poor, but there is no inherent nobility of the poor.

The poor are no more inherently virtuous or superior than those who are not poor. Human frailty, faults and shortcomings are evenly distributed across the entire population. There is no exception to human faults based on economic status. Human failings are no more or less concentrated anywhere across the spectrum of financial net worth.

If you are poor during a chapter of your life, do not allow yourself to become seduced by the tribe of the poor and the myth of its inherent nobility and moral superiority to those who are not poor.

330. Honor Among Thieves

I've known some thieves in my life. I've known some petty thieves and some king-sized thieves. I've known thieves from the lowly and downtrodden to the highest reaches of professional and social status.

I can say without reservation that there is no honor among thieves. Given the opportunity, a thief will steal from anyone, including another thief.

There is no honor among thieves.

331. Critical Mass

Some people are only a stray encounter, a happenstance event, a random word, one perceived slight from reaching critical mass. These people are usually well known in work and social environments for frequent emotional eruptions and verbal explosions.

They are often given a wide berth or coddled to avoid a repeat performance.

They are, almost always, using this behavior as a manipulative control mechanism. Anger is easy. It intimidates other people and enables the achievement of agendas and goals.

Critical mass people are unreliable as friends and co-workers and generally dangerous on multiple levels. They should be avoided.

332. The Wrigley Field Bleachers

One beautiful summer afternoon I took my wife to a baseball game at Wrigley Field, the Mecca of baseball.

We sat in the centerfield bleachers where she had a fine, up-close view of the ivy on the walls.

We sipped Old Style beer in plastic cups as the game unfolded.

The cotton ball cumulous clouds drifted across the dark blue sky as hit and runs, pickoff plays and pitchouts were executed on the field.

At the stretch we stood and sang "Take Me Out to the Ballgame" with all the lust and gusto demanded in such a hallowed setting.

As the last notes of the organ died out, we settled into our seats. I glanced over, checking to see if the overwhelming beauty and romance of baseball had completely enveloped her.

"No one can resist this setting, this place," I thought. "She is powerless before the seductive power of the glorious game at Wrigley on a summer afternoon."

She turned to me and asked, "How much time is left in the game?" She looked bored to tears.

The moral of this story is that when it comes to passion for an interest, osmosis doesn't work. Either someone else shares your passion or they don't. No amount of dipping, immersion, steeping or drenching in the subject of your passion will change someone else into a true believer.

333. Perspective

It is very important to remember that for essentially everyone you know, or will ever know, there is only one perspective: their own.

People generally have a very self-centric view of the world. Most view the world through the drinking straw of their own experiences, biases, cultural conditioning and expectations. It is very, very rare to find a person who can view any aspect of the world from a wider or broader perspective.

334. Money and Bitterness

Money can do a lot of things, but it will never assuage bitterness. No amount of money spent, obtained, saved or squandered will ever change a bitter person.

335. The Ugliest Side of People

If you want to see the ugliest side of people, lay out a bunch of your stuff you want to give away and tell the group of them to take whatever they want.

336. The People of the World

The people of the world are all basically the same. Most of them are just trying to raise their families, build strong communities and develop opportunities for their families, tribes and nations.

Everywhere in the world there are good people and bad people. Fortunately, there are more good than bad, almost always by a wide margin.

337. The Director of Dotting

You will often come across people, mostly lowly functionaries working for countless layers of bureaucrats, who seem inordinately obsessed with what seem to you to be trivial matters. They are insistent that forms be filled out properly, that processes be followed to the letter, etc., while all you want to do is get this dreary bit of officialdom completed and be on with your day. The more impatient, sarcastic or angry you get, the more insistent, entrenched and unmoving they become.

What is happening is a classic confrontation with the Director of Dotting. They are in charge of dotting that particular "i" and nothing is going to happen until the dot appears on that letter. Why are they so unreasonable? Usually it is because that dot is their entire domain of influence and control. They are in a work position of zero prestige and even lower prospects for advancement. They are going nowhere and they will more than enjoy your accompanying them on that journey.

How do you survive the encounter? Put yourself in their position. Show respect. Practice deference. Follow the rules.

Above all, remember that tomorrow you will be someone else, but this person will be right back there, being the Director of Dotting. Forever.

338. Award Politics

Every award, no matter how small or large, from the "National Plumbing Association Best New Gate Valve, Brass, 2 inches and Larger" to the Nobel Peace Prize, is political.

The higher the prestige and wider the press coverage, the more political the selection of the winner is. Entertainment awards, in particular, are almost always blatant political statements, endorsement, protests, snubs, etc.

I've sat on many judging panels. Every award is political.

339. The Power Rookie Rule

Any individual or group who attains power for the first time will always, without exception, misuse and mismanage it. This is true in personal life, business life, society and local, national and international politics. The only question is how bad the damage will be and if they will survive their misapplication of power to have a chance at it again.

Be very, very wary of people, tribes, groups or parties who are in power for the first time or the first time in a long time. They will, always, misuse that power and you do not want to be a victim of their incompetence.

340. Affirmation via Attack

Many people make themselves feel better by attacking others. For them, the only way they know how to make themselves look better is by denigrating those around them.

People who are attacking and nasty are by far the most insecure people. They live by the adage "The best defense is a good offense."

341. Three Acts

Human storytelling in western civilization is structured into a drama. The classic form is three acts.

The acts consist of first, introduce the characters; second, introduce conflict; third, resolve the conflict.

The story of human existence is related in terms of drama. Drama is how human life is explained, taught, remembered, codified and represented. From your trip to the store to geopolitical events, the story will be told within a dramatic framework.

It is very important to understand how drama works, and how you are influenced and manipulated by human events shaped into dramatic renditions for your consumption.

342. Horses and Water

"You can lead a horse to water, but you can't make them drink." – American folk wisdom.

This is true not only of horses, but people too. You can lead your family, your children, your friends, your co-workers, your company, your customers, your community and even your nation to water, but you can't make them drink.

There will be times in your life when you will be faced with this challenge. If you become a consultant, this will be the first lesson you learn. In either case, you must come to terms with this reality or it will destroy you.

343. The Human Exception

Humans are exception based. Our minds are amazingly efficient at spotting exceptions, regardless of the context. Whether it's examining a data set or looking at an image, humans will spot and hone in on an exception, be it an outlier in a data sample or a white speck in a field of black.

Humans are much less adept at spotting the subtle shift, the slow movement and the slight changes that, over time, lead to tectonic displacement.

Keep this in mind as you move through life. It is especially relevant in child rearing and business management where exception is easy, but the real rewards come from awareness of, insight into and appreciation of the subtleties.

344. Fish Dinner

"Give a man a fish, you feed him for a day. Teach a man to fish, you feed him for a lifetime." – Chinese Proverb.

Giving people fish dinner every day does nothing but kill ambition, aspiration and desire. It breeds complacency and a sense of entitlement. Feeding people fish dinner every night yields nothing but a bunch of people doing nothing but waiting for their free handout and complaining about the service.

Individuals, families, tribes, races, countries and entire continents have been laid waste by handouts. Entire generations have grown up not knowing what it means to wake up for a purpose, interview for a job, prepare themselves for work, be on time and take responsibility for their lives. Handouts, and their inevitable follow-on, entitlement, have destroyed more lives than anything the handout was designed to alleviate.

Learn how to fish.

345. Validate Concern / Issue

A human with a grievance will verbalize that grievance until it is received, understood and validated. A human who feels their grievance has not been listened to, comprehended and stamped as legitimate will repeat that grievance until they feel it has been. That is normal human behavior.

If their grievance or issue has been listened to, comprehended and validated, and they continue to repeat the same grievance or issue time after time after time, you have entered the realm of abnormal psychology and you are dealing with someone who has a psychological issue.

346. Changing People

You cannot change people. You can coerce them, motivate them or reward them, but you cannot change them.

Change only comes from within.

347. Negative People

Extended exposure to negative people does incalculable damage to your psyche, spirit and soul.

Tribes

348. Tribe

The fundamental social unit of humanity is tribe. Tribe is the single most important element in global human interaction. All humans belong to tribes, and if they feel tribe-less, will form one, or coagulate one or search out one they can identify with and join.

In other cultures, tribe is not only completely understood, it is as ingrained into the cultures as the intake of oxygen. Americans do not understand tribe, as the United States is a truly polyglot society. As such, it is very, very challenging for America, and Americans, to relate to the rest of the planet, where the fundamental social unit is tribe. We don't understand tribal loyalty, which is understandable when the closest we get to it is Cub Nation.

You will belong to multiple tribes in your lifetime. You will be a member of many different tribes in your lifetime, from the pre-school sandbox tribe to the retirement afternoon shuffleboard tribe. The tribes will be based on interests, activities, alignments, affiliations, location, aspirations, avocations, etc. These are societal tribes of convenience. It is very important to both understand that you are in a tribe when you are in one, and to give yourself permission to leave a tribe and move on with your life.

You will never know what tribe is and means to the rest of the world, but knowing that you don't know is, in and of itself, important.

349. The Tribe Rules

All tribes operate on the same basic set of rules, so it is important to understand them.

Language - Admission into the tribe requires language. You must speak the language or code, whether that means acronyms, colloquialisms, buzz words, relevant street slang or a human language.

Symbols – Tribes require tribal symbols. These are typically physical things, such as merchandise brands, decals, tattoos, clothing, accessories, devices, hair styles, etc.

Bona Fides – You must earn acceptance into the tribe by your bona fides, the things that qualify you for admission. These can be material goods, but are more often required experience, ranging from professional stature to performing a specific act.

Endorsement – You must endorse the actions, standards, beliefs, attitudes, faith(s) and outlook of the tribe to be admitted, and especially, to remain a member.

Compliance – You must comply with the tribe and its dictates to become and remain a member. Independence of thought and action is not tolerated.

Exit – Your exit from the tribe will always be accompanied by vilification by the remaining tribal members. From the tribe's perspective, you do not ascend from a tribe, you always descend.

350. Self-Selective Groups

Most voluntary tribes are self-selective groups. They usually coalesce around a common interest or cause. It may be something as innocuous as a brand or model of a material object or a social movement or goal. But, regardless, the members of the group are self-selective.

This means that you cannot gain a statistically valid sample set within the group on any topic or issue even remotely related to the reason they clustered.

Be very wary of opinions, conclusions or assertions from self-selective groups. They are, due to their inherent nature of self-selection, almost always skewed.

351. The Power of Peers

Nothing will influence you more than your tribe, your peer group, who you associate with. They become the group that forms a vernacular, a code of ethics, a set of acceptable behaviors, a framework of reality and the common goals that all tribal members will strive towards.

Thus, it becomes extremely critical to choose your peers wisely. This is the reason that your network, the group of people you know and associate with, the people you have relationships with, can and will largely determine who and what you become.

Your peer group can motivate you to become all you can be, or can willfully hold you back from becoming more than they are or can achieve. It requires extreme strength of will to break away from a peer group and set out on your own path. No choice is more lined with loneliness, and none yields more rewards in fulfilling your potential.

352. Sinking to a Level

You will always rise to or sink to the level of your competition. This is why it is so important to make good choices about your peer group as a teenager, which college you attend, the friends you associate with, your team at work and what you do with your time.

If you are always striving to find the best at whatever you are interested in, you will grow and achieve at a highly accelerated rate. You will find yourself among the elite in whatever field of endeavor or interest you pursue.

On the other hand, if you hang with losers, if you associate with underachievers, you will never have a role model or anything to aspire to that will advance you in life.

Put yourself among the very best at whatever you choose to do.

353. The Immutable Law of Bureaucracy

The mission and goal of the bureaucracy is the survival and expansion of the bureaucracy.

354. Communities of Complaint

Beware communities of complaint. Regardless if they are virtual communities or as physical as the local watering hole; misery loves company and miserable people will cluster into communities. Avoid miserable people and their communities of complaint at all costs.

355. Passionate Peers

Seek out and sustain relationships with peers who are passionate about their interests, professions, etc. People who are passionate about their interests bring energy to life and to those around them.

356. Alpha Dogs

In every group of humans you will find both male and female Alpha Dogs. They are driven to dominate the pack, and will use whatever means required to achieve control. If they cannot achieve control, they will destroy the current leader, destroy the pack or destroy whatever goal the pack is trying to achieve. If they cannot control their current pack, they will roam until they find a pack to dominate.

Humans, being oriented to abdicating leadership and the responsibility that accompanies it, are hard wired to follow, usually blindly, an Alpha Dog.

Be aware of the Alpha Dogs in your personal and business life. Know your position in the pack.

357. Unknown People

In his book *One Man Caravan* Robert Fulton, Jr. tells a wonderful anecdote of his encounter with two tribes in Central Asia.

As he pulled into a dusty village in the middle of nowhere on his Douglas Twin motorcycle in 1933, the locals greeted him with a mixture of awe and trepidation. After the usual greetings, exchanges and a ceremonial meal, they asked where he planned to venture to the following day. Robert informed them that he intended to ride over the next mountain range and continue his journey around the world, the first solo circumnavigation by anyone on a motorcycle.

The entire tribe recoiled as one. The women wailed and threw themselves on the ground. The men pounded the earth. The elders beseeched him, "Do not go there! Those people are all thieves and murderers! They will steal what you own and then kill you!"

Somewhat taken aback by the intensity of their message, Robert thanked them for their advice, but gently insisted he would continue his travels. The tribe begged and cajoled, but he persevered.

The next morning he was treated as a dead man walking, with women in mourning and men looking deeply into his eyes, all believing his fate has been sealed.

Robert rode over the mountains that day into a new territory, occupied by a different tribe.

As he pulled into another dusty village, he was greeted with great curiosity.

The locals asked him, "From where did you come?"

When he pointed behind him to the mountains and replied, "From there, over the mountains," they were incredulous.

"From there?" they asked, "From over the mountains?"

"Yes," Robert replied.

"But that is impossible!" their wise men exclaimed. "No one can come from over those mountains alive! Everyone knows that the people there are all thieves and murderers! They would have stolen everything you own and then killed you!"

As Robert Fulton learned in 1933, and we are reminded today, we all fear the unknown, we all fear other people that we know little to nothing about. We are usually sharing the same fears about each other, and are usually mutually unworthy of those fears.

In our travels we have met, mingled with, broken bread with, visited the homes of and shared adventures with people from all stations in life, from the poorest of the poor to the richest of the rich. We have spent time with people of all walks of life, from most of the corners of this planet.

So far, we haven't met a single one who was worthy of the fears that most of us harbor towards the unknown people of unknown lands.

Nation States, Cultures and Societies

358. All Politics Are Local

In 2004 we spent some time with an extended Bedouin family. We met them in their compound of goat-hair tents where the families lived. The area of the Syrian Desert we were in was pretty close to the Iraqi border, where the war was raging.

When the topic of geopolitics came up, and specifically the war in Iraq, the patriarch of the family spoke at length regarding the issue. In his long discourse, he barely mentioned anything apart from the hardships the war placed on his tribe, as they customarily herded their goats across the vast desert that stretched from Syria through Iraq. The war made it harder for his tribe to migrate their herds of goats across the border with the changing seasons to traditional grazing areas.

In my lifetime, this was perhaps the ultimate example of Tip O'Neal's immortal maxim, "All Politics Are Local."

All politics, regardless of scale, are local. It all comes down to how the issue affects individuals in their individual lives.

359. Centuries

From the time of the reformation, enlightenment and renaissance until the end of the 19th century, the known world belonged to the Europeans.

The 20th century largely belonged to the United States.

The 21st will belong to the Chinese. Teach your children Mandarin.

360. What America Does Best

America does one thing better than anyone else and anything else – overcompensation. It is the defining national character trait.

361. Tombstone Governance

Governance in the United States is by tombstone.

Nothing happens until a bunch of tombstones pop up, then suddenly, overcompensation and overreaction abound.

362. Zero Sum Petroleum

There may or may not be a finite amount of known reserves of petroleum. There may be extensive reserves yet undiscovered. But one thing is certain, geopolitics consist of not much more than a zero sum game for petroleum.

If you want to understand how the geopolitical world works, just look at the main economic players - Europe, U.S., China, India and Japan - and see who they depend on for their petroleum.

Geopolitics hasn't evolved much since the Europeans invented the Great Game. Now it is played for the biggest prize of all, access to petroleum to fuel developing and developed economies.

Everything else that surrounds or is layered over that issue is just political theater.

363. Diversity = Strength

In our diversity lies our strength.

A piece of metal formed from pure iron lacks strength, is brittle or both.

The combination of iron and carbon makes steel, which is stronger than any of the elements combined to form it. The addition of chromium forms stainless steel, which is both strong and resists corrosion. It is the combination of materials that creates the unique strength of steel.

The diversity of the U.S. is what created the world's largest economy, a land of endless, boundless opportunity. The energy and cornucopia of new ideas and innovation that is formed by the mixing of cultures, backgrounds, races, ideals and dreams is what made the U.S. what it is today.

America's diversity is the primary and only sustainable competitive differentiator compared to the other developed nations of the world, all of which are predominately pure representations of their native tribes.

Just like our nation, and like steel, diversity of the components of life - experiences, outlooks, relationships, locations, destinations, journeys and education - creates strength.

364. Media Mortgages

While we were traveling in India, I noticed a huge difference in how the media there reported events of the world and how U.S and European media reported those same events. While in the Middle East, I personally witnessed events that were subsequently completely distorted and misrepresented by U.S. and European media.

In speaking with working reporters in the Middle East, I learned why they filtered and distorted what they reported. Every organization in today's politically polarized media had a particular slant on the news and served an audience that shared that perspective. That audience wanted to be told what it wanted to be told, and anything other than that message was going to be rejected. Publishers, news directors, editors and managers are the operating filters of the news. If the reporters in the field submitted stories or reports that didn't match the view of the organization they worked for, they wouldn't have a job for very long. If the reporter wanted to make their mortgage payments, they'd better be submitting work that matched the agenda of the news organizations for which they worked.

It's an ugly and ironic truth, but the truth that there is no truth in news reporting is the undeniable, undisputable truth. As long as the reporters in the field are still making their mortgage payments, you'll always know that what you are reading and seeing is, by the nature of the process that produces it, skewed and filtered to match the agendas of those producing and distributing it.

365. $500 Million and 00/100ths

It is estimated that the United States 2008 presidential race will cost the winning candidate $500 million. You don't raise that kind of money with bake sales and car washes.

By the time someone is elected president, senator, representative, governor or state legislator, they have sold their soul and prostituted their values to raise the required cash. They have traded their last vestige of integrity to get elected. And, they will sacrifice it again and again to stay elected.

Their time in office is spent doing the bidding of those who paid the $5,000, $500,000 or $5 million to get them there. All other issues, activities, messaging, causes, etc. are merely window dressing and political theater used to entertain the true believers of their party, convince the constituents that they are "working for them" and keep the media occupied.

I've been inside of politics and seen up close and personal how it works. You don't want to know.

Until the United States adopts publically-funded elections and bans non-public money from politics, the U.S. will have the best government money can buy.

366. Do and Say

Politicians and political parties will do and say anything to obtain and retain power. And I mean absolutely *anything*.

367. The Nation Comes First

"No nation is to be trusted farther than it is bound by its interests." – George Washington.

A nation state always operates in its own best interests. Any alliances and affiliations, or regional or global organization priorities or agendas, come after the nation state takes care of its own interests. There is no exception to this rule.

368. Be My Hero

America is hero-based. Its history, its morality tales, its very identity is wrapped up in heroes. Every American is indoctrinated into the lexicon, roles and drama of the hero epic.

As you watch how people act, interact, lead, achieve and execute power keep this in mind.

Understanding heroes is a prerequisite to understanding the personality of America.

369. The United States of Aspiration

America is all about aspiration. The desire to better one's self, to build a better life for one's children, to achieve greatness, is the very core of the American character.

Today, aspiration is the button that marketers push to create the perception of need, to drive materialism. But, it goes deeper than that in the national character. Materialism is the shoddy, trampy, wrong-side-of-the-tracks, moral-less, crack-addicted cousin of the aspiration that created the nation.

Understanding aspiration is a prerequisite to understanding the character of America.

370. Misandry

Misogyny, the hatred of women, is a very well-known word. There is not an American woman of any age who hasn't seen it, read it and been indoctrinated by the industry that surrounds it. Since the early 1970s American society has been immersed in a non-stop, mass immersion of social programming to stamp out misogyny. The primary method has been a society-wide adoption of its counterpart, misandry: the hatred of men.

Misandry is not a well-known word. For instance, misogyny is recognized by Microsoft Word's built-in dictionary while misandry is not. The word itself is equally unknown in society, academics and popular culture. But, its implementation, through systematic demeaning, discrediting, diminishing and unrelenting negative stereotyping of men, is pervasive in those areas and beyond.

Attempt to find a positive male role model in popular music, sports, television and movies. Attempt to find a positive or heroic depiction of males in academics, especially in college-level material. If you manage to find a few, compare the ratio of positive male references and role models to negative references and role models. The consistent message our society drums into every little boy's and girl's head from childhood through college graduation is that men are lying, cheating, conniving, brutal, violent, emotionless, abusive, ignorant, impulsive, base and repulsive creatures.

Attempt to find a state that is as concerned about divorced fathers' visitation rights as about divorced fathers' child support payments. Attempt to find a state that considers divorced fathers equal parents with equal rights and abilities for full-time placement. Instead, you will find a family court system that views fathers as nothing more than a source of funds.

You would be hard pressed to find an instance of any family court, in any county, in any state, that vigorously enforces visitation rights for fathers. I challenge you to find a single county jail cell containing a mother who refused to abide by the court's ruling on child placement. The American family court system has one, single overriding orientation, and that is to serve the needs, wishes and desires of divorced mothers and their advocates.

Misandry, the hatred of men, is now enshrined in our culture, while the merest hint of misogyny is stamped out with quick and ruthless action. Visit the greeting card aisle of a large store. Read through a few dozen cards that reference men and mentally replace every male reference with a female one. Imagine the consequences if that happened physically, and greeting cards were produced with such phrases and references directed towards women. The store would be picketed within 24 hours, if not burned to the ground.

A few decades ago there were misogynist aspects of the American culture. The pendulum has now swung and a thoroughly misandrist society has taken its place. The long-term, negative effects on children and on society of a completely emasculated population are difficult to imagine, but America shall bear that bitter fruit.

Be aware of how you have been subtly and brazenly indoctrinated by misandry. Take a critical, detailed look at your attitudes about men and women as genders. What assumptions and preconceptions do you carry? How many are truly accurate and how many reflect the repeated messaging of popular culture? Do you truly view men and women as equal?

371. Cultural WD-40

American culture is the universal penetrating oil of the planet. It seeps into every crack and crevice in every society and culture on earth. It is pervasive. It is unstoppable. It is often not welcome.

The rest of the world judges Americans and American society primarily by our popular culture. If you wonder what the other 6.3 billion people on the planet think of you, watch some American television and movies. That is what they think you are.

372. Greed's Own Political System

Communism, and its grotesquely malformed, poor red-headed stepchild, socialism, is the ideal system except for its fundamental flaw, its Achilles' heel: communism never accounted for human greed.

You must have a way to account for, contain, funnel, channel and leverage human greed or your political and economic system is doomed. You can't shame greed into abeyance. You can't keep it corralled with idealistic, altruistic thought and indoctrination. It will rise up and consume any system in denial of greed that gives it even a tiny crack of breathing space.

Capitalism has its flaws, but it's the only system that has a fundamental aspect that incorporates and leverages human greed. Until human greed goes away, capitalism is the best we've got.

373. Society's Hierarchy of Needs

Take a look at Maslow's hierarchy of needs and compare it to who society rewards the most.

Think of the people who work every day to keep the fundamental systems of the society functioning: water, electricity, fuel, food, etc. How are they regarded and rewarded?

Think of the people teaching children how to achieve knowledge, confidence, problem solving, morality, creativity, etc. How are they regarded and rewarded?

Now think of the people who are regarded the highest and rewarded the most: athletes, entertainers, actors and celebrities. Where are they on the hierarchy of needs? You won't find them anywhere. They don't provide a single element of need, instead, they provide false drama.

As a modern, developed society, we regard the highest and reward the most those who provide false drama, not those who fulfill any element of the hierarchy of needs for our society.

When viewed against the span of history and the innumerable faded and failed civilizations that have preceded ours, this is a troubling similarity. It speaks of decadence, not of endurance.

374. The Opportunity Loop

In America's formative years, a combination of hope, struggle, hard work, adventure and risk created a self-reinforcing opportunity loop.

The more people who believed in a better future and worked hard to achieve it, the larger the opportunity loop became. More opportunity created more opportunity, and it became the largest human magnet in the history of the world, all of them drawn to opportunity.

Aside from in Western Europe, just about every person we have met in the entire world wanted to come to America for the opportunities.

375. The Victimhood and Entitlement Loops

In modern America the opportunity loop still exists only for the first and second generation immigrants and a small percentage of the general population, the risk-taking entrepreneurs. Those two groups continue to leverage the opportunity loop to change their lives, the lives of their families and to create innovations, companies and jobs.

The rest of America has been seduced by the self-reinforcing victimhood and entitlement loops. In those loops, there are no consequences for choices, everyone who created a better life for themselves did it dishonestly, everyone is owed a living and a life and everyone is being mercilessly persecuted by an oppressive overseer class.

In the victimhood and entitlement loops, the mantra has been codified by academics, shouted by money-grubbing opportunists, formed into iconic, society-wide indoctrination by popular culture and drummed into the heads of willing believers from the time they are infants until they are lowered into the grave.

The victimhood and entitlement loop believers warmly embrace the opportunity to be responsible for nothing, live a consequence-free life and always have someone else to blame for every single aspect of their world and their lives.

376. Demographics Drive History

Politics drives policy, but demographics drive history.

Short-term politics, almost always local politics, at best national politics, drives social policy. But, policy doesn't determine, or drive, history. Demographics drive history.

History shows no examples of long-term peace, growth and stability when there are huge demographic disparities in income, education, marriage status, quality of life, etc., between age cohort segments, economic segments, geographic segments, nation-state segments or macro-religious segments. The disparities are always changed or shifted in usually abrupt balance and equilibrium-seeking corrections.

Because those doing the perceived oppressing are loathe to give up their position, the change usually comes after much resistance and arrives as a rapid, sharp transition, almost always accompanied by copious amounts of violence.

All that is required to initiate the shift is the enablement of the downtrodden / disadvantaged by a new empowerment. The empowerment can be a new political alliance, a new form of communication, a new weapon or even a new strategy.

Terrorism, often referred to as the poor man's nuclear weapon, is just the latest example of this phenomenon. It is merely the modern manifestation of the inevitable equalization between disparate demographic groups.

The end game generally results in the imposition of a new set of disparities to replace the old. This pattern is repeated throughout history, from ancient Egypt and China to the modern day communist revolutions in China and Russia and the Islamic revolution in Iran, all of which simply replaced one oppressive set of disparities with another.

377. Fixing the Blame vs. Fixing the Problem

American culture is almost exclusively interested in fixing the blame instead of fixing the problem.

378. Racism, Inc.

Racism has become institutionalized in America. But, it has not been institutionalized in the form it existed in as government and social policy prior to the civil rights movement. In its current form, it is institutionalized in academia, education and business.

There are college degree programs in racism. There are organizations and businesses that exist on the merchandising of all aspects of racism and its effects. There are people who have massive wealth and huge influence because they have perfected the art of turning the specter of racism into a business model.

Racism is no longer a cultural attribute; it is now a business segment; it is Racism, Inc.

The primary product of that business model is an entire population group, indoctrinated in victimhood, which is incapable of viewing any life attribute or experience through any perspective except racism. This population group is fanatically loyal to their leaders, regardless of how the leaders' mantra of victimhood keeps generation after generation locked into a downward spiral.

Racism, Inc. has the ability to crush all who oppose it, even members of its own community who have the vision and courage to stand up and point out that America is the epicenter of most of the world's opportunity for growth, advancement and achievement.

Racism, Inc., regardless of its lip service to the topic, does not want growth, advancement and achievement for its community. If there was growth, advancement and achievement, Racism, Inc. would lose its constituency and business model. Instead of growth, advancement and achievement, Racism, Inc. wants to perpetuate the belief that racism is interwoven into every single aspect of life and Racism, Inc. is the only route to salvation.

There is, without doubt, still racism in America. It is very doubtful, however, that the remaining racism in America is even one percent as damaging to its victims as Racism, Inc. is to its constituency.

379. Competition is Good

Competition drives success. Where would Coke be without Pepsi, Ford without Chevrolet or the Red Sox without the Yankees? Without a competitor, it is impossible for individuals, teams and organizations to maintain a high level of performance over time.

Competition drives innovation and efficiency. An individual, tribe or organization that has no competition always produces sub-standard output. Compare the state of consumer goods in the U.S.S.R. at the time of the collapse of the communist Soviet Union with comparable products in the capitalist West. Everything from Soviet toasters to Trabants, a truly horrible car produced in East Germany during that era, were substandard compared to Western counterparts.

In the Soviet communist economy, all decisions were made by central control. There was no competition, no voice of the consumer or market demand-driven decisions. In the capitalist economies of the West, products lived and died based on the market's demands and desires. If a product or service answered an unmet need in the market, it prospered. If it did not, it died. It is this Darwinian survival of the fittest products and services that keep innovation and efficiency alive.

This sharp edge of competition, its life and death nature, fosters efficiency. The co-location of competitors ensures that every player is as efficient as possible to remain competitive. Note the proximity of competing drug store chain retail stores. Compare the distance between major competitor's locations in all retail segments. Close proximity competition exposes inefficiencies. It ensures that prices are low and each operation remains innovative and runs as efficiently as possible.

Without personal and organizational competition, human activities quickly grow stale, static and lifeless. Competition is good.

380. Europe

"They are old over there, older than we are.
They fathered our speech and mothered many a document we hold dear.
We came from there in the seeds of our forefathers.
We are in debt to them, we owe them much.
Yet we came away from them because we wanted no more of what they held out to us.
We are the same as they and yet not the same.
And in the turn of the wheel of time we shall not be the same nor shall they." –
Carl Sandberg

It is very easy to be a Europhile. Europe is most Americans' heritage. The history is relevant, the faces familiar, the foods common. It is easy to reflexively genuflect to the older and wiser Europe, always leading the way with the correct answer to every question.

Compared to Europe, America is usually cast as the adolescent society, an immature culture trapped in Puritan psychosis. America is often viewed as a 16-year old just handed the keys to a very powerful automobile, juiced on early teen hormones, armed with a fat wallet and incapable of making the mature judgments required to manage such armament without casualties.

Some of that may indeed be true, but if that analogy is applied, then Europe is surely a third-year university student with no conception of the bills that have been paid to provide the coddled and protected life they enjoy, insulated in a single-mindset cocoon, nurturing dreams of utopia and shouting platitudes that sound heroic to fellow believers, but ring hollow to those out in the real world paying the bills and keeping the bad guys at bay.

Europe is no more the center of enlightenment and advanced civilization than America is the source of all evil. Anyone who believes either of those maxims is dangerously naïve.

381. Island America

One of the biggest factors impeding Americans in effectively relating to and interacting with the rest of the world is the simple scale of America itself.

The U.S. is geographically so large you could spend a lifetime exploring it and never see and experience all it has to offer. Why should anyone care about the rest of the world when there's so much right here to see and do?

The U.S. economy is so large and so chock full of opportunity, you could spend a lifetime starting and building businesses and never run out of market segments and unmet needs. With that amount of economic upside, why would you need to worry about the rest of the world?

This massive, overwhelming and insulating scale leads to American media and Americans being almost entirely isolated and self-absorbed. Stories from the outside world only pierce the barrier wrapped around the U.S. if they are spectacular, concern mass death, contain huge amounts of drama or directly threaten Americans. Consequently, Americans know very, very little about the reality of the outside world. All they know is the distorted and selective version that makes it through the media filter.

Most Americans spend their lives learning about, and having their media report on, America. Most Americans spend their entire lifetimes within the borders of America. At most, they may venture to Canada or an isolated, walled beach resort in Mexico or the Caribbean. Most Americans go to their graves never having interacted with a foreigner in a foreign land, never having learned about another culture, never having experienced any way of living life other than the American way.

Thus, America is a self-absorbed nation, a nation with a distorted sense of uniqueness, an isolated nation and a nation with very little incentive or ability to interact with or truly learn about the rest of the world.

Unfortunately, the world is genuinely getting smaller. World problems affect every American. The World economy touches every American.

It is no longer an option to consider America an island - insulated, a safe cocoon - where you can live your life and never have to worry about or interact with the rest of the world.

America is no longer an island. It is just another boat on the ocean of the world. And very, very few Americans know how to sail those seas.

382. The American Immigrant Pattern

The first generation immigrants to America sacrifice everything for a better life for their children. Two jobs, three jobs, whatever it takes, the children will be educated and achieve a better life.

The second generation usually attends college and achieves a much higher standard of living than their parents. They usually achieve the American Dream.

The third generation often becomes completely Americanized and loses the drive and commitment demonstrated by their grandparents and parents. They often become just like other underachieving American children.

In many American immigrant cultures, second- or third-generation teenage and young adult immigrants develop a strong identity with, and attachment to, their family's country of origin. They have no knowledge of the real conditions there that drove their parents or grandparents to emigrate to America. They often romanticize or gloss over conditions in the home country and cherry pick cultural aspects to manifest in their adopted country.

383. The Puritan Factor

The United States was founded by Puritans. The legacy of that founding philosophy and outlook still exists, and in many ways, permeates the society.

While difficult to notice from inside the U.S. fishbowl, it is readily apparent when compared with other nations, in particular other developed nations.

384. America's Way

America's way of life is only one among many possible ways to live your life. If you never get out of the country and experience other alternatives, you will never know the possibilities.

You will also never know the relative strengths and weaknesses of America's way of life.

You will, however, be very susceptible to those who claim America's way is the best way, the only way.

385. The People

Who shall speak for the people?

Who knows the works from A to Z

      so he can say, "I know what the

      people want"? Who is this phenom?

      where did he come from?

. . .

Who shall speak for the people?

who has the answers?

where is the sure interpreter?

who knows what to say?

Excerpted from "The People, Yes" by Carl Sandberg

The most dangerous politicians are populists, those who claim to speak for the people. Look closely at them, and examine everything about them in detail. Without exception, they are almost all opportunists, pandering for support.

386. The Bi-annual Bear

Back in the days of the cold war, the United States Defense Department budget came up for review every two years. Consequently, every two years, about six months before the congressional hearings started, the newspapers and television would start to fill with tales of the Soviet threat.

Slowly and steadily, the public was fed the story of the threat of nuclear vaporization via long-range bombers, submarine-launched or silo-based intercontinental ballistic missiles; idling fleets of Soviet tanks ready to thunder through the Fulda Gap and overrun Western Europe; and the slow creep of communism to our very doorstep through puppet regimes in South and Central America.

Sure enough, by the time the first congressional defense committee hearing gavel fell, the public and their elected officials were salivating at the opportunity to pour more money into programs, systems and technologies to fend off the burgeoning Soviet threat to the very existence of western civilization.

The way of the world has not changed much in the years since the fearsome Soviet Bear was trotted out like a circus act every two years.

When a nation needs to justify its means to advance the nation state agenda, it will always feature, accentuate and exaggerate, or create from whole cloth if necessary, a foreign threat.

When there are times of increased international tension and sabers are rattling, always keep the bi-annual bear in mind. Be very careful to evaluate how much of what you are being told is real and how much is simply designed to facilitate and advance an agenda. It is much more important to perceive and understand the underlying agenda than to know the details of the real or imagined threat.

387. The Empty Schoolyard

During our travels in Japan, we discovered a troubling symbol of modern Japan and, with Japan being the most developed nation in the world, the iconic symbol of the end-state of the current model of human development: the empty schoolyard.

About mid-August 2006, Japan had fewer people than it did the day before. Japan is literally dying. Its birthrate is less than 1.32, while a rate of 2.1 is required to maintain a static population size.

The challenge is children. When humans become educated, successful, comfortable and coddled in modern conveniences, they stop reproducing. The number of children in Japan has fallen for 25 straight years.

The existential challenge is that children are required in order create a new group of workers in the economy. They not only fill the jobs, they support the economy and feed the retirement funding system for the preceding generations. Without a new crop of workers as large or larger than the retired population segment, taxes must rise to meet the society's obligations. Eventually the tax rate becomes crippling, social benefits are slashed, the entire system breaks down and the economy and country collapse.

The empty schoolyards are not limited to Japan. Western Europe is also experiencing this phenomenon, as are other fully developed economies. From Singapore to Germany, governments have created financial bonuses and other rewards to encourage young couples to reproduce. The programs have not met with much success. Wherever humans live in a fully-developed economy, where they are educated and successful, they make the choice to put their energy into self-gratification rather than the personal sacrifices inherent in parenting.

Japan provided us with a unique opportunity to witness and experience the apogee of human societal and economic development. But for all its "best in the world" attributes, Japan, as we have seen it and known it, is dying. Soon, Japan, as we know it, will be dead, and its demise will mark the end of humankind's long development-based climb from the cave to the condominium.

Japan's death marks the death of development, the death of the model of species, societal and economic development that has defined the last few million years. Mankind will, from this point forward, be in a post-development phase, struggling to define a new evolutionary model that enables ongoing economic and societal viability for developed nations in an era of self-absorbed, shrinking, native working populations.

388. Map Reading Skills

In totalitarian countries it is very rare to find people who know how to read a map. The government does not want their people to know where they are, where anything else is and especially how to get there.

389. Germany vs. Japan vs. China

Germans believe they are the best, and thus, obviously, deserve to rule the world. The Japanese work diligently, every day, striving to be considered worthy of being the best, and to earn the responsibility of running the world. The Chinese simply know, to the depths of their souls, they are the best and are divinely destined to rule the world.

If the U.S. is smart they will stick to what they do best and secure the global marketing rights to the upcoming cage match.

390. The Charity Model

After 50 years and $600 billion worth of giving, according to the United Nations there has been close to zero rise in living standards in Africa. There is no better example in human history that the charity model, simply giving, does not work. All it accomplishes is the destruction of initiative, ambition, desire for achievement and, in the end, the human spirit.

The only model that works is investment and ownership. The local population must be invested in the initiative. They must select it as a priority. They must invest time, energy and wealth into the initiative. They must have ownership and responsibility for success.

Simply giving, simply distributing a *hand out*, does not work. What works is helping a people or a person achieve via offering a helping *hand up*.

391. Judging a Society

You don't judge a society by how its rich people live. You don't judge a society by how its middle class lives. You don't judge a society by how its poor live. You judge a society by how it treats its prisoners.

392. National Purpose

As I write this, I have visited 40 countries. In 39 of those countries there has been a palpable sense of national purpose. In those countries, people know what the country is striving to achieve, what direction the country is headed, and what each person is asked to do to achieve those goals. The less developed the nation, usually, the stronger the sense of national purpose.

The 40th country, the one with no sense of national purpose, no unifying theme, no common goal, no shared values, no unifying identity, is the United States of America.

393. Consequences

One way to evaluate a political candidate or party is to view them through the prism of consequences. Is their message one of essentially no consequences for peoples' choices? If people make poor choices over and over and over again, does this candidate or party advocate that there should be no consequences?

Do you enjoy the same luxury in your own life, or do you pay consequences for your actions?

Should society enable, allow and encourage people to spend their lifetimes making bad choices with no consequences?

394. The Last Path to Power

The path last taken by those who seize power will always be sealed off to prevent anyone following the same course and deposing the current rulers.

For instance, in China, the communist regime came to power via a peasant and worker revolution. Consequently, there are no unions except the official party unions allowed. The party remains the only voice of the people. If anyone deposes the communist party, it won't be via the path of peasant and worker revolution.

If you want to change things, you will need to take a fresh course, not the one taken by those currently in control.

395. Educate the Girls

During our travels in 2004, I interviewed three different Non-Government Program (NGO) program managers in different regions of the world, two of whom worked for the United Nations. All three gave the same assessment, unprompted, as to the single most important factor in changing the potential outcomes for a developing country's society: educate the girls.

If girls are educated, even to a sixth grade level, the rate of population growth drops dramatically and the standard of living for families increases significantly.

If you educate them to the eighth grade level, the results are measurably better still.

No number of aid programs, free handouts, hospitals, etc., can match the impact of simply educating the girls.

396. Democracy

Democracy requires an educated, informed, engaged and motivated electorate. If any of these prerequisites are lacking, the form of government is a democracy in name only.

This applies to all so-called democracies, especially the United States of America.

397. The Challenge of Divestment

Modern developed societies are structured to encourage and reward acquisition. By the time people are young adults they have very highly developed and attuned product evaluation and acquisition skills.

Conversely, almost no one divests themselves of material goods except to throw them away so they can buy the next, newer replacement thing. Large scale divestment of material goods is essentially unheard of, so there are few to no common skills, systems, processes or infrastructure to facilitate it.

One of the most challenging things I ever accomplished was to give away a complete, turn-key corporate headquarters. It took me over a year to locate a suitable non-profit that would or could accept it.

It was even more challenging for us to divest ourselves of essentially all the worldly goods from our personal lives.

Ironically, in modern, developed societies, it is much easier to acquire things than it is to give them away.

398. Bad Guy Glue

Watch what happens when a leader needs to unify his team, company, state or nation. The most powerful glue to hold disparate or unhappy people together is a common enemy.

Watch what happens when China is experiencing a lot of internal dissent. The party will trot out Taiwan or WWII Japanese atrocities to unify the population in hatred of an external factor.

America or another artificial external "Bad Guy" threat are also regularly featured by ruling families, oligarchies and tin-pot dictators who want to divert the attention of their seething masses away from their failed policies or societies.

Entities in the United States also rely on Bad Guy Glue. When the government, politicians, activists or personalities want to rally the troops and unify their supporters for action, they will feature a common enemy.

A fundamental rule of drama is that the story's success is directly proportional to the depravity, fear and loathing of the bad guy in the story. For example, the market triumph of the original Star Wars franchise was directly related to the specter of Darth Vader.

If you can personalize the common enemy as an individual human Bad Guy, the glue gets even stronger. That's why Islamists, Anti-American Europeans and the despots running the Middle East were so overjoyed when George W. Bush was re-elected in 2004. He made such a wonderfully pre-packaged foil for them, it was easy to keep their constituents' attention diverted and from pointing out that their current or would-be emperors lack a single stitch of clothing.

Watch how Bad Guy Glue is used in the world around you, in families, at work, in politics and in popular culture. It is the most common tactic used to unify disparate factions, and, if personalized, is highly energizing for groups.

399. The Victor's History

The victor writes the history. We have no way of knowing if past kings were really wise, princesses beautiful or warriors brave. Our history is the product of the public relations machines of their eras. A historian, storyteller, poet or minstrel didn't live long if they didn't relate the version of history that glorified their patrons.

The telling of today's history and current events is equally skewed by political partisanship, world views and topical trends. Be very wary of wholesale adoption of any view of current events or recent history by yourself or especially groups.

Only by personal investigation, in-depth research of many different points of view and a broad range of experiences and perspectives can you hope to have any feel for what is actually currently happening or happened in the past.

400. Childhood Disease vs. Female Education

In a developing country, the prevailing birth rate is primarily driven by two factors: childhood disease and the state of female education. International aid organizations generally focus on childhood disease. It is possible to make significant impacts on childhood disease rates in relatively short timeframes and the resulting charts, news stories and accolades are highly desirable.

Educating females takes time and requires sustained investment of money and resources. Modern, developed societies are much less interested in, and less well equipped structurally and culturally, for anything that requires long-term commitment. But, if it becomes a reality, educating females has a very significant attenuating affect on birth rates.

In practical terms, the population growth rate for developing countries usually reflects rapid acceleration as a result of successful programs related to childhood disease. It then becomes a race to educate the females soon enough to slow that population growth rate before the expanding population outstrips the available resources.

401. Goal and Result Timelines

A fundamental difference between American business and governmental management and Asian business and governmental management is that American business and government management is measured against the next quarter's goals and Asian business and government management is measured against the next decade-, 20 year-, 50 year- and century-goals.

The short-term, myopic American focus on immediate results has resulted in disastrous, ruinous, game-over strategic and tactical management errors in American business and governmental leadership.

American business and government management teams often have long-term, multi-year plans and goals but you would be hard pressed to present more than a handful that are not completely symbolic in nature, form and function.

In a world of rapidly decreasing economic deltas the luxury of American market uniqueness has disappeared. The legacy of short-term American goals is an ongoing burden in a rapidly developing, long-term world.

God, Faith and Religion

402. The Monochrome World

Is there a God?

Take a walk through a botanical garden or look out over a valley filled with spring flowers. This world could all be monochrome, in black and white.

You tell me.

403. Religions vs. Cults

One definition of a cult is any religion other than your own. It is extremely difficult for humans to respect the legitimacy of any religion other than their own.

Why is your religion the exclusive owner of salvation? What makes your religion the only genuine religion, the only possible route to the one true understanding of God?

Why is every other religion a cult and yours isn't?

404. Faith <> Religion

Faith does not equal religion.

Faith is the manifestation of the seeking of God.

Religion is the codification of faith.

As in any codification, religion attenuates, categorizes and creates orthodoxies of faith. In doing so, it creates arbitrary lines that define faith. Often, these lines are about little more than creating ownership and claimed exclusivity. Over time, religion becomes more and more about human desires, traits and needs and less and less about faith, except to the extent it can be used to draw out support from the faithful.

On Friday nights in Portland, a Christian group goes to an area where the homeless live. There, the volunteers wash, cleanse and bandage the feet of the homeless. That is faith.

In Sikkim, we saw two elderly women who were prostrating themselves on the ground, then drawing up their knees like an inchworm, then stretching out prostrated again, all the while never lifting their eyes. With each cycle they advanced their bodies about 18 inches. They had traveled all the way from their village in this manner to pay honor to a visiting Buddhist holy man. Their village was 50 kilometers (31 miles) away. That is faith.

While in Mississippi for a month doing Katrina relief work, we saw scores and scores of volunteer teams digging out homes, shoveling debris and rebuilding homes. Every single one of them was from a church group. That is faith.

Faith does not equal religion.

405. Faith vs. Belief

Faith is unassailable, unquestionable and inviolable. Faith cannot be debated, swayed by logic or influenced by facts.

Belief is open to debate, can be questioned, is determined by factual evidence and can be empirically tested and changed based on the results.

Be aware of those things you espouse which are faith and those which are belief. Be extremely aware of the choices you make based on faith versus those you make based on belief.

406. Atheism and the World

There is a school of thought which maintains that religion is destructive and negative. Their position is that religion has caused so much strife and destruction in human history that it must be stamped out and eliminated. It is argued that atheism, and its modern PR counterpart, rationalism, is the only pure and informed school of thought and world view, and that religion's adherents are simple-minded, ignorant, uninformed lemmings who would be laughable if they weren't so dangerously misguided.

The flaw in this thinking is its inherent arrogance. Most of the world's people, and by a wide margin, believe in some form of God or religion. Most of those who profess to not be religious, especially in developed economies such as Western Europe, have simply replaced classic religion with ancient and modern superstitions. The truly atheistic, without superstitious artifacts, are a tiny, tiny percentage of the human population.

Could it be possible that a low, single-digit percentage of the people alive today have truly figured out what humans are supposed to be and how they are supposed to think?

I don't know the answer to that question, but it would help a lot if they would keep in mind that their low numbers relative to the world's population are not reflective of an exclusive, transcendent club as much as a rounding error in calculating the membership of the world's belief systems.

Atheists and rationalists showing some respect to the vast majority of people who live on this planet who, for whatever reason, believe in God or religion would go a long way to establishing reciprocal respect instead of hostility.

407. Exclusivity of Salvation

In 325 CE (AD) somewhere between 250 to 318 bishops (depending on whose count you accept) accompanied by over 1,000 priests, deacons and acolytes, met in Nicaea, Bithynia (present-day Iznik, Turkey), at the behest of Roman Emperor Constantine I. Their meeting was the first council of Nicaea.

The council lasted from May 20 to June 19. Over the span of that month the bishops debated and resolved several critical theological challenges for the early church. The council was primarily called to decide on the Arian controversy concerning the nature of Christ, as he related to the nature of God. In the course of history, however, that issue became just another footnote in the long list of Christian theological debates.

By far the longest lasting and notable outcome of the council was the doctrinal statement, or oath, that defined the Christian faith. That oath described, exactly, the beliefs of the Christian faith. It became known as the Nicene Creed, and was recited by priests and the laity at every subsequent mass across Christendom.

In 381 CE (AD) the First Council of Constantinople met to again debate matters of theological and doctrinal concern, primarily the divinity of the Holy

Spirit. Arguably, its most notable achievement was the official confirmation and endorsement of the concept of the Trinity.

Another of its actions, considered relatively minor compared to the Trinity, was the insertion of five words into the Nicene Creed, "…and in the Holy Ghost, _who proceedeth from the Father_,"

In 1054 CE (AD), 673 years later, the Christian church, what we now know as the Catholic church, split into two parts in the Great Schism. The two segments became the Roman Catholic Church, centered in Rome, and the Eastern Orthodox Church, originally centered in Constantinople (modern day Istanbul, Turkey).

The Great Schism was an inflammatory event, stoking great hatred and resentments. Both sides clung tightly to their positions and eventually claimed that since the other side didn't exactly follow the proper beliefs, practices, liturgies, ceremonies and rites they were heretics and every one of their members would consequently burn in hell.

The reason for the Great Schism of 1054? There were many aspects, but the most commonly cited reason are those innocuous five words from 673 years before: _"who proceedeth from the Father."_

Each side of the Great Schism claimed to have an exclusive claim on salvation. Only by following their exact beliefs and practicing their exact rites, in this case either including or excluding five words, could a believer achieve salvation.

This difference of five words may seem trivial, but to those highly invested, those who believed they represented an exclusive claim to salvation, they were worth dying for, as many did when Roman Catholic Christian Crusaders murdered thousands and sacked Christian Constantinople in 1204.

Every one of those crusaders believed that their religion, their tribe of believers, had the only true path to God and salvation, and that they alone possessed exclusivity of salvation.

To those highly invested in exclusivity of salvation, no price is too high to defend or enforce that exclusivity.

The Nicene Creed was decreed in 325 CE (AD). The Great Schism happened in 1054 CE (AD). In 2005 I learned of a sect of the Protestant Church of Christ denomination that believed every other member of the Church of Christ, every other Protestant, every other Christian, every other person in the world except the true believers of their small sect, was doomed to damnation. This tiny subset of the Church of Christ had determined they were the only believers in the world, out of more than six billion people, who had the secret to salvation. This small group determined they had exclusivity of salvation and everyone else, all six billion men, women and children, were going to burn in hell.

Exclusivity of salvation is used to differentiate almost every form of belief in the world. It forms the bright line that separates the tribe of true believers from all others.

It is used to create a fundamental perception of need in those who are outside the line. Exclusivity of salvation states if you don't join our tribe of believers, and practice belief, rite and ritual exactly our way, then you are doomed to damnation.

Exclusivity of salvation is primarily used to create the perception of need, the need by those outside to join the tribe of believers to achieve salvation. The definition of marketing is creating the perception of need. Exclusivity of salvation, when used to drive recruitment, is nothing more than marketing.

Can anyone prove exclusivity of salvation?

Can anyone prove it is anything more than commonality reinforcement within the tribe of believers, simply a way to make everyone feel better that they have all made the right choice, the only true choice?

Can anyone prove it is anything more than arrogance, the maximum manifestation of hubris? How can any person, any group of believers, have the fundamental arrogance to claim only they will achieve salvation and every other sect, every other denomination, every other religion, every other seeker of God, every other person on earth will suffer eternal damnation?

I have tremendous respect for seekers of God. I try to spend time with them and learn from them wherever I meet them, anywhere in the world, regardless of their Gods, their beliefs, their practices, their idols, their rites or their rituals. True seekers of God, in my experience, are seeking enlightenment and peace of spirit. To true seekers of God, in my experience, rite and ritual, while familiar and comforting, are secondary to that pursuit.

Unfortunately, true seekers of God are rare, and they are almost always superseded by, and overwhelmed by, those more interested in tribal and community association, relationships and networking, dogma, ritual and conformity than enlightenment. Part and parcel of that package of dominance is exclusivity of salvation.

Should you choose to seek God, you must make your own choice on how to do so. But, when you do, be careful of, and aware of, the reasons you do so. Is it more about tribal and community association or relationships and networking? Is it more about the comforting nature of rite and ritual? Is it more about exclusivity of salvation? Or is it all about enlightenment and seeking God?

Along the path of seeking God you will meet many. Beware those who feature and tout exclusivity of salvation. No one has an exclusive lock on salvation or an exclusive guarantee of salvation. It is all based on faith. And nobody's faith is demonstrably more pure or effective than anyone else's.

Nobody can claim exclusive rights to salvation.

408. True Believers

While in Turkey, we visited the ancient Ottoman palace on the Bosporus. It was the seat of power for the Ottoman Empire, once the most scientifically, medically and militarily advanced civilization on the planet. The Ottoman Caliphates, the political and religious rulers of the Muslim empire, gathered all of the most notable religious artifacts from their empire and era in their palace.

When the palace was converted to a museum, one wing was filled with those religious artifacts. Among the artifacts were objects, bones, markers, etc. associated with the shared prophets of the Jews, Christians and Muslims, and those of the prophet Mohammad, the founder of Islam.

As we walked respectfully through these rooms with our guide, Kazim Uzunoglu, I noticed a group of elderly Muslim women, fully covered, slowly, fearfully, approaching a glass-enclosed island case containing artifacts of the prophet Mohammad. Their hands extended outward, palms out, shaking. Their cheeks were lined with tears. They were overcome with devotion and reverence.

We passed out of the room onto the terrace outside overlooking the Bosporus. Once outside I turned to Kazim, a Muslim, and asked, "What chain of evidence exists to prove conclusively that those artifacts are indeed the bones, the cane, the footstep, of the prophets?"

Kazim replied, "To the true believer, no evidence is required. To the non-believer, none will suffice."

409. Going to Heaven

"If I could not go to heaven but with a party, I would not go there at all." – Thomas Jefferson.

Jefferson's remark related to political parties, but is equally applicable to groups in general. If you seek a heaven it is important to understand the context of your quest.

Does your personal vision of heaven require others? Or can you imagine a paradise alone, devoid of others?

Can your soul be at solitary peace?

410. A Faith vs. The Faith

I have tremendous respect for people seeking God. Most of them operate within a structured religious context of one type or another. They manifest their seeking of God through a faith.

The danger is when they move from having *a* faith to believing they have *The* Faith, the *one* and *uniquely* true way to seek and find God.

Respect people of faith. Be wary of those who believe they have *The* Faith.

411. Religion

People are involved in religion, the human codified, structured reflection of faith, for three primary reasons:

1. Convenient, pre-packaged answers to questions
2. A built-in tribe providing shelter, protection, support and networking
3. To seek true enlightenment

Of these, the third, seeking true enlightenment, is the rarest reason. Those who become involved in religion for that reason are often disappointed, usually disillusioned and sometimes very, very bitter.

412. God Is – Or Isn't

God is either omniscient, omnipresent and omnipotent, or isn't.

God is either all things, or isn't.

God is either the creator of the universe, or isn't.

God is either the alpha and the omega, or isn't.

God is either the arbiter between eternal peace and eternal damnation, or isn't.

God is either the path to enlightenment, or isn't.

God is either a fabrication of man to provide easy, pre-packaged answers to the unknowable, or isn't.

God is either a response to existential anxieties, or isn't.

God is a ruse, an opiate, used by elites to control the masses, or isn't.

God is a patrimonial framework used to perpetuate and extend the subjugation of women, or isn't.

God is a manifestation of hard wired, pre-programmed mental modules used for survival response in early humans, or isn't.

God is a mass of neuron connections in a dedicated portion of the human brain, or isn't.

Either way, at some point in your life, you will need to determine your individual perceptions and beliefs about God.

God is pervasive throughout all human societies and cultures, from newly discovered tribes in the Amazon basin to the oldest and most developed societies on earth. God, and how man relates to God, permeates all of human history, from the earliest cave paintings to the most modern forms of human expression.

Just like every other human, from individuals to tribes to societies to the entire population of the planet, you will, at some point, need to determine your fundamental relationship to the human concept of God.

And, when you do, keep in mind that your relationship to the human concept of God can, and probably will, change and evolve over time as you move through the chapters of your life.

Travel

413. The First Rule of Travel

The first and most important rule for successful travel is: Don't mess with the locals.

414. Travel Yields Perspective

The outcome of travel is perspective.

You will never gain true perspective of another place, people or culture by skimming a magazine, reading a book or watching a television show or movie.

To truly gain perspective, or instill it in your children, you must travel.

415. Travel Learning

The Germans have a phrase that translates loosely to "travel learning." Their philosophy is that you learn more by traveling than any amount of television, movies or books could ever teach you, or teach your children.

You will teach a child more by traveling with them, taking them to places, near or far, than by any other method.

416. The Gut Rule

When traveling and in life, establish and maintain a no quibble, no discussion, no debate "gut rule."

If you feel anything in your gut, or anyone you are traveling with feels anything, and I mean anything, even the slightest little tingle, you all turn around and leave. There is no board meeting, no conference calls, no Roberts Rules of Order, no proxy vehicle for unresolved relationship issues, no debate.

One tingle, everybody bails. Now.

417. The Next Place

"Never assume the next place will be better than where you are now." – Fredy Baumann.

When traveling, don't always be in a rush to get to the next place. Instead, fully explore, enjoy and get to know the place you are in now.

Just because it is the next place does not guarantee it will be a better place.

418. Ride Your Own Ride

The tourist walked up to the restaurant, stopped, glanced at the exterior, looked over the menu on display and smiled, apparently finding something he liked. He started to enter but then stopped.

He pulled his travel guidebook out and leafed through the well-worn, dog-eared pages until he came to the city's restaurant listings. He traced his finger down the reviews again and again. When he didn't find the restaurant before him listed in his book, he turned and walked away.

Meanwhile, we sat inside and enjoyed one of the best meals we'd had in weeks.

The tourist had fallen into the trap of becoming dependant on his guidebook. He was unwilling to take a chance on any experience, even a meal, without the explicit endorsement and recommendation of the authors.

In reality, the tourist was not on his own trip. He was recreating a version of the guidebook's trip. He was just like so many of the other travelers we see moving around the big tourist areas in clumps and packs, never deviating from the prescribed route, the advised stops and the recommended activities.

And, that is a real shame, because our best travel experiences, by far, are the ones we stumble into ourselves.

Whether it was wandering around the Byzantine back alleys of the cities in the Middle East or the small fishing villages of Japan, the best discoveries, the most authentic experiences and the best new friends, have always come due to our own discoveries, not by following the lowest common denominator recommendations of a guidebook.

A guidebook is written to appeal to the broadest possible audience while presenting the lowest possible risk profile. That guarantees if you follow a guidebook you will experience the same white toast, vanilla journey as the other 500 shuffling zombies thumbing their guidebooks around you.

In addition, guidebooks are generally targeted at a specific market segment. For instance, Lonely Planet guidebooks are the bible for early 20s (and those who still wish they were) backpackers. That's great if you want to know which hostel is less than $1 USD cheaper than the next, but not very relevant if you are looking for a different type of travel experience, such as a really nice, once-in-a-while, dinner in a decent or upscale restaurant, much less where you can experience something of the local culture without sharing it with 100 other backpackers.

When you base your trip on a guide book, you are not living your experience - you are living theirs. You are not on your unique journey, you are walking down a well-worn path established and defined by people you have never met and likely never will.

At a minimum, it is less rewarding to live someone else's journey. In some situations it can be dangerous.

When I learned how to ride off-road motorcycles at the ripe old age of 37, I had the good fortune to fall in with a group of guys who were all above average to excellent to regional champion to national champion to world champion class riders. The upside to that experience was that for the few brief seconds I could keep them in sight, I could pick up a few pointers. A few of them also took mercy on me and coached me in specific techniques for specific challenges.

I spent a few years riding very hard trying to keep up with them, all the while crashing on a regular basis when riding over my head attempting to stay within the same area code as their rapidly disappearing dust clouds. That chapter of my life is most accurately described as long periods where my velocity exceeded my abilities alternating with the consequences thereof. My yield was a good collection of broken bike bits, bruises, scars, etc.

I finally came to the conclusion that no matter how hard I tried, I was never going to compensate for the fact that these guys, almost to a man, grew up with a dirt bike between their legs and the endless, infinite expanses of the 60s and 70s American West to ride it in. It finally sunk in that if I wanted to really enjoy the experience and take in the incredible scenes of nature around me, I needed to stop riding their ride and start riding my own.

At that moment, my enjoyment of the sport increased by several orders of magnitude. I stopped trying to take someone else's journey and started to experience my own.

The same goes for travel. Don't get trapped into following someone else's journey, especially a guidebook's.

Ride your own ride.

419. The Call to Prayer

When we traveled in the Middle East, one of the most foreign, intrusive and initially discomforting things in the environment was the five times daily call to prayer from the minarets of every mosque in the region. The wailing, warbling Arabic was completely unfamiliar, unintelligible and very offsetting.

Over time, however, it became part of the background of every day, and we eventually began to critique the quality of each performance, rating them against our favorites.

Now, as we travel in other areas of the world, we still miss the daily rhythm of the call to prayer.

It is testament to the fact that even the most foreign and unfamiliar can become a part of the fabric of your life. You can and will miss the unfamiliar.

420. Local Knowledge

When sailing in new or unfamiliar places, one imperative for success is to seek and obtain local knowledge. By asking local sailors and fishermen you can gain insight into unique local conditions and hazards that would take you years to learn on your own.

The same is true for all forms of travel, and for that matter, any life situation in which you are in unfamiliar situations or surroundings. Find someone who has local knowledge and ask for what you need.

421. Travel Pack

Always pack for travel the day or night before you leave, even if your departure is scheduled for late the following day, and especially if you are not a professional business traveler.

Sleeping on it overnight will give you a chance to remember the things you forgot to pack.

422. Bad Roads

"Bad roads bring good people. Good roads bring all kinds of people." – Mama Espinoza.

Bad roads, by their very nature, weed out the idiots, the unprepared, the uncommitted, the casual, the negative, the transients and the lost. It takes perseverance, ingenuity, adaptability, commitment and a durable positive attitude to arrive.

If you make it to the end of a bad road, you've not only earned it, you'll find others there like you.

Conversely, good roads bring anyone who can manage to drive a car.

The more challenging path in life – the bad road – will deliver you to a place filled with people of good character.

423. Growing Up Black

I grew up white. I've had some black friends through the years, but know little about their culture.

After Hurricane Katrina in 2005, we spent a month in Mississippi doing relief work. For most of that time we lived with and around black families. We slept in their yards, ate meals with them, played with their kids and worked long, hot, sweaty days with them cutting fallen trees out of homes.

While sharing meals and working alongside them, I learned what it was like to grow up black in the segregated South and have only 175 feet of beach available to you along the entire Gulf of Mexico coastline. I learned what it was like to get an education in segregated schools, find a way to work your way through college, build a life and raise a family. I learned what it was like to be a black man, in a black community. I learned some history, learned some tales and learned some songs. I learned a lot. But I'll never, ever, really know what it was like to grow up black.

There is no substitute for actually going somewhere and living amongst the people. You will learn much. In fact, you will learn what the reality really is. Not the glossed over news version, or the skewed drama used to advance someone's political agenda, but the actual, on-the-ground, reality.

But, in the end, just like for me, you will never know the full and complete measure of their lives. But, you will know more than anyone who has never actually been there. It is important to understand the difference.

424. One Thing

When you are traveling, schedule one thing per day. Americans tend to cram their travel days like they cram their daily schedule. They attempt to see and do as many things as humanly possible, sometimes even more than humanly possible, every day. This short-changes every experience, guarantees a superficial experience and leads to burn out, frayed nerves and irritability.

Schedule one thing per day. You may see less, but you will truly experience what you do see.

425. Cultural Goggles

The biggest challenge in travel is to do it without wearing cultural goggles. If you look at everything around you, and all of your experiences, through the filter of what you were raised to think is normal, what you think is right and wrong, you will miss at least 90 percent of what the world has to offer.

It is very challenging to experience new places, people and things without overlaying them with your cultural expectations.

Take off your cultural goggles. Although it will be very challenging and uncomfortable, it is the only way to see the full bounty and beauty of the world and its people.

426. The Journey is the Destination

If you focus on a destination, you are setting yourself up for disappointment. No destination can live up to what you want or expect it to be.

Instead, focus on the journey. Keep your mind open to its lessons. Take the time to savor the journey. You will never pass this way again. And, besides, the true rewards lie along it, not at the destination.

427. International Travel

The most important key to survival and enjoyment in international travel is to always remember that when you are in a foreign country, you are a guest.

Act like one.

Practicalities

428. The First Immutable Law of Email

Without exception, wait overnight before replying to any important, life-altering, career-impacting or emotional email message.

429. The Second Immutable Law of Email

It is impossible to express emotion in an email. Emoticons do not, and never will, effectively communicate emotion. If you've got something to say in which the emotional content is important, could be easily misunderstood or you need to read the emotions of the respondent, then pick up the phone or walk over and talk to them face to face.

430. The Third Immutable Law of Email

Almost every major company in the world monitors their employees' email. Never put anything in an email you wouldn't want on the front page of tomorrow's newspaper.

431. The Negotiation Walk

If you are not prepared to walk away from the table, you've already lost.

432. The Negotiation Talk

The first person who speaks after the initial offer of price in a negotiation loses.

433. The Negotiation Clock

Whoever is under time pressure or a deadline in a negotiation has already lost.

434. Never Live West of Work

Never live West of where you work. If you do, you will be driving into the sun in the morning and into the sun at night. Squinting into the sun twice a day greatly increases the chances of having an auto accident. If at all possible, live North, South or East of where you work.

435. Cut Away

"Always cut away from yourself when using a knife. Always push the blade away from your body." – Clarence Hackney.

You will work with and around numerous dangerous tools in your life. You will be in many different types of dangerous situations dealing with dangerous people.

Always be aware of where the danger lies, and keep it isolated from yourself.

436. Let the Saw do the Work

"Let the saw do the work." – Clarence Hackney.

When you are cutting metal or wood with a saw, you must let the saw do the work. It won't help if you try to bear down on the saw and add weight, or you'll most likely just get a crooked cut. It won't help if you invest a few dozen strokes in a big cut and then start another one because the saw isn't cutting fast enough. The saw will do the job if you just let it do its work using steady smooth strokes. Just keep at it.

This is the same in life. If you make a plan or choose a course, you need to let that choice play out. It won't help if you try to force things. It won't help if you keep getting impatient and repeatedly change course or start over. You need to keep at it, and give your plan, your choice, a chance to do its work.

437. The High Cost of Poverty

Poverty is expensive.

As bizarre as that sounds, it is a concrete rule of the economic landscape.

When you are poor and have no or bad credit, you pay more for everything.

You pay more for housing because you can't afford to buy real estate and build equity. At the extremes you rent by the day or week, and pay orders of magnitude more for shelter than homeowners or even renters.

You pay usurious interest rates for any type of credit you are able to obtain, thus any item purchased on credit costs many times more than if purchased with cash or with normal interest rates.

If you can't even qualify for that credit, and can't afford to buy anything, you rent it for sky-high rates that cost you many times more in rentals in a short period that it would cost to buy the item.

You don't have much cash, so you are consistently late paying your bills. This adds large late fees and penalties to what you already owe.

You can't afford a reliable car so you pour huge amounts of money into patchwork repairs of unreliable junkers.

Poverty is incredibly expensive. And, once you start down the poverty spiral, because of these very high recurring costs, it is extremely challenging to escape.

This is another reason why building and protecting a good credit rating, one that yields access to capital and affordable interest rates, is your most precious financial asset.

438. Noise Fatigue

Loud noise, loud sound, is incredibly fatiguing and its effects are not widely appreciated. Wear earplugs when riding motorcycles and when operating loud equipment. You will arrive at the end of the day much stronger.

439. 2AM vs. 8AM

When you are working late, stop working when you realize that you just spent 15 minutes on something that you could do in 45 seconds in the morning. Get some sleep and start fresh. You will accomplish more and make fewer mistakes.

440. The Russian Toast

I offer a toast.

I toast to the day I carry the coffin at your funeral. Your funeral will be vast, with countless friends gathered from distant places to honor your life.

I toast to the day I carry the coffin at your funeral. It will be the finest coffin, richly appointed, lined with the softest silk.

I toast to the day I carry the coffin at your funeral. Your coffin will be made of oak, strong oak, sturdy oak, from an oak tree 100 years old.

I toast to the day I carry the coffin at your funeral. I will carry your coffin made from 100-year-old oak, from an oak tree I will plant tomorrow.

A toast!

441. The Black Hobby

When it comes to vehicles, black is not a color, it is a hobby.

442. Speed Doesn't Kill

Speed doesn't kill. Difference in speed kills.

The most dangerous moments are not at high speed, properly trained, on or in a suitable vehicle at a suitable venue. The most dangerous moments are any time and place you are at a significantly greater or slower speed than the other vehicles around you.

For this reason, always be at freeway speed when you get to the end of the entrance ramp. If you are going faster than you need to be, you can quickly, with a tap of the brakes, slow to a matching speed. But, if you arrive at the end of the entrance ramp going too slow compared to the freeway traffic, it will take a very long time to accelerate to a higher speed.

Be extremely cautious when you are moving quickly next to a line of slow moving or stopped traffic. If there is a gap between cars in your lane, vehicles in the stopped or slow line of traffic are very likely to jump out into your lane and cause a crash.

Remember the immutable law of street motorcycling: It isn't the crash that hurts; it's the sudden stop at the end.

Speed doesn't kill. Difference in speed kills.

443. Total Cost of Ownership (TCO)

Every capital investment, whether it is a manufacturing plant, a production line, a server rack, a boat, a home, a car or a television has three categories of costs in its total cost of ownership.

- Acquisition
- Utilization
- Divestment

When calculating the cost of a capital asset, you must consider and include all three elements.

Acquisition costs include research, consulting or other evaluation costs, travel, trade shows, dealer visits, demonstrations, test rentals, inspections, certifications, shipping, taxes, fees, professional services (legal, accounting, etc.), cost of capital (financing costs) and the asset cost (purchase price).

Utilization costs include operational costs, consumables (fuel, consumable parts, etc.), repair (labor and parts), upgrades, renovations, operating fees, taxes (property, asset, etc.), storage, etc.

Divestment costs include upgrade or repair to make salable, inspections, certifications, taxes, shipping, professional services (legal, accounting, etc.) and the costs of sales (sales commissions, transaction fees, etc.).

It is all too easy when considering a capital asset purchase to only consider the asset cost. While you may be able to easily afford the purchase price and the cost of capital, the other elements of the TCO may add up to more than your free cash flow can support.

Every asset purchase from a toaster to a manufacturing plant involves all three TCO categories of costs. Whatever capital asset you are considering purchasing, regardless of size or cost, perform a complete TCO analysis prior to purchase and after divestment. It is the only way to fully understand the true cost of ownership of an asset.

444. Gravity

In motorcycling and body shape – gravity always wins.

Respect gravity.

445. Two Types

There are two types of motorcycle riders: those who *have* gone down and those who *will* go down. There are no exceptions to this rule.

Dress appropriately for the sport, and be ready when your time comes.

446. Preparing

Always prepare for events, tasks, activities and obligations the day before they are scheduled. There is always time to do something the day or night before, but never time to do things the day of, especially the morning of, the task or event.

447. Common Grammatical Errors

If you want to advance yourself in life, you must be able to write effectively. In order to communicate credibly, you must eliminate common grammatical errors.

- To, too, two
- Its, it's
- They're, their, there
- Your, you're
- Who's, whose
- No, know
- Sight, site
- Light, lite
- Lose, loose
- Affect, effect
- Break, brake
- New, knew
- Threw, through
- Accept, except
- Write, right, rite
- Capital, capitol
- Principle, principal
- Weather, whether
- Lie, lay, laid, lain

- Insure, ensure, assure

You must know the proper usage for these words and use them appropriately.

448. Spandex

"Spandex is a privilege, not a right." – Anonymous.

Know where your current body shape and condition fits in the fashion and style universe. Wear things that complement your body instead of accentuating its weakest attributes.

449. Sell the Dream

The first lesson you learn in the boat business is that you never sell a boat. You never talk to the prospective buyers about buying a boat. You don't paint a story about fulfilling the ultimate boat purchase.

In the boat business, you never sell the boat, you sell the dream. You don't sell the boat, you sell the dream the boat represents: idyllic day sails, racing glory or a circumnavigation filled with adventure and discovery.

Boats aren't the only thing sold in this manner. Always be aware which you are buying. Is it a tangible purchase or are you buying a dream?

450. Building Fires

A fire requires three things:

1. Heat
2. Oxygen
3. Fuel

If you quiz them, most people don't get the first of those elements, but it is crucial. You must build your fire in a place that reflects heat back into the fire or you will struggle to build and sustain it.

Almost everybody remembers oxygen and fuel as requirements. You need a steady supply of fresh air and you've got to have fuel that will burn.

If you don't have all three of these elements, your fire is not sustainable. You may be able to get it going, but you won't be able to keep it going, and that leads to a lot of frustration.

Another rule of fire building is that to have a big fire you must first have a small one. You must start very small, get a small fire going, then build a medium fire on that, then a large fire, if you want one, on top of the success of the medium fire. If you get impatient and try to go directly from kindling to a large fire, all you will reap is some smoke and failure.

Steps for building a fire:

1. Gather the driest fuel you can find, especially plenty of small to medium twigs and sticks. You will need kindling (dry grass, dry leaves, paper, etc.), small and medium twigs, small and medium branches (rolled up newspaper can be substituted for these sizes), small and medium logs or large branches. Get all the fuel before you start. You need to pay attention to the fire and if you are off searching for additional fuel it is likely to collapse or go out in your absence.

2. Break or cut the small to medium material to working length - 12 to 18 inches / 30.5 to 45.8 cm is good.

3. Form a U with three medium to large size logs. Keep one end open so air can reach the fire. The U will reflect the small fire's heat back onto itself and enable a medium and large fire. Keep the closed end of the U fairly narrow, around 8 to 10 inches / 20.3 to 25.4 cm, and be certain it is shorter across than the length of your small and medium size logs.

4. Make a small pile of your driest kindling near, but not against, the backside of the U. Use crumpled newspaper if that's all you have.

5. Build a cribwork (interlaced structure) of small twigs over and around your kindling. Leave an opening so you can get a match or cigarette lighter into your kindling without toppling the cribwork. Leave plenty of air gaps in the cribwork to ensure good airflow.

6. Build a cribwork of larger twigs or small branches over and around the cribwork of twigs. Be sure to leave an opening so you can light the kindling and feed in more if necessary. Leave plenty of air gaps in the cribwork to ensure good airflow.

7. Inspect your kindling and cribworks. Your goal with the kindling, twigs and small branches is to build a bed of coals from them as they burn.

The bed of coals provides the heat to ignite and sustain the medium and large fire.

8. Light the kindling. If necessary, blow gently to get a solid yellow flame going.

9. Be patient and let the kindling fully ignite and burn.

10. If required, feed in additional kindling to get the twig cribwork burning. Don't stuff them in or you will put out the fire. Put it in one small piece at a time. Let each piece ignite and burn before inserting another.

11. If required, feed in additional twigs to get the small branch cribwork burning. Don't stuff them in or you will put out the fire. Put them in one small piece at a time. Let each piece ignite and burn before inserting another.

12. Carefully place small branches over the twigs to form a grid or cribwork without collapsing the burning material. If possible, prop them over the twigs on the big U logs. Maintain good air gaps. Do not pile them on or lay them on side by side or you will suffocate the fire.

13. Once the small branches are burning steadily, lay larger branches or small logs over them to form a grid or cribwork. Lay them over or prop them on the U logs.

14. Add additional feed stock of small branches or rolled up newspapers into the fire as required to keep it burning steadily. DO NOT cram them in or pile them on or you will suffocate the fire.

15. When the larger branches or small logs are burning steadily you can proceed to make as big a fire as you want following the same principles.

16. When you are done with the fire, be sure your fire is completely out. That means multiple buckets of water or completely buried with a shovel. DO NOT leave a burning fire or hot bed of coals unattended. Ever!

Using accelerants such as lighter fluid or other fuels is the mark of a fire amateur. These people are dangerous and you should avoid them. It demonstrates a willingness to endanger themselves and others because they are too lazy to do a job correctly.

The epitome of fire building is a one-match fire. If properly constructed, you can go from one match to a large fire without adding a single twig.

Now read back through those instructions and think about your life. To build a successful life you need exactly the same things as building a successful fire.

Are you fully prepared for the fire of your life? Do you have a full and sustainable supply of all required elements? Do you have fuel of the proper sizes? Do you have supportive structures that will reflect your energy back? Have you properly constructed the architecture? Are you starting small and building from there?

Are you mindlessly stuffing fuel into the fire and smothering it? Are you using accelerants and doing nothing more than wasting fuel and demonstrating your ignorance?

Or, do you have a one-match fire?

451. The Old Car Hobby

The old car hobby is very rewarding. It includes a tremendous sense of accomplishment, a built-in tribe of fellow hobbyists, social events and networking, interesting quests and colorful personalities.

Requirements for the hobby include:

- Sustainable disposable income
- Tools
- Clean, warm, well-lighted place to work
- Readily available parts
- Solid, worthy vehicle to invest your time in
- Perseverance
- Willingness to learn

If you don't have these components, then owning an old car will be an exercise in frustration and a slow spiral downward into financial oblivion.

452. Measure Twice

"Measure twice, cut once." – American folk wisdom.

Whenever you are using material of any kind, always measure two or three times before you cut it. You will take a little more time preparing for the cut, but you will save yourself a lot of grief and material.

453. Estimating Sunset

To estimate how much time you have before sunset:

1. Hold your hand out at arms length
2. Bend your wrist and turn your palm towards your face, with your fingers parallel to the horizon
3. Raise or lower your arm until your little finger is just touching the horizon

Each finger between the horizon and the sun is about 15 minutes

454. The Unneeded Banker

It is a rule of business and life that when you don't need money, banks are more than willing to lend it to you. When you desperately need it, the opposite is true.

For this reason, it is critically important to establish banking relationships when you don't need the money. Go and meet your bankers now. Establish and maintain personal relationships with them.

At some point in your business or your life you will need a line of credit or other financing tools to grow your business or survive a financially challenging period. That's when the relationships you built when you didn't need the money will save the day.

455. Banks Sell Money

The fundamental business model of a bank is selling money.

Banks don't make a significant profit on checking accounts or their other retail banking products and services. Banks make a profit by selling you money, that is, by loaning it to you and charging you interest. Typically, they will borrow the money from another bank at a lower interest rate and loan that money to you at a higher interest rate; the difference between the interest rates is the bank's profit margin. Check the numbers, it isn't much.

Remember how small that profit margin is when you are wondering why a bank is so picky about loaning you money.

456. 0 Percent vs. Cash Back

If you are faced with a choice between 0 percent financing and receiving a cash rebate at the time of purchase, always take the 0 percent financing. Zero percent financing is equal to a free cost of money. It allows you to spread out the capital costs of the asset over time with no cost of money.

A cash rebate is a waste. You will spend a cash rebate within days or weeks and be left with nothing to show except the interest charges for the duration of the financing contract.

Always take the 0 percent.

457. Opportunity Cost

For every choice you make in life there is an opportunity cost.

In financial terms, this is what you could have done with the money if you had not invested it in the choice you made. For instance, if you didn't buy a $50,000 car, but instead put that cash into investments, your opportunity cost is the value of those investments at the end of the service life of the car, plus the negative depreciation of the car.

A $50,000 investment for five years at 5 percent yields about $64,000. Conversely, the $50,000 car would be worth about $20,000 at the end of the same five years after you subtract the depreciation. Your base opportunity cost is the $64,000 value of the investment you could have made. The total opportunity cost is $64,000 + the $30,000 depreciation = $94,000. How does that $50,000 car look now?

If you finance the $50,000 car on a five-year loan at 7 percent you will pay $9,404 in interest over the life of the loan. Your $50,000 car is now a $59,404 car, so you need to include the finance charges in your opportunity cost calculations. That's an opportunity cost of $64,000 + the $30,000 depreciation + the $9,404 in financing costs = $103,404. How does that $50,000 car look now?

There is also an opportunity cost for life choices you make. You can spend four years doing exactly what you are doing now. Or, you could spend four years earning a college degree. If you spend the four years doing exactly what you are doing now, at the end of the four years your opportunity cost is the lifelong lack of opportunity and life experiences that would be enabled by the degree.

When you are evaluating financial and life choices, put the opportunity cost at the top of your decision criteria.

458. Managing Debt

Avoid debt.

Only use it for durable capital assets whose lifetime will exceed the duration of the loan used to purchase it. In other words, never buy something with debt that won't outlast the time it takes to pay it off.

But, most importantly, avoid debt.

459. Spreadsheets <> Reality

No spreadsheet or financial modeling projection beyond a few days or weeks ever exactly matches the resulting reality.

This is true in both business and personal financial planning.

Do not confuse numbers plugged into a financial model with what is going to happen. At best, it is what is likely to happen. At worst, it will lead you to make decisions that result in very negative financial consequences.

460. Finding Flaws

In any purchase decision it is important to know the strengths and weaknesses of what you are considering buying. One effective and efficient way to learn the shortcomings of a potential product or service is to talk to the competitors.

A lot of what they tell you will be designed to create fear, uncertainty and doubt (FUD), but there will also be some elements that will be true weaknesses and other factors good to know.

461. Backup

Have you ever had your computer crash? Have you ever had a computer stolen?

What was the most important loss when that happened? Was it the hardware or the software?

No, it wasn't either of those things. What was most important was the data you lost. The most important loss, indeed the only loss that mattered, was all of the unique, irretrievable, irreplaceable work and information that you stored on your computer.

When you lost all of that irreplaceable, invaluable data, were you hoping to lose it? Were you planning to lose it? Were you willing to lose it?

There is only one thing that would have changed your loss - a backup of your computer's data.

When it comes to information - to data - there is only one rule: Don't back up what you are willing to lose.

462. Ethnic Restaurants

The best ethnic food restaurants are the ones where you are the only one in the place who isn't a native speaker of the relevant language.

463. The Path of Progress

When buying a home or property, buy in the path of progress.

Visit the local city offices. Talk to the planning director. Examine the city's master growth plan. Discover where the areas of planned growth are located. Drive around the areas and identify buying opportunities near where new businesses, schools and residential areas will be located. Those are the areas that will experience the highest, fastest rates of growth and, consequently, the fastest appreciation in property values.

464. The Smallest House

When buying a starter or builder home, in other words, your first or a stepping-stone home, buy the smallest house in the nicest neighborhood.

America is an aspiration-based society. Potential buyers will aspire to live in the nicest neighborhood, so buy the smallest or most affordable home in the nicest neighborhood.

Invest sweat equity in the home by improving it in ways that most affect its desirability and resale value, and then sell it. Repeat.

Before long you will build up enough equity to purchase whatever property you want, wherever you want.

465. The Coastline Factory

They are not manufacturing any more coastline. Land fronting water is the one, single, best real estate investment. It will always be desirable. Over the mid- to long-term, it will, nearly without fail, increase in value.

466. The Last Moment of Control

When you make a major asset purchase, the last moment you have any control is the millisecond before you sign the contract.

Treat the time before you sign with due and commensurate respect. Ensure that you ponder, long and hard, all aspects of the transaction prior to signing.

Negotiate with resolve, with full and complete knowledge that once you sign you trade all negotiating power for the gratification of the purchase.

The person selling you the asset will use every technique at their disposal to rush you through the signing process, because they know that they are most vulnerable at that very second.

The last moment you have any control in a major asset purchase is the millisecond before you sign. Use those moments well.

467. Kill the Darlings

When I was a kid I used to sit at my grandparent's house and read *The World Book Encyclopedia*. When I went to Chicago to manage a media production house, World Book was one of our clients. That was very cool.

I once asked Esther Zimmerer, a senior editor at World Book, how she could take a subject like gravity or airplane and cut it down to a manageable size that would allow enough space to include the other thousands of subjects in the encyclopedia. She replied simply, "Edit ruthlessly."

When I was a professional photographer, and later a film and video director and producer, one of the biggest lessons I learned, and by far the toughest to implement, was "Kill the Darlings."

The darlings are all the shots and scenes that we have tremendous emotional investment in. We may have worked for weeks to gain access to a site, or spent hours waiting for the right light. Or we may have shot hundreds of images or hundreds of feet of film or video of a young girl seeking just the right interplay of sparkling eyes, flashing smile and sunlight glowing in her hair. But, without that emotional investment and context, the shots or the footage really don't work.

Every photo, every scene, must tell a story, on its own, with no narration or caption. It must communicate something to the viewer, with no supporting, gripping tale of struggle and strife of what it took to get that shot. If the shot or scene cannot stand on its own, it must go.

The same is true of your life. How many things, elements, relationships and recurring commitments do you retain because of your emotional investment in them instead of their actual value and relevance to your life?

Edit ruthlessly. Kill the Darlings.

468. Mr. Sawzall is My Friend

Some years ago I embarked on a major renovation project. It involved an old Victorian estate home, associated out-buildings, many contractors, wheelbarrow loads of money and, many would say, a certain pre-disposition toward masochism.

During the initial stages of the project, I escorted legions of contractors through the home and other buildings so they could build quotes for the project. The majority of the contractors were polite enough not to question my sanity for undertaking the project directly in front of me, which I greatly appreciated. However, I was surprised when several of the most promising and professional contractors didn't call me back.

When I contacted them they informed me that they wouldn't take the job on, as they preferred "new construction" jobs over renovation. I couldn't believe they were walking away from a huge project when we were heading into the winter season, a quiet time for construction in our little piece of the frozen tundra.

They explained that, all in all, they'd rather shut down for the season than get involved in a project that was impossible to estimate accurately due to the amount of hidden surprises inherent in renovation work. They preferred the clean, secure, reliable world of new construction, where they knew exactly what lay in wait around every corner. They weren't even interested in doing the project on a time and material basis, saying it just wasn't worth the grief they knew they'd encounter. Mystified, I turned to several contractors who were willing, and we began the project.

With every room, we found some new mystery. Using their ubiquitous Sawzall, a powerful reciprocating electric saw that can literally cut through anything known to man, the contractors removed plaster, lathe and anything else that stood in their way, only to reveal old gas lines, fabric covered wiring from Edison's era, re-located walls, boarded up windows, etc.

The project was like an archeological dig, uncovering layers of past lives. With each new find, our plans had to change to reflect our new reality. Design alteration after design alteration, change after change, we rolled with the punches of new discoveries and unexpected challenges.

In the end, we wound up with a beautifully restored 14-room home and associated buildings that was a wonderful accomplishment, even if it was significantly different from what we originally planned.

The lesson here is that it is impossible to accurately estimate the cost in money and time of home renovation work. That beautiful "fixer upper" you keep driving by and lusting after is much more likely to be a money pit than a semi-neglected jewel.

Renovation projects usually cost one-and-a-half to three times more than your initial, back of the envelope, estimates. They usually take at least twice as long as you or your primary contractors estimate.

But, it's not the cost and time that wear you down and grind you into dust on a renovation project. It is the constant setbacks, the endless new discoveries requiring a complete change of plans, the very, very expenses surprises and the ever-receding finish line that break your spirit.

Before you take on a major home renovation, be sure to work through a few modest "renovate and sell" house projects first. Start with a home that just needs some new drywall in a few rooms or a new kitchen to be marketable. Those experiences will show you how many surprises lurk within each wall - surprises that can only be revealed by your new best friend, Mr. Sawzall.

469. The First Three Rules of Photography

Photography was my first real career. I started young, at 16. My boss and mentor, Steve Willard, spotted me along the sidelines of a high school football game, gave me my big break and taught me all the essential rules of professional photography, including the first three.

The first rule of photography:

Never leave a camera strap hanging over the edge of a table, counter or any horizontal surface. The camera will inevitably be pulled off onto the floor.

The second rule of photography:

Physically separate your exposed images from your camera equipment. This means once you expose film or fill a memory card, put it in your shirt or pants pocket, not in your camera bag. A thief may steal your camera bag, but it can be replaced. The images are unique and irreplaceable.

The third rule of photography:

Capture lots of images when you shoot. Film or memory is extremely inexpensive compared to recreating the experience.

470. Taking Better Photos

Basics

- Hold your camera properly.
    - o Spread your legs about shoulder width
    - o If you are using a "point and click" digital camera, hold it with two hands
    - o If you are using a Single Lens Reflex (SLR) camera, create a three-point support system by holding your camera body and lens with your left hand and pressing it against the bones around your eye socket. You should have three points of support: your left hand, the bone above the eye and the cheek bone below the eye. Press the camera up against your face firmly so your neck and head, as well as your left arm, wrist and hand, are actively supporting the camera. For the best support put your left elbow firmly against your ribs.
- Press the shutter properly. Don't jab at the shutter button. Slowly push your finger down until the shutter releases. The smoothest release is realized by rolling your finger across the shutter button.
- Use the proper camera mode. For basic photographers, keep your camera in "automatic" mode.

- Keep lighting consistent. Place your subjects in one type or level of lighting. For an outdoor people shot, get everyone into the sunlight or everyone into the shadow. Do not have a little shadow and a little sunlight mixed on the same subject.

- Avoid harsh sunlight. Bright sunlight will make your subjects squint. Put everyone in the shade if possible, the lighting will be more even and "soft."

- Use over the shoulder (OTS) lighting. Keep the light source over your shoulder, behind you, with the subjects in front of you. Avoid shooting into the sun or into a bright light source.

- Use proper camera orientation. Holding your camera normally, or horizontally, will produce a "landscape" oriented image. Landscape orientation is best for horizontal subjects such as a family group or a photo of a low, wide house. Holding the camera turned 90 degrees from horizontal will produce a "portrait," or vertically-oriented image. Portrait orientation is best for strongly vertical subjects, such as a single person or a tall tower. Use the camera orientation that will fill the majority of the frame with your subject.

- Keep your camera level. Look at your viewfinder or view screen and compare the horizon line or the lines of buildings, rooms or objects to the edges of the viewfinder or view screen. The lines should be parallel.

- Check your framing. Before you shoot, look around the edges of the viewfinder or view screen. Do you have even spacing around your subject? Are you cutting off the subject's head or feet? Is everyone or everything in the photo that you want to be in?

- Check the focus point. Your camera will probably beep and display an icon in the viewfinder or view screen where it is locking focus for your photo. Before you shoot, confirm that the focus point is on your subject.

- Don't center your subject in the middle of an otherwise empty frame. A photo with a small subject exactly in the center of the frame is the most common framing error and rarely makes a good photograph. Make use of "Rule of Thirds" framing by placing your subject and/or the point of interest (eyes, key object, brightest point, etc.) on one of the thirds lines or intersection points of the frame.

Intermediate

- Know your camera. Read the manual and try every function on the camera. Know what every button does. Know what every setting does. Know what every menu option does. You cannot advance or improve your photography without knowing how your primary tool, your camera, operates.

- Know your camera and lens combinations. If you are using a Single Lens Reflex (SLR) camera that enables the use of different lenses, you must understand what each camera / lens combination is capable of creating. In particular, get a feel for the lowest light levels you can effectively utilize with your fastest lens wide open and highest usable ISO settings. Also, experiment to discover the slowest shutter speeds you can use at your longest possible focal length.

- Know your flash. Read your flash unit's manual or the flash section of your camera's manual and try every function on the flash. Know what every button does. Know what every setting does. Know what every menu option does. In particular, you need to know how to alter your flash output down 1/3 to 3 stops for fill-flash purposes.

- Use the proper fully automatic mode. Understand what your camera's additional automatic operating modes (portrait, landscape, night, etc.) do and what conditions they are optimized for. Don't be afraid or ashamed to use fully automatic mode. The idea is to get the shot, not worry about how you got it. Start with automatic mode to get the "record shot," then experiment with other automatic modes that you think would be appropriate for the situation.

- Use the proper priority mode. Understand fully what TV (time value or shutter priority) and AV (aperture value or aperture priority) modes do and what shooting conditions and desired creative outcome are best for each mode.

- Use fill flash. Soften shadows and create a catch light (pinpoints of light in a subject's eyes) by using fill flash. Fill flash to soften the shadows is mandatory for shooting in blazing, direct, harsh sunlight.

- Use bounce flash. Direct flash is harsh and will often wash out your subject. Use a dedicated flash with a rotating head and bounce off a ceiling or a card.

- Use under exposure to protect highlights. Digital cameras have limited dynamic range, so it is easy to overexpose highlights. Once the highlights are gone, you cannot get them back. Conversely, digital cameras can create files that have good resiliency for underexposure. Bracket down a third and a full stop to create some files that will preserve your highlights.

- Understand panning. Practice panning with your most likely camera/lens panning combination. This will probably be your longest telephoto lens. Understand the effects of the different Vibration Reduction (VR) or Image Stabilization (IS) settings on the lenses you own and how they affect panning. Determine what visual effects different shutter speeds produce at different panning rates.

- Adjust your subjects to the available light conditions. Leverage the "golden hour" moments of sunrise and sunset for spectacular, large scale scenery and settings. Use those same moments for subjects you can schedule and control. In the harsh light of a sunny mid-day, wait for a cloud, shoot in the shadows or concentrate on macro photography. On cloudy or rainy days, concentrate on the richness and subtlety of color that is released and accentuated by the soft lighting. For interiors, use tripods and existing light where possible, softening the lighting by using bounce flash where it is not possible.

- Get the angle. Move away from the standard, eye-level point of view. Get down on the ground, get on your knees, lay down, get down to children's eye level, get a puppy's point of view, get up and elevated, get over people's shoulders. In short, create an image that is different than the standard view.

- Get small. The small details of a place or event often tell the story in a way and scale that is more approachable and understandable. Keep your eyes open for the small things, the everyday objects, the human scale things that make your story compelling.

- Capture the peak of the action. In any activity, movement or sports shot, capture the moment of highest drama, stress or effort. This requires anticipation and the ability to time your shutter release with the precise moment required.

- Use leading lines. Compose your image to use leading lines to draw the viewer's eye into the subject.

- Use patterns. Use patterns to define the creative space of the image and accentuate the difference of the subject.

- Use light levels. The human eye is drawn to exceptions and brightness. Ensure your subject has a higher light level than everything else in the frame or is accentuated by exception.

- Use selective focus. Isolate your subject by making it the only thing tack sharp in the frame. Use aperture priority mode to control depth of field. Use shutter priority mode and panning to make your moving subject the only thing in focus against a blurred background.

- Create emotion. Successful photographs create, invoke or spark emotion in the viewer. Strive to generate wonder, fear, excitement, anticipation, awe, trepidation, tension, comfort, contentment, etc., in the viewer. Your image must create an emotion to be successful.

- Tell a story. Each photograph you create should be able to stand on its own and tell its own story without the luxury of a caption. As you look through the viewfinder or at the view screen, ask yourself, "What story is this image telling?"

- Capture the establishing shot. Shoot overall scenes, the exterior of buildings, signs and markers that describe the subject and place your photographs in the context of locations and events.

- Establish the context. Shoot signs, calendars, newspapers, notes, etc., that will establish the context of the images you are shooting. These images will greatly aid the process of cataloging the images now and understanding where and when they were created at a later date.

- Understand the different types of images you create.

  o Record shots. These are an overall view of the castle, city, place, thing, etc. It will look like a postcard image. Its purpose is to establish the record that you were there or record the status or existence of a place, person or object.

  o Grab shots. These are images you create by grabbing and shooting. You may or may not capture the quickly passing event, object or person in the fleeting moment.

  o Controlled shots. These are images you create when you control the setting, subject, time and place.

  o Experimental shots. These are images you create while exploring the capabilities of your tools.

  o Creative shots. These are images you create by applying your creativity and vision to the world that you encounter. Your creativity is primarily limited by your knowledge of your tools. If you fully know what your tools (camera, lens, lighting, etc.) are capable of, then your results will only be limited by your imagination, inspiration and freedom of thought.

Work and Business

In your lifetime, you will spend more time at work than with your family or your friends. You will invest most of your life energy into your work. Because work is such a large portion of your overall life experience, it makes sense to understand the basics of work, business and entrepreneurship.

At its most fundamental levels, work and business are very simple. But, as you attempt to be a success in work, build a career or create and sustain a business of your own, you will soon discover that it is also infinitely complex.

Work

471. How to Succeed

When you start out in your working life, you will be working for others. It is nearly the only way to begin, and the smart way to learn and to make your inevitable mistakes.

While working for others, no matter if you do so for a time and then work for yourself or if you spend your entire working life working for others, there are some universal truths about work and how to succeed that are relevant no matter where or how you work.

I have never seen or heard a more succinct compilation of those universal truths than from Chapter Three of the 1917 Army Officers' Manual.

Excerpted from:

Officers' Manual
By Major J.A. Moss
United States Army
Sixth Edition (revised May, 1917)

Being a service manual consisting of a compilation in convenient, handy form, of "Customs of the Service" and other matters of a practical, worth-knowing nature – things of value and assistance to the inexperienced – most of which cannot be found in print, but must be learned by experience – often by doing that which we should not do or by failing to do that which we should do.

[Pages 67 – 69]

CHAPTER III

HOW TO SUCCEED IN THE ARMY

155. **Make yourself useful** – that's the way many of our most prominent men in the army and in civil life have succeeded.

HOW TO MAKE YOURSELF USEFUL

1. Whatever You Do, *it matters not how unimportant*, DO THOROUGHLY – WITH ALL YOUR MIGHT – WITH YOUR WHOLE HEART AND SOUL – *as if your very life depended on it* – and then look for something else to do.

Almost any officer can do a thing fairly well. Many can do a thing very well. A few can do a thing superbly well. *But the one who, through zeal, energy, enthusiasm, patience, and persistence,* STAMPS EVERYTHING HE DOES WITH HIS PERSONALITY, MAKING IT INDIVIDUAL AND DISTINCT, *is the one who, in the Army, like in every other field of human endeavor, will succeed.* Such a man can't help but succeed – you might as well try to stop the waters of Niagara as to stop him from succeeding.

2. DO NOT CONFINE YOURSELF TO DOING ONLY WHAT YOU ARE TOLD TO DO – only what your captain, your commanding officer, the Army Regulations or general orders tell you to do – DO MORE THAN YOU ARE TOLD TO DO. There are always other things to be done – HUNT FOR THEM (you'll be able to find them) AND DO THEM.

3. DO NOT PROCRASTINATE – whenever you have something to do, DO IT *and* DO IT *at once – don't put it off!* Make it an invariable rule at the very beginning of your career never to put off until tomorrow what you can do today.

4. *Always endeavor to* ANTICIPATE THE WISHES OF YOUR SUPERIORS, putting yourself in their place and doing what you would have your subordinates do for you.

5. When directed to do a thing, if you can't do it at first, do not then report you can't do it, but TRY SOME OTHER WAY, and keep on TRYING SOME OTHER WAY until you have either succeeded or have exhausted every possible means you can think of. *It is really astonishing how comparatively few things in this world cannot be done, if one only tries hard enough to do them.*

And when given a task by the commanding officer or any other superior, do not pester him by continually reporting what you are doing, the difficulties that are being encountered, getting his opinion about this and that, etc. Remember, it is the RESULT that your superior wants – *the result that it is "up to" YOU to accomplish* – he doesn't want his time taken up and his patience tried in the manner stated, by sharing your troubles, etc. – probably he has some of his own. So, unless absolutely necessary in order to get some point cleared, which can be cleared only by the superior himself, or to have some obstacle overcome which can be overcome only by the superior himself, keep away from him until you are ready to "deliver the goods."

6. Do not confine yourself to THINKING, to DREAMING. It is not enough to have ideas – ideas alone mean nothing – they must be put into effect. One idea that is carried out, that is given body and form – one idea that assumes definite, tangible form and bears concrete results, is worth a million ideas that are born but to die.

Get into the habit of following things up, of "camping on a fellow's trail." If, for instance, you wish to get something from the Quartermaster's Corps, or if you wish to have the Quartermaster's Corps do something for you, don't stop when your request goes in, but keep the matter before you as "unfinished business" until you have gotten what you went after, or it becomes very evident that the article can not be gotten or the thing can not be done – and remember, as stated before, *that there are comparatively few things in this world that can not be done, if you only try hard enough*. The making of a request is only the beginning – unless you *follow it up, it may,* (and often does) *mean nothing*.

7. Last, but not least, don't allow yourself to get into the unfortunate, annoying, pestiferous mental attitude of always finding reasons why things can't be done. There are some unfortunate human beings in this world who, as soon as a thing to be done is mentioned, at once and *instinctively* begin to think up and advance reasons why it can't be done. Such an attitude is a mental condition – a form of mental disease that stamps the man as "a dead one," a pessimistic creature

whose mission in life is to obstruct and retard progress, and annoy, hamper and pester "the live ones" – those who DO THINGS and PRODUCE RESULTS in the game of life.

If you haven't [done] it already, cultivate and develop the opposite mental attitude – that is, as soon as a thing to be done is mentioned by a superior begin at once and *instinctively* to think up different means and ways in which it can be done, bearing in mind "Stonewall" Jackson's motto, *"Any man can do anything that he REALLY wants to do."*

Remember, the man who succeeds in this world is the man who ATTRACTS ATTENTION and the man who ATTRACTS ATTENTION is the man who DOES THINGS – not the man who TALKS about doing things.

It is safe to say any young officer who follows the above principles will not only, in the course of time, become generally and favorably known throughout the Army, but he will also ultimately rise to a position of prominence and influence. It may be a long time – perhaps five, ten, or even fifteen years – before your efforts are fully recognized and rewarded, but don't be discouraged – remember this has been the experience of some of our greatest generals and our greatest railroad presidents, merchants, bankers, and other recognized leaders, but that's the way they succeeded.

[All emphasis duplicated from the original text.]

472. Job Grief

Every job has grief. It doesn't matter if you are a dog catcher or the president, every job has grief. Therefore, find a job that is intrinsically rewarding so the inevitable grief is worth it.

473. Sustainable Rewards

Work for sustainable rewards. Money is not a sustainable reward. Sustainable rewards include, but are not limited to, fulfillment, growth and discovery.

474. The Employee Prime Directive

The prime directive of survival for any employee is to never, ever let their direct supervisor get blindsided.

475. Everyone is Replaceable

Immutable law of corporations: Everyone is replaceable.

In a corporate environment, the minute you start to believe that you are so special that no one could ever do what you do, know what you know or be as essential as you are, you are doomed.

Everyone in a corporation, every single person, is ultimately viewed as expendable and replaceable. You may be considered valuable, a prime contributor and a key team player, but no matter what, you will never be irreplaceable.

476. Pick Your Hill

In the workplace, in your personal life and especially in relationships, be very careful to pick a hill you are willing to die on.

This is one of the most important lessons you will ever learn about the corporate world. Be very careful about signing up for causes, missions, crusades, etc., that pit you against powerful political forces. Be very, very careful about being willing to sacrifice your career, job or client on a hill.

There will be many hills in life. Be very careful when picking a hill you are willing to die on.

477. Losing Yourself in Work

If someone, including you, is losing themselves in their work, they are doing nothing more than using their work as an escape. They are hiding from the other aspects of their life and using work to shelter themselves from other challenges.

It may be because they consider themselves better at work skills than life skills; are actively running from a painful memory, situation or reality; or are seeking affirmation at work when they find none outside it - but they are all hiding.

People who are hiding are already being dishonest with themselves. It is a very small step from there to being dishonest with others. Be very wary of people lost in their work.

478. Good Glove

"Good glove, no bat." – Anonymous baseball scout.

Once you get a tag such as "good glove, no bat" in baseball you are done. You will never shake that evaluation, no matter how long you play the game.

The same is true in your career within a company. If you start in one role, you will always be perceived as being in that role. If your goal is to advance your career by moving upwards through various roles, you will probably need to move to different companies to have a real chance in those new roles, otherwise you'll always be viewed as the former analyst, former entry-level worker, former project manager, etc.

479. When to Resign

"Every business has problems. When you feel you can no longer be part of the solution it is time to leave." – Richard Tanler.

You will often be frustrated by things in your workplace. If and when you get to the point that you cannot contribute to making your workplace, your company, better, then it is time to seek new opportunities.

Don't be cavalier or casual about this decision. Give it some time. But, if after due consideration, you truly feel you cannot contribute positively, then move on.

480. A One-Trick Pony

As you become successful in a career, the work, career, project, team leadership, business management and travel develop their own rhythm and they become their own song. They can become the dominant, even the only, song that plays in your head. They can become the only tune you really know how to play well. The better you get at performing it, and the more applause you get along the way, the easier it becomes to limit your repertoire more and more to that song and its variations.

Beware of becoming a one-trick pony, a one-song band. At some point, the music will stop, and where will you be then? Will there still be a chair to sit down in at that point in the game? Or will you be left standing?

When you enter the peak years of your working and career life chapter, it is incredibly easy to get sucked up into the day-to-day rhythm and minutiae of that existence. One day, by your choice or by that of others, that song will cease.

To what end are you living this life? What ultimate goal are you working towards?

What lighthouse are you rowing towards?

During my career I worked on literally thousands of projects. I could not name more than a handful of them for you now. I attended or led countless thousands of meetings, seminars, workshops, etc. I delivered literally hundreds of keynote speeches. I could not tell you the details of more than a few of them now.

I spent thousands of nights in business hotels and flew more than a million air miles, almost every single one of them domestic, the hard way.

I couldn't begin to recall the details of any of them.

Someday, there will be a life without work, after work, beyond work. When that day comes you will still need a life, a purpose and a way to find fulfillment, on that day and those that follow.

As you grow in your career and continue to experience success and increasing levels of responsibility, there will be tremendous pressure to sacrifice the non-work, non-career parts of your being to demonstrate that you are "all in" for your company, job and career. Resist the easy path to give up all to show that you are as committed as anyone else who is climbing the ladder.

During the fantastically wonderful, enriching and rewarding peak years of your life and career, remember to invest in yourself and in preparing yourself for that day when the music stops. Ensure you are more than your work. Ensure you have a life rich with interests, investments and accomplishments outside of your career.

When the company, job and career are all over and your life begins again, none of the projects, the promotions or work accolades will matter. What will matter are the small investments you made along the way to prepare for that day.

Enjoy the peak of your career. It will never come again. Savor the exotic experiences, the relationships with people from around the world, providing real solutions and building successful, value-add solutions for your customers and your business. Work hard. Never, ever compromise your integrity. Build your career, your accomplishments and your business.

But, don't ever stop asking yourself every step of every mile along the journey, "Am I just a one-trick pony? Am I more than my work? What is my end goal? Is this choice advancing me towards my lighthouse?"

481. Life Out of Balance

There are many people who live their adult, professional, business lives in a completely out-of-balance state. They live a life devoid of purpose and meaning outside of their work.

Common characteristics of these people include:

- An average work week of 60 or more hours

- No non-work related relationships they consider friendship other than salespeople and distant, childhood, youth or college age friends

- An inability to maintain an intelligent, informed conversation about any non-work related topic

- A majority of non-work related activities devoted to relieving work-related stress

- An internal value and reward system skewed towards work achievement, status and materialism

- Shallow, dysfunctional and/or non-existent personal relationships

- High to pervasive levels of anxiety, angst and anger

- Persistent physical and mental health manifestations of stress-related disorders

- A lack of hobbies, interests and avocations outside of work

- Minimal to no non-work related tribal memberships
- Non-work related tribal memberships devoted almost entirely to business networking, achievement and advancement
- Short-tempered, irritable
- Deteriorating health

Do you know any people who match some or all of these characteristics? Are they your workmates? Are they your friends? Are they you?

482. The Heart Surgeon

When I was still a young man, my father had a mild heart attack. His diagnosis was severely clogged arteries that fed blood to his heart muscle. The treatment was heart bypass surgery, in which healthy, unclogged blood veins were harvested from his leg and transplanted to his heart to bypass the clogged arteries. By that era, it was a routine surgery, but not without its dangers since the surgery required the use of a heart/lung machine and his heart would be stopped for a portion of the procedure.

A normal part of the process involved the surgeon briefing the family on the procedure and providing reassurances immediately prior to the surgery. My father's surgeon dutifully outlined the impending procedure and reassured my mother, siblings and immediate relatives in the surgery waiting room. As he confidently nodded and turned, he crooked a finger towards my brother-in-law and myself, and motioned for us to follow him into the hallway towards the surgical suites.

As the doors swung shut behind us, he turned towards us, nearly pinning us to the wall with his radiating aura of power and doctor-god presence.

Looking each of us alternately in the eyes, he said, "I do 200 of these a year. I've been doing them for many years. In all that time I've never had a single patient look up from the table and say, "Gee doc, I sure wish I'd spent more time in the office."

He paused and again looked each of us in the eyes, long and hard, then said, "You don't have to end up on that table. You two are still young enough to change before you do."

With that, he turned and strode through the next set of double doors. We both stared after him, dumbfounded, the sweeping of the spring-hinged doors rocking back and forth the only sound.

We finally looked at each other and walked solemnly back into the waiting room.

I never forgot those words, but it took me more than 20 years to put them into practice.

If you are still young enough to change, do it. Don't end up on that table.

483. Moving for $

Never take a new job solely for more money. You will very quickly be just as unhappy as you were before you moved for the money.

You cannot escape the immutable law of increased salary: as soon as you make more money you will spend more money. All the net extra money you thought was going to buy you a better life won't be there. You'll just have a few more things. Things won't make you happy.

Soon, very soon, you'll discover that the new job has just as many bad attributes as your last one, along with added expectations because you are being paid more money.

Increased compensation does not equate to job satisfaction. In surveys it consistently ranks near the bottom of the list of factors that determine job happiness. If you want to be happier in your job, look for one that provides you with a sense of self-determination, flexibility and fulfillment.

484. Workplace Influence

It is nearly impossible to overstate the importance of your workplace environment. You will spend more waking hours at work than anywhere else in your life.

Who you work for and with makes all the difference in your work life. No amount of money, perquisites or benefits will make up for a negative, corrosive manager, co-workers or employees.

If your workplace is filled with negative, bickering, unhappy people, you will inevitably become one too.

Find a good, positive, rewarding place to work. That is much more important than money.

485. Spelling Assume

It is easy to remember how to spell assume. Just remember what happens whenever you assume, especially at work. You make an ASS out of U and ME.

Don't assume.

486. A Message to Garcia

Many a modern business person bemoans the lack of self-initiative and work ethic among their employees and subcontractors. Many attribute it to recent declines in the education system or degraded moral fiber of the society. The following excerpt shows that this challenge is not limited to the current era, but is one business people have been struggling to overcome for nearly 100 years.

At a personal level, its moral is simple: Are you a person who can be trusted and counted on to deliver a message to Garcia?

Excerpted from

    Officers' Manual

    By Major J.A. Moss

    United States Army

    Sixth Edition (revised May, 1917)

    Section written by Mr. Elbert Hubbard

In all this Cuban business there is one man [who] stands out on the horizon of my memory, like Mars at perihelion. When war broke out between Spain and the United States, it was very necessary to communicate quickly with the leader of the Insurgents. Garcia was somewhere in the mountain fastnesses of Cuba – no one knew where. No mail nor telegraph message could reach him. The President must secure his co-operation, and quickly.

What to do!

Someone said to the President, "There's a fellow by the name of Rowan [who] will find Garcia for you, if anybody can."

Rowan was sent for and given a letter to be delivered to Garcia. How "the fellow by the name of Rowan" took the letter, sealed it up in an oil-skin pouch, strapped it over his heart, in four days landed by night off the coast of Cuba from an open boat, disappeared into the jungle and in three weeks came out on the other side of the island, having traversed a hostile country on foot and delivered his letter to Garcia, are things I have no special desire now to tell in detail.

The point I wish to make is this: [President] McKinley gave Rowan a letter to be delivered to Garcia; Rowan took the letter and did not ask, "Where is he at?" By the Eternal! There is a man whose form should be cast in deathless bronze and the statue placed in every college of the land. It is not book learning young men need, nor instruction about this and that, but a stiffening of the vertebrae which will cause them to be loyal to a trust, to act promptly, concentrate their energies; do the thing – "carry a message to Garcia!"

General Garcia is dead now, but there are other Garcias.

No man who has endeavored to carry out an enterprise where many hands were needed, but has been well-nigh appalled at times by the imbecility of the average man – the inability or unwillingness to concentrate on a thing and do it. Slip-shod assistance, foolish inattention, dowdy indifference, and half-hearted work seem the rule.

You, reader, put this matter to a test: You are sitting now in your office – six clerks are within call. Summon any one and make this request: "Please look in the encyclopedia and make a brief memorandum for me concerning the life of Coreggio."

Will the clerk quietly say, "Yes sir," and go do the task?

On your life, he will not.

He will look at you out of a fishy eye, and ask one or more of the following questions:

> Who was he?
>
> Which encyclopedia?
>
> Was I hired for that?
>
> Don't you mean Bismark?
>
> What's the matter with Charlie doing it?
>
> Is he dead?
>
> Is there any hurry?
>
> Shan't I bring you the book and let you look it up yourself?
>
> What do you want to know for?

And, I will lay you 10 to one that after you have answered the questions, and explained how to find the information, and why you want it, the clerk will go off and get one of the other clerks to help him try to find Garcia – and then come back and tell you there is no such man. Of course, I may lose my bet, but according to the Law of Averages, I will not.

Now, if you are wise you will not bother to explain to your "assistant" that Correggio is indexed under the C's, not in the K's, but you will smile sweetly and say, "Never mind," and go look it up yourself.

Advertise for a stenographer, and nine out of 10 who apply can neither spell nor punctuate – and do not think it necessary to.

Can such a one write a letter to Garcia?

"You see that bookkeeper?" said the foreman to me in a large factory.

"Yes, what about him?"

"Well, he's a fine accountant, but if I'd send him uptown on an errand, he might accomplish the errand all right and, on the other hand, might stop at four saloons on the way, and when he got to Main Street, would forget what he had been sent for."

Can such a man be entrusted to carry a message to Garcia?

I know one man of really brilliant parts who has not the ability to manage a business of his own, and yet who is absolutely worthless to anyone else, because he carries with him constantly the insane suspicion that his employer is oppressing, or intending to oppress him. He cannot give orders, and he will not receive them. Should a message be given to him to take to Garcia, his answer would probably be, "Take it yourself."

My heart goes out to the man who does his work when the "boss" is away, as well as when he is at home. And, the man who, when given a letter for Garcia, quietly takes the missive, without asking any idiotic questions, and with no lurking intention of chucking it into the nearest sewer, or of doing aught else but deliver it.

Civilization is one long, anxious search for just such individuals. Anything such a man asks shall be granted; his kind are so rare that no employer can afford to let him go. He is wanted in every city, town and village – in every office, shop, store and factory. The world cries out for such; he is needed and needed badly – the man who can carry a message to Garcia.

Business Fundamentals

487. The Essential Value Proposition

You will never succeed in business until you fully understand and can succinctly articulate your essential value proposition. What is the essence of your service or product offering? What do you provide in exchange for payment? The answer to this question becomes a short clause in your elevator test statement.

488. The Elevator Test

Get on an elevator and push the button for the next floor up or down. Count how many seconds it takes from the instant the doors close to when they open again.

Repeat the test. This time imagine that the CEO of your company or a prime customer prospect asks you, just before the doors close, what it is you do and why that is important.

You have the length of time between the floors to clearly and completely articulate your reason for business existence and how and why you, your team, your project or your company, is better than the alternatives and deserves support and investment.

That is the elevator test.

Until you can pass that test, you are not ready for the marketplace.

489. Leadership vs. Management

Management is not leadership. It is possible to be a manager and be an ineffective leader.

Leadership is not management. It is possible to be a leader and be a completely ineffective manager.

A successful business requires both leadership and management. Know the difference between the two.

490. Leaders Hire Managers

Leaders hire managers, not the other way around.

If you want someone to lead a group, organization or company, don't pick a manager, pick a leader.

491. Tenderness

Paul Simon has a great song from his first solo effort called "Tenderness." The signature line in that song is "But there's no tenderness beneath your honesty."

A first-time entrepreneur asked me to review the business plan for her startup. I gave it an honest review.

She emailed me back and was obviously hurt. She said, in essence, she wanted the truth, but not if it hurt. She wanted tenderness instead of honesty.

She launched her startup and, unfortunately, it soon folded.

Business is not about tenderness.

492. The Gold in the Gold Rush

Aside from a very small number of people you could count on your fingers, the miners in the California gold rush did not make the money.

At the top level, the manufacturers of the clothing, shovels, picks and supplies made a lot of money during the gold rush. At the middle level, the hardware stores and outfitters made a lot of money selling supplies to the miners. At the bottom level, the miners, almost nobody made any money.

In times of a gold rush, don't be a miner, be the person making or selling supplies to the miners.

493. The Power of Will

Having the will to succeed is very important in business; in fact, it is a prerequisite for success.

However, no amount of will can ever overcome a flawed business model, a fundamentally changed market or some catastrophic circumstances.

494. Never Compete on Price

Price is not a sustainable differentiator in the market. If the market segment provides profits, there will inevitably be a lower cost supplier attracted to that segment.

Price competition is always won by the business with the most capital assets available to invest in the price war. You will never win a price war with a larger business unless they lose interest, which very rarely happens.

Competing on price attracts the worst customers. Customers who make a purchase decision primarily based on cost will abandon your business the instant they find a lower price.

Compete on quality and uniqueness of product and service.

Never compete on price.

495. A Good Contract

A good contract is fair to all parties. If you think having a contract that is great for you but bad for the other parties is a fantastic outcome, you are new to business and naïve about life.

A ruinous contract is not good for anyone, no matter who stands to profit initially. A ruinous contract does nothing but create enmity and enemies. Business is tough enough without creating legions of people bent on revenge.

A good contract is fair to all parties, provides protection to all parties and provides reasonable business risk for all parties.

496. In Panic There is Profit

The most advantageous position in business is to have customers in panic and be perceived as the solution.

497. Ask for the Business

Although lack of sufficient capital is certainly the number one reason businesses fail, the second leading cause is probably lack of asking for the business.

Many entrepreneurs have a very difficult time asking potential customers, in a simple and direct way, for their business.

If you can't ask for someone's business and feel good about doing it, you don't belong in business.

498. The Brand

In building a career or a business, after honesty and integrity, nothing is more important than your brand.

Everything you do, every aspect of your actions and of your business, impacts your brand. Consequently, you must be very focused on carefully nurturing your brand, and growing it into a strong and durable entity.

Every interaction with you or your company is representative of your brand. Consequently, you must ensure that every single interaction, of all types, enhances the perception of your brand.

Every single product or service delivered encapsulates and symbolizes your brand. Consequently, you must deliver products and services that create a positive experience, resulting in an aura of quality, dependability and trust around your brand.

Every negative assertion, allegation or evaluation of your products and services, your team, your company or yourself negatively affects your brand. Consequently, you must be ever vigilant and rigorous in defending your brand.

Your brand is the sum total of everything you work for and hope to achieve. Your brand reflects your standards, expectations and requirements. Your brand is you.

499. Talking to Levels

Managers run teams and projects. Directors run programs. Vice presidents run functions. Presidents run discreet business entities, usually companies. Chief Executive Officers, Chief Financial Officers, Chief Operating Officers and other C-level people run groups of discreet business entities, usually companies.

When you are talking to a manager, talk about tactical things related to their specific project and/or deliverables. When you talk to a director, talk about tactical things related to their program and how that program fits into its strategic goal or process. When you talk to a vice president, talk about their function(s), their programs, the strategic context and the challenges and opportunities of those functions and programs. When you talk to a president, talk to them about the strategic directions, challenges and opportunities for their discreet business entity or company. When you talk to a C-level person, talk to them about the strategic challenges and opportunities for their group of discreet business entities or companies.

Always match your topics to the level of the person you are talking with, tactical for tactical, strategic for strategic.

Never talk about a tactical subject with a strategic person unless they specifically ask you about it. If they do, keep your answer very succinct (use your elevator test response) and always tie the tactical subject to the stated strategic goals of the organization and how it measurably advances the agenda(s) of the strategic person.

In all cases, regardless of whether you are talking to the janitor or the CEO, always talk to them within the context of their stated and unstated agenda(s). Your fundamental value proposition, your core offering, whatever it is, must advance their agenda(s) or you are a waste of their time.

Never waste anyone's time by having nothing relevant to say to someone at their level. It is better to not have an interaction than to have one that wastes someone's time, especially that of a strategic player.

500. The C-Band

Over the years I worked with a lot of C-band executives: CEOs, COOs, CFOs, CIOs, etc. As a group, they were, almost without exception, a pleasure to work with. At the VP level you could get some challenging people, but by the time a person had ascended to the C-band, they had things well in hand and had been through enough to keep things in perspective.

The same attributes applied to most of the board of directors members I worked with. If they had a real business pedigree, and were not a showpiece or political appointee, they generally were a credit to their group and were capable of making positive contributions.

In large companies, most VPs were still climbing, still aspiring to the C-band, so you had to be very careful to not get caught in the cross hairs of a high-powered vendetta or range war. But, as long as you were careful about the typical VP level corporate politics, VPs were usually good to work with.

Most people at the director level, and worse, manager level, were clawing their way to the top. The most common method of climbing the ladder at those levels was by using a knife in each hand to stab in the back whoever was in the way and kick them off or climb over them as they slid down to their doom. The director and manager ranks are rife with intrigue and opportunity. Careers hang in the balance on most days and on most deliverables. It is a brutal competition for the highest stakes available: survival and advancement. You must learn how to thrive and survive among the manager and director classes to endure, much less advance, in a corporate environment.

People at the team level are generally set in their roles. If they are qualified, a few are looking for promotions to manager. Others are looking to advance a skill set so they can move to a higher paying position. Others are coasting along, just looking to survive another day with the fewest possible responsibilities. There are always a few who get almost everything done, they are the doers, the real worker bees who make all the honey. They are overworked and underappreciated. Identify and avoid the martyrs among them, then get the remaining doers on your team.

Always keep in mind that tomorrow's C-band person is somewhere along the path, somewhere in the VPs, directors, managers and team members of today.

501. FUD

When the mainframe computing model was threatened by client / server architecture and the rise of the personal computer, IBM fought back with one of the most successful and effective marketing campaigns ever devised: Fear, Uncertainty and Doubt (FUD).

By raising fears, encouraging uncertainty and planting the seeds of doubt about every alternative to mainframe architecture, IBM fought a very effective rear guard holding action against the inevitable forces of a changing market.

In any dynamic, evolving or rapidly shifting market, representatives of the status quo will almost always use a variation of the FUD strategy. Be aware of what it is and how it is used, regardless of which side of the equation you are on.

502. The Consultant Effect

A consultant often says the same things and offers the same recommendations as staffers have been saying and recommending for years, but the consultant is listened to and the consultant's recommendations acted upon.

The reason for this disparity is that the consultant is recognized as an expert and is charging a lot of money for their services. When a company pays a lot of money, they tend to want to show something for the investment, so they will act on the consultant's advice.

503. Projects vs. Programs

Projects are discreet applications of defined resources, for a specific and limited time, to accomplish a particular tactical objective. Programs are a series or collection of projects designed to accomplish or advance a strategic objective.

Projects are run by teams and managers, programs are run by senior managers or directors, or rarely, vice presidents.

504. The Magic Bullet

Businesses will often throw money at a technology "magic bullet" solution in an effort to avoid the difficult cultural and process issues that lie at the heart of their challenges.

It is much easier to live through repeated technology project failures than face the real challenges. Technology managers can be fired and new ones sacrificed, all the while avoiding the real, underlying issues.

Culture and process issues require change on everyone's part, and that requires very high levels of sustained leadership skills to execute. There are few business leaders willing to take on that challenge.

505. The Newsletter

The most dangerous thing in life and business are recurring commitments. For that reason, avoid commitments that sound effective and easy, but involve infinite recurring commitments.

The classic example is a newsletter. It sounds easy, everyone is initially enthusiastic and there seems to be plenty of content. All of that lasts for the first couple of issues. After that, finding the content and the resources to produce it becomes a burden. Ceasing publication is an admission of failure and the worst possible message to send to the recipients of the publication. You are thus trapped.

Avoid recurring commitments when possible. If you consider pledging to a recurring commitment, think very carefully about the required resources, especially the time requirements.

506. Scalability in All Things

The easiest way to spot a company that is built for growth is their overall scalability.

Most business leaders and managers consider scalability to be a technical issue, limited to information, manufacturing and logistical systems. But, to be fully scalable, capable of orders of magnitude growth, a business must be scalable in all aspects of the organization.

The scalability mandate is critically important to processes and culture. A business can have high levels of scalability available in its technical systems, but if its documented processes and its culture are not scalable, then the business is not going anywhere.

507. The Customer Diamond

A customer is like a diamond, it has many facets. Every way you touch that customer, every way they interact with you, every way they view you, is a facet of that diamond.

You must ensure that every facet of that diamond reflects a consistent image and experience. Every possible way your customer touches, interacts and views your company must reflect the same level of quality, capability, responsiveness, engagement, execution, commitment and integrity.

If one process, function or component of your customer experience is flawed, then the diamond is flawed and it is devalued, almost worthless.

Ensure each facet of your customer diamond is flawless.

508. Culture & Process Dependence

Never make your success dependent on culture or process change in any individual, human group, organization or company.

Humans hate change. They especially hate change imposed on them from external forces. Even more, they hate externally forced change to their daily routine, the way they go about things and the way they interact with each other.

If your success depends on others changing their behavior, you are almost certain to fail.

509. Five and Five

"It takes five years to build a reputation and five minutes to lose it." – John DeSalvo.

In any profession you will quickly discover that it is a small, insular and usually inbred group of people who populate that world. Everyone knows just about everyone else, and regardless of whether it is software or plumbing parts, it's the same 200 to 300 people, year after year, who make it up.

The core group will move from job to job within the industry, while a few new people filter in as a few transients drop out. Within five years in an industry, if you have any interest or desire at all, you will know all the key players, they will know you and everyone will know everyone else, if not personally, certainly by reputation.

When I produced media in Chicago, I knew another producer who did not realize this rule, even after being around the industry for at least five years. One day, after working long hours for over a week, he exploded in anger and threw a slide projector at a client.

Within a few days just about everyone in the industry heard the story. He was permanently tagged, like the scarlet letter, as the guy who threw the slide projector at the client. His reputation never recovered.

Regardless of the profession you choose, never forget the Five and Five rule. It will take you at least five years to build a reputation. You will need to work hard every subsequent day to maintain that reputation. And, most importantly, you can throw it all away, as the producer did, in less than five minutes.

510. The Reflection

A business, for good or for ill, will always reflect the personality of the person who is truly in charge.

A business that does not reflect the personality of the titular leader, i.e., CEO or President, is a business in the midst of a leadership struggle.

511. First Class Education

One of the perks of traveling a lot is that you accumulate a lot of hotel points and airline miles. If you concentrate your efforts on a few, or even better, a single airline, you can start to earn admission into the upper tiers of the airline rewards programs.

I flew on United Airlines steadily since the early days of their mileage program, so I reaped the benefits of that loyalty as I slowly piled up over a million miles with the carrier. Of all the rewards the airlines offer, probably the nicest perk for the professional traveler with loyalty status on an airline is the enhanced ability to upgrade from coach to business- or first-class.

The typical things people focus on with these upgrades are that business- and first-class seats are wider, sometimes there is power for your laptop, often the service is more attentive and generally the food is better, which can be pretty important when it is your only meal of the day. However, all of these pale in comparison to the most important aspect of an upgrade - who you meet and what you learn while talking to them.

I've met and conversed with countless CEOs and senior executives on upgraded flights in business- or first-class. In each of those conversations I endeavored to learn one thing, to take away one lesson, to glean one bit of wisdom, to harvest a single hard-won management maxim.

Once you earn your way up into the business- or first-class section you face a choice. You can slip on your noise-cancelling headphones and bury your nose in your laptop, or you can take a few minutes, usually during the meal, and respectfully converse with your seatmate. You may find that some of the most important things you learn about business come in those few minutes of conversation.

512. Priorities vs. Budgets

As a business management consultant I heard a lot about priorities. In the introductory meeting and group management team interviews, senior executives would drone on endlessly about the organization's priorities. Top priority this and critical priority that; it was all I could do to keep my eyes from rolling back in my head.

If the senior executives started down that same path in my personal, one-on-one, interviews I would usually cut them off and say, "Don't tell me about your priorities, show me your budget."

People, teams, groups, tribes and organizations often make a big show of pontificating about their priorities. Very rarely does the investment of their resources reflect their stated priorities.

It comes down to fundamental honesty - honesty with yourself, with your team, with your organization, with your business. It is one thing to spout about priorities. It is another to live them.

Show me your budget.

513. The Dying Business

How to identify a dying business:

- Limited or no response to changing market conditions

- Cutting research and development (R&D)

- Cutting marketing, advertising or Public Relations (PR)

- Infinitely deferred maintenance or upkeep

- Fully utilized or lack of formal banking line of credit

- Fully utilized informal financing channels (credit cards, etc.)

- Personally fully leveraged principals

- 90-150+ days on accounts payable (AP)

- Factoring (selling invoices)

- Delayed or partial payroll

- Degraded standards of integrity, honesty and character

If your business or the company you work for exhibits some or all of these characteristics, it is time to move to another opportunity.

514. The 1st National Bank of AP

A business in financial trouble will always turn to their accounts payable (AP) for their first source of financing or cash. If you have a customer that suddenly alters their payment schedule from a regular, short-term payer to a long-term, reluctant payer, you know they are in trouble.

If your own business is using its AP as a credit line, you know you are in the first stages of financial failure. If this is the case, you must immediately, without hesitation, institute a crisis plan for recovery. When you are leveraging your AP, you have much less time to survive than you think, usually by at least one order of magnitude.

515. One Face

The marketplace presents a myriad of ways your customers can interact with your business. They may interact with the business face-to-face at retail, by phone, through print, through television, through radio, through mobile devices or via the Internet.

It is essential that, regardless of how your customers interface with your business, you are presenting one consistent face to those customers. Ensure that all of your corporate identity is consistent. Ensure that all of your user interfaces have the same look and feel. Ensure that all of your print materials match in quality, color, design and materials.

Your customers need to feel as if they are relating to and interacting with one company, your company, not a different company for every different form of interaction.

Present one face to the customer.

516. Marketing Defined

Marketing creates the perception of need.

517. Marketing Execution

"Marketing is 95 percent execution." – Stephanie Hackney.

Most of the attention in the marketing profession is given to the big ideas, the innovative techniques, the splashy and the new. But the reality of marketing is that the ideas are a very small part of what makes a successful marketing campaign. The truth is successful marketing is at least 95 percent execution.

Ensure your marketing team reflects this reality. If your marketing people are full of great ideas but lack the ability or resources to implement them, you will fail.

518. Marketing Basics

The immutable laws of marketing:

- Marketing's purpose is to create the perception of need. That is its only purpose. Everything else associated with marketing is just an aspect of that mission. Creating the perception of need works on all levels. From the tactile feel of your business card to the execution of the processes around welcoming new customers, it's all about creating the thought: "I need to use this company's products and services."

- Ideas are great, but are worthless without execution. Your marketing ideas will help you stand out, but they must be flawlessly executed, within the context of documented processes, to be effective over time in the marketplace.

- Marketing is holistic. It's not just a splashy advertising campaign or a catchy slogan. Marketing is the sum total of every point of contact with the external world. Every single way your business interfaces with and interacts with the outside world is part of marketing.

To create a holistic marketing aura around your business you need to:

Create the Perception of Need

Methods to create the perception of need include:

- Identify need, e.g., efficiency, economic savings, reduced downtime.
- Identify driver, e.g., regulation, legal requirements, cultural expectations, societal assumptions ("be green"), recruiting and retention factor ("good place to work").
- Identify norms, e.g., industry best practice, common business practice.
- Identify aspiration. This is more common in consumer advertising, for example, "This bike will make you a better, more successful, sexier rider," but is also applicable in business-to-business (B2B) situations when used to present a model of success that others can aspire to.

Overcome Objections

Once the perception of need is created, you need to close the sale. That implies you must overcome objections. You do that by presenting features and benefits. These are comparative to, first, the existing state (Why should I do anything other than what I'm doing right now?), which is overcoming objections to need; and, secondly, your competition, which is overcoming objections to utilizing your company instead of a competitor (Why shouldn't I use Everything4Less, Inc.?).

Mitigate Perceived Risk

The key to overcoming objections is usually to focus on risk reduction. Demonstrate why using your company reduces the risks versus any other alternative.

There are many aspects to risk, and don't be afraid to leverage any of them. You are basically using the fear leverage point, which is what risk management is rooted in. Think about what your customers fear and how your products and services can eliminate or minimize those fears. Focus on those points.

Establish Your Value Proposition

You must establish your fundamental value proposition. What is it you are proposing to do for the customer? This is normally and most effectively couched in answering the customer's question: "What's in it for me?" You must persuasively and convincingly answer that question.

Deliver the Call to Action

Finally, your marketing message must include a clear call to action. You must explicitly ask the prospect to do exactly what you want them to do, e.g., buy a product or service, participate in an activity, etc.

519. Marketing Pull vs. Push

Pull is creating market demand via advertising, couponing or other means. Resulting demand pulls products out of the distribution channels. Pull incentivizes customers.

Push is loading product into the distribution channels and relying on your sales channels to distribute it into the marketplace. Push incentivizes distributors.

520. Marketing Basics – The Story

Customers make purchase decisions based on different criteria. Some customers require "the story" in order to make a purchase decision. The most common example of "the story" is restaurant menus, which often include the background or history of the restaurant, its cuisine, its key leaders, etc. Some are complete fiction, but that is not important. What is important is that the menu includes "the story" for those customers who require it.

Ensure that "the story" for your business is available to your customers who require it.

521. Marketing Basics – Logo Design

When evaluating potential business and product logo designs look for a design that:

- Is inherently scalable. You need it to "read" in sizes from business card/matchbook to billboard.

- Is memorable. Is the design visually unique? Will humans inherently remember the shape and form, or will it be registered as a variation of a known shape?

- Is contemporary but timeless. Avoid trendy design flourishes or techniques that will date your logo and company within a year or two.

- Is media friendly. The design must be suitable for all forms of print, screening and electronic media. Just requiring a Pantone color isn't enough. You need a color that works for everything from web to television to silk screen to CYMK to sRGB.

522. Marketing - Web Site Basics

A business's web site is an important part of its overall marketing program. In some cases, the web site may be the only point of contact for customers. In many cases, it is the primary point of contact for customers. Consequently, the web site must reflect the highest possible levels of investment and execution.

The web site must reflect current web technology, clean and understandable design and a flawless user experience.

The web site's minimum content is:

- Mission / Purpose
- Market(s) Served
- Products and Services
- Differentiation vs. Competition
- Features and Benefits
- Overcome Objections
- Authentication / Endorsements / Certifications (usually a subset of features and benefits)
- Purchase Process (how a customer buys a product or service)
- Call to Action (ask for the business)
- Testimonials (from current and/or former clients)
- Contact information

523. "What's in it for me?"

The only question that matters to most customers is "What's in it for me?" Your marketing must, above and beyond anything else, answer that question.

Review your marketing messages. Are they primarily or exclusively about your markets served and product offerings? If so, they are missing the mark by a mile.

Your marketing messages must, without exception, first and foremost, answer the customer's question, "What's in it for me?"

524. Marketing for Marketing's Sake

Do you remember New Coke? Not many other people do either. New Coke and Coke Classic are the poster children for the disaster of Marketing for Marketing's Sake. They were a catastrophe that nearly crippled the Coca-Cola Company and were a marketing driven change for no other reason than to serve the needs of the marketing department.

Conceived in the unholy marriage of reaction to competition and customer focus groups, New Coke was a reformulation of one of the world's best known, crown jewel brands. Driven by a marketing regime intent on making a name for themselves, it was pure change for change's sake. It was a change that was unnecessary except by those seeking to build their own careers and resumes, regardless of the risk to the brand or the business.

Marketing professionals are, by their very nature, oriented to what is new, what is exciting, what is fresh and what is different. They are never content to exist in a static environment. For this reason, they will always seek to freshen, to repackage, to alter, to change. It is their character, their nature and their destiny.

However, as in the case of New Coke, the marketing department's compulsion to change can be at the cost of a product, a brand or even a company. Beware pure change for change's sake - marketing for marketing's sake - championed by the marketing team, lest you and your product become the next New Coke.

525. Public Speaking Basics

To succeed in your business career you will probably need to be an effective public speaker. The process and experience can be daunting for some. However, with good preparation and by following some basic rules you will find that public speaking can be very rewarding.

1. Prepare well in advance. Do not wait until the week or day before your presentation to prepare your materials and yourself. Meet or exceed all materials submission deadlines of the event organizers.

2. Present a relevant message. Research and learn the demographics of your audience. Build a message that is relevant to their challenges. Present a solution to an existential challenge for your audience.

3. Present a concise message. Do not try to cover more than one major topic in your presentation, especially in a keynote. Introduce your key points early, cover them in detail in the body and repeat them in your summary.

4. Understand your audience's limitations. Your audience will usually remember, at best, three things that you tell them. Don't overload them with information or they will remember even less.

5.   Present your key information in different ways. People learn by sound, sight and touch/motion. That means you need to teach the key elements of your presentation in three different ways: by voice, by visual and by a memorable motion or body movement.

6.   Keep visuals simple and direct. A good billboard has seven words or less. Your visual support materials are your billboards. Keep them simple and straightforward. Limit or eliminate flashy animations, graphics, etc. They do little but distract your audience.

7.   Limit the number of visuals. The maximum rate is around one visual per minute. One visual per two to three minutes is better. A higher rate of visuals simply ensures your audience will become overwhelmed and stop paying attention.

8.   Be professional, tasteful, tactful and relevant. The content of your presentation must meet the utmost standards of professionalism. It must always, without exception, reflect the highest professional standards, good taste and tactfulness. And, most importantly, be relevant. Avoid inside jokes, politics, cultural issues, snide comments, satire, denigration or negative messaging. Don't put anything in your presentation you wouldn't feel comfortable appearing on the front page of the next day's newspaper with your name and photograph beside it.

9.   Prepare walk-in and walk-out visuals. Prepare images to display as the audience enters and leaves the room. These visuals should contain the name of your presentation (as it appears in the event marketing and schedule materials), your name and your relevant contact information.

10.   Prepare your cue cards / bullet points / script. The worst possible thing you can do is stand in front of an audience and read your presentation. The best possible thing you can do is maintain direct eye contact with your audience for the entire duration. You will probably

fall somewhere in between those two options, especially early in your public speaking career. Strive to present from cue cards or bullet points. Avoid reading.

11. Prepare your introduction. Many speaking venues provide a master of ceremonies or a presentation room host who will introduce you. Keep your introduction brief and ensure its content is relevant to the audience. Never, ever read your own introduction.

12. Rehearse your presentation. Read it through several times aloud. Practice it in front of a mirror. If possible, practice it in the presentation room.

13. Do a site check. Visit your assigned presentation venue before your presentation, the day before if possible. Allow plenty of time to correct technical issues. Familiarize yourself with the physical layout of the area. Test the power, sound and visual systems to ensure all elements are compatible with anything you are providing (visuals, technology, etc.). Be sure to test all technology (laptop, etc.) you are providing with the systems available in the presentation space. Do not accept any verbal commitments or promises that it will work – test it. Meet and coordinate with the room supervisor/monitor to confirm schedules, room turnover, house light control, etc. Stand at the podium or presentation position with the room lights in presentation mode. Familiarize yourself with the lighting controls and coordinate audio, lighting, media and technology cues with the technical crew(s).

14. Arrive early. Arrive in plenty of time to set up your presentation and ensure everything is in order long before the scheduled presentation time.

15. Restroom. Visit the restroom before your presentation begins. Check all aspects of your personal appearance in the mirror.

16. Water. Make certain you have a pitcher and glass of water at the podium. Pour a glass of water before you begin. Do not over-hydrate and do not allow yourself to become dehydrated.

17. Sound and visual check. Do one final check of the sound and visual systems before the audience enters the room. Test all systems you will use in your presentation.

18. Cue check. Do one final check with all technical personnel to confirm the cues for house light, walk-in/walk-out music, special media segments, etc.

19. As the audience enters the room, greet them and, depending on the venue and circumstances, engage some in small talk.

20. Start on time. No exceptions.

21. Never apologize. If the roof is leaking or the venue is nearly freezing, that is not your responsibility. All apologies are the responsibility of the group organizing the event. If there is a venue issue, insist the organizers take a few minutes to deliver any relevant messages. Your presence must be limited to your content. Apologizing lowers your credibility.

22. Stand with both feet on the floor, about shoulder width apart.

23. Keep your hands out of your pockets.

24. Use your hands to emphasize a point, illustrate a visual or as a tactile/motion learning device. Do not shuffle papers, play with paper clips or otherwise distract your audience with your hands.

25. Make eye contact with the audience. Start with people in the front rows and keep making eye contact with other people in the audience for the duration of your presentation. Some venues will use very bright lights on you, the presenter, and the audience will be in the dark, so you can't

see them. Keep making eye contact anyway. Look directly into where you know their eyes are based on your venue site check (step 13).

26. Speak slowly, directly, clearly and with purpose. The number-one mistake public speakers make, especially those with little to no experience, is speaking too quickly. Rushing through your presentation because you are uncomfortable will just make things worse. Stop and take a sip of water if you have to. Wait two beats. Begin again. More slowly this time. Repeat if required.

27. Move. Do not stand rigidly in one position, frozen behind the podium. If at all possible, be mobile. Move around on the stage. Stride over to address your audience at an important point. Be expansive when appropriate.

28. Pause for effect. After making a key point or asking a critical question, pause for effect. Let your most important messages soak in.

29. Variation. Nothing puts an audience to sleep faster than an unvarying monotone delivery. Vary your cadence and intonation. Watch a televangelist or two to see the masters of this craft in action. For your own presentation, stop well short of turning single syllable words into six syllable words, as they often do, but use them as an example of one end of the verbal presentation style spectrum and as examples of the verbal power of variation in cadence and intonation.

30. Involve the audience early. At the beginning of your presentation, ask some simple "raise your hands" or "say your answer" type questions. Audience response creates an emotional commitment to you and your presentation on their part. It is the presenter's version of the door-to-door salesman's trick of asking you how you are today - any response creates a fundamental human bond. Build in audience response points

in a few places in your presentation to reinforce and extend the bond. Treat the bond with respect.

31. Emphasize your key points early, cover them in detail in the body and repeat them in the summary. Remember, your audience will usually remember, at best, three things you tell them. Emphasize those three things.

32. Always give your best. Regardless if you are presenting to 10,000 or to 10 people in a nearly empty room prepared for 1,000, always, without exception, give your best possible effort. I have presented while sick, while bleeding, while distracted with personal and professional crisis and tragedy and in every manner and description of challenging to horrible venues. Always, always give your best.

33. End on time. No exceptions.

34. Thank the audience for their time and attention. Always. No exceptions.

526. The Smartest Guy

I spent many years as a public speaker presenting on technical and business management topics. At some speeches I would allow time for questions and answers at the end. Inevitably, somebody would stand up and present a three to four-minute monologue filled with assertions and a five or six word question tacked onto the end. Their performance was not about asking me a question, it was about proving to everyone they were the smartest person in the room.

In every human gathering, there is almost always somebody in the room whose insecurities demand they prove they are the smartest person there. If you are a manager or a team leader, this can be a regular part of your life. If you are a public speaker, you are likely to get at least one in every crowd.

It is important to recognize this behavior and know how to defuse it. Never let the smartest guy seize control or shift the agenda of the session, meeting or event. If possible, let them strut their feathers a little bit so they can get it out of their system, then suggest you take their question "off-line" or away from the general session. The promise of one-on-one attention will feed their undernourished ego while also enabling you to keep things on track.

527. Trade Show Basics

The most efficient way to research a market segment for startup opportunities is to attend at least two trade shows for that segment or a related segment.

Your strategic goals in attending trade shows for startup research are:

- Market sizing data
- Market direction and trends
- Identify market leaders in various segments
- Identify industry thought leaders / gurus
- Identify market opportunities targeted by new startups
- Identify potential strategic relationships
- Identify or confirm unmet market needs

- Establish relationships with trade show organizers for future marketing and speaking opportunities

Your tactical goals in attending trade shows for startup research are:

- Identify and sample all relevant industry magazines, periodicals, web sites, etc.
- Survey and understand the offerings of all the small booths around the periphery
- Network with other entrepreneurs and startups
- Attend the major keynote presentations to get a read on industry direction
- Walk every inch of every aisle
- Collect and review marketing collateral

528. Trade Show Efficiency and Survival Tips:

- If at all possible, stay at the hotel directly connected to the convention center. It is worth the extra money to save the time in transit. You will also have exponentially more networking opportunities staying at the show hotel than elsewhere.
- Know the trends, technologies and companies you are interested in researching prior to arrival.
- Only pay for attending the show conference sessions if you are on your second or third trade show and/or have already determined this is a viable market segment. On your first show or during initial research

you will learn more by an in-depth canvassing of the show floor than the conference sessions.

- Bring an empty suitcase or budget space in yours for the collateral you want to take home.

- Bring a pocket notebook and several good pens.

- Bring a highlighter.

- Bring three times as many business cards as you think you will need.

- When you arrive at the show entrance, get a current show guide, show floor booth map and vendor index. Find a table where you can sit down and review the show guide. Highlight the company names and the booth locations for your "must see" technologies and companies.

- Develop a plan for covering the show floor.

- Consider going directly to your highest priority booths first.

- The booth workers will be most helpful, most energetic and most responsive on the first day of the show. They will be completely burned out by the last day. Keep this in mind when planning visits to your critical, highest priority booths.

- If you see a booth giving out heavy duty bags with wide carrying handles, grab one. Keep your eyes open for cloth bags with long handle straps. You can loop those straps over your shoulder, which is a key capability as you gather a load of collateral.

- If you want a copy of specific collateral or technical documents, get them early in the show as vendors may run out by the last day.

- If you have a technical question, approach the nerdiest-looking person in the booth.

- Wear comfortable walking shoes; you will cover many miles.

- Stay hydrated.

- Take regular breaks to sit down and rest your legs and feet.

- Stay fresh. You will be very inefficient when you get tired. Go back to your hotel room and rest if you need to. You will get more done in an hour being fresh than in four being tired.

- Take notes. You will not remember much once you leave the show.

- Be polite but firm in not getting drawn into time-sucking interactions with booth workers. You have many miles to cover and a very limited amount of time to do it in.

- No booth worker wants to ship anything back home that they can dispose of at the show location. If there are things you are interested in that are displayed or featured in the booth, you can often make a good deal on the last show day.

- Consider shipping home your conference proceedings and show marketing collateral. There are usually shipping booths set up on the last day of the show for this purpose.

- Most importantly, never, ever talk about your business idea at a trade show. Ever.

It is easy to get distracted by the hoopla of a trade show, especially for first timers. Stay focused on your goal. Remember you are there to determine if a business idea is viable.

Don't be afraid to walk away from a business concept if your research at the trade show demonstrates there are fundamental flaws in your proposed business model.

Management

529. How to Lead

1. Establish and communicate a unique vision.

2. Require vision endorsement. Only include on your team and in your organization members who endorse and support your vision.

3. Define and clearly articulate a challenging, but achievable plan to realize the vision.

4. Initiate and reward discrete, definable, quantifiable and measurable work to accomplish the plan.

5. Compensate and reward only on measured results that advance the agenda of the plan.

6. Regularly update the plan to reflect changing realities and maintain an ongoing challenge.

7. Develop and instill process rigor throughout the organization.

8. Be fair, but absolutely firm - never compromise values.

9. Communicate often, completely and honestly.

10. Maintain absolute honesty and integrity.

530. Jack Welch's Six Rules for Managers

1. Face reality as it is, not as it was or as you wish it to be.

2. Be candid with everyone.

3. Don't manage, lead.

4. Change before you have to.

5. If you don't have a competitive advantage, don't compete.

6. Control your own destiny, or someone else will.

These six rules are bedrock principles for success in business and in life. If you have to pick only one to live by, choose number one.

531. The Work on the Table

My first job as a manager was in 1979 at a media production company in Chicago. I was fresh out of the corn fields of Iowa and, while I knew the technical side of media production, I knew little to nothing about managing people.

A few weeks into the job I was sitting in my office when I heard a loud commotion from down the hallway in the art department. As I ran down the hallway I couldn't make out any words among the screams and shouts. I had no idea what was going on. But, whatever it was, it was my first management crisis and from the sounds of things, it was a big one.

When I reached the scene I found our art director and one of our lead artists going at it hammer and tong. As I started to decipher the words and phrases I realized they were fighting over a woman, which wouldn't have been remarkable in my former, isolated, Ozzie and Harriet Iowa world, except both my art director and my lead artist were also women.

As we got them separated and calmed down, I had to make a fundamental personal decision.

How was I going to manage these people? How was I going to judge their performance? How was I going to relate to them as people?

In those few seconds, as we got them separated and sorted out, I decided I would manage them, evaluate them, reward them, motivate them and interact with them just like everyone else who worked for me – based on the work they put on the table.

In the years following I managed people of nearly every race, creed and orientation and I followed the same principle. The only thing that mattered was the work they put on the table. Anything that compromised the excellence of that product or negatively affected the organization was a problem; otherwise, it was not a work-related issue.

Evaluate, incent, reward, motivate and interact – in other words, manage – based solely on the work on the table.

532. The Point of Pain

If you want to make a recognizable and meaningful difference, find a point of pain, life-threatening pain, and relieve or eliminate that pain. If you are relieving life-threatening pain you will never be short of resources and energy to accomplish that goal.

This is especially true when attempting to drive change in an organization. The change will never be endorsed, accepted and implemented unless it is viewed as relieving significant pain.

533. A, B and C Players

Participants in business can be divided into three classes of capability: A, B and C players.

C players are low-level implementers. They are marginally to somewhat focused on their jobs and reasonably efficient if closely supervised. C players can be fiercely loyal, but will most often move between jobs for marginal differences in pay, work roles or conditions. C players can advance from C- to C+, but require a large dose of self-motivation and investment by the business to do so. Be very careful of committing to this investment as the incremental delta in capability is relatively small.

B players are intelligent, motivated and highly focused. They are capable of self-direction and self-initiation with minimal guidance. One B player is worth five to 15 C players. You can advance a B- player to a B+ player with sustained long-term commitment from you, the business and the player. The delta in capability can be significant, but retention is unlikely without a contractual agreement. B players are active climbers and will change jobs regularly to advance their careers. Some B players would otherwise be an A player, but have a fundamental flaw, an Achilles' heel, that prevents them from reaching that level of capability and performance.

A level players are born, not made. You cannot create an A player from a B player, no matter how much time and effort you invest in the task. A players are attracted to A player environments. A player environments are staffed with other A players where high achievement is the norm and great accomplishments are expected. A players are capable of both vision and execution, are excellent communicators, are natural leaders, initiate self- and group-action, are flexible and adaptive, are capable of high levels of focus and commitment and are at the top levels of all aspects of capability and performance.

A players are highly sought, thus challenging to recruit. A players need fresh challenges as they get bored easily and will move to a new job if their current one becomes stale. A players do not often ascend to the top positions of their organizations since the B players are much more practiced and adept at the Machiavellian political intrigue required to ascend with their comparatively limited skill sets. Because they often get frozen out of the final selection process for the top positions, many A players become disaffected in the prime to latter stages of their careers.

A commitment to A players requires a commitment to the process of A players. Because of their unique attributes, it is unlikely you will retain an A player for the entire run of your business unless you are a high technology play on an IPO fast track. Because of this, you need to develop, implement and sustain a process to recruit, nurture and leverage the series of A players that will pass through your business. It's not about identifying and hiring a single A player who will be the magic bullet for your business; it's about identifying and hiring a series of A players who will add value to your business over its entire lifetime.

There is no substitute for an A player. It doesn't matter how many thousands of C players you amass or how many hundreds of skilled survivor B players you pile up, you can never match the unique capabilities of a single A player.

An exceptional business requires all three types of players, A, B and C. You can have an ongoing business with Cs and Bs, but you will never ascend to the top tier of businesses that are innovative, make a difference or leave a mark without A players.

534. Employees vs. Friends

Employees are employees, not friends. Don't confuse the two. The same goes if you are an employee. Your manager, your employer, is just that, not your friend.

Confusing those roles from either perspective always eventually results in negative outcomes.

535. Hiring for $

Never recruit or entice an employee solely with remuneration.

Recruiting by money is fundamentally flawed for two primary reasons:

1. First, an employee who moves to your opportunity for money will just as quickly leave for the same reason.

2. Second, money provides motivation for only a very short time and is the poorest of all workplace motivational factors. It is a fundamentally short-term motivational tactic and attracts only the most materialistic and shallow people.

536. Life Drama

Do not allow workers to import their life drama into the workplace. You must enforce a policy that makes it imperative to leave the drama at home.

Child care issues, relationship struggles, family fights, he said/she said battles, etc., are the primary fuels for a blazing personal life drama bonfire. Personal life drama belongs in the personal side of life. Work is about work, not about resolving personal life issues.

Personal life dramas belong at home. If you have a worker who cannot leave them there, you must terminate them, lest they infect your entire organization.

537. One Budget Cycle

In a corporate environment, your project or program must deliver measurable, incremental value within one budget cycle.

538. Parallel Advance

In a corporate business environment you, your project and your team must be operating parallel to the stated strategic goals of the business. In addition, you must measurably advance the stated and unstated agenda(s) of those who control your corporate destiny.

539. The Three Variables

In any project, given that quality work is required and cannot be compromised, there are only three variables: scope, resources and time.

Scope defines how much is going to be accomplished or delivered. Resources are the available capital, manpower, tools, etc.

In general, everyone except very experienced project managers dramatically underestimates the required amount of work to accomplish a goal.

You usually will have communicated or agreed to a set scope, so any reduction in that scope will destroy your credibility and trustworthiness.

There is a finite amount of additional resources you can add to a project, surprisingly small in fact, before you get to a point of diminishing returns where more people added actually slow things down.

The only remaining variable is time. Thus, most projects are late - and over budget.

540. The Pride of Authorship Trap

If you create something personally, you will always, without exception, have pride of authorship in that creation.

Pride of authorship distorts your ability to manage that creation in a dynamic environment.

Typically, you will be unable to recognize when the creation has outlived its usefulness or relevance, or should be replaced with an updated, freshened, current or more professionally executed example.

Therefore, as a manager, executive or entrepreneur, it is almost always better to procure and approve instead of personally create assets.

541. The Endurance of Functions and Processes

In business, people come and go, but functions and processes remain.

Never identify anything in business, e.g., an asset, a function or a process, with a person's identity. The person will eventually, for some reason or another, move on. The function and process, however, will remain.

542. Documented Processes

A business must have documented processes to reach its full potential.

Documented processes enable training and re-training, are essential to scalability and are required for certification.

In an undocumented business, most business process knowledge is carried in the heads of the executives and employees. Every time someone leaves, the process must be re-created or re-innovated. In a documented business, every single process, from procuring light bulbs to managing cash flow, is fully documented. Thus, no matter who leaves, the process remains.

In an undocumented business, scalability decisions, especially related to automating business processes, are conducted in a vacuum. In a documented business, processes can be illustrated and discussed, and informed decisions made regarding the potential efficiencies and returns on investment for process automation.

In an undocumented business industry certification such as ISO is a distant, unattainable dream. In a documented business, industry certification is a straightforward and very achievable goal.

No business will ever reach its full potential without documented processes.

543. Perfect Someday

You will never become an effective manager or rise above that level unless you learn the difference between good enough today versus perfect someday.

Perfectionists will either never initiate a task because they fear they cannot deliver perfection, or will be caught in an endless loop because they believe they can deliver perfection with just a little more time and resources invested in the task. In either case, their ability to manage tasks, teams or projects is severely diminished or crippled.

An effective manager knows the difference between good enough today versus perfect someday. They can make the determination of when to deliver what they have instead perpetuating an endless loop of procrastination or delaying delivery of what they fear is less than perfect.

544. Long Hours - Managers

When evaluating the performance of managers, working 60 or more hours a week does not correlate to competence or dedication, it correlates to inefficiency and inability. If someone at a manager level or above cannot accomplish their normal work responsibilities within 45 – 50 hours they are not suited for the role.

545. Tin Cupping

Project managers often beg for funding by making the rounds of the business holding out their "tin cup" for budget contributions for their projects. These project managers believe that if only they can collect enough money to get their project built then they can demonstrate the value of their efforts and their brilliance as managers.

In fact, they are setting themselves up for almost certain failure.

When you put together a project budget by tin cupping, you have immediately abdicated scope control. There is no way you will ever be able to refuse a request for an enhancement, additional capability or a change in delivery date from any of the people or departments from which you have obtained funding.

Scope control is challenging enough when you are only working to please one stakeholder. When you have an entire collection of people, departments and functions from whom you have taken funding, you have nowhere to go but disappointment. No matter what, you will fail to meet the majority of your investors' expectations.

It is almost never worth the risk to tin cup for budget. Instead, find a single person or business entity with life-threatening pain that can be relieved through your project, and get them to be the sole funding source. It is the only path to meeting expectations, sustainable political will, ongoing funding and project and career success.

546. Managing People of Grief

There will be times when you will be required to manage people of grief, e.g., prima donnas, complainers, the chronically late, borderline lunatics, etc. For resource, political, strategic or tactical reasons, you may be precluded from arbitrarily disposing of them immediately.

Three approaches to gaining productivity from people of grief while maintaining management control are to a) Allow flexibility of delivery, for instance, "I don't care if you want to work from 10 PM to 6 AM, just get it done;" b) Demand excellence, for example, "Whatever you do must be excellent, top-quality work that reflects your superior abilities;" and c) Cut immediately on non-delivery, such as, "I gave you the opportunity to deliver excellent work on your own schedule, but you put it off until the day before it was due and then delivered sub-standard, compromised work that is beneath your capabilities."

Prima donnas and creative types love flexible schedules. You must obtain superior quality work from these people of grief to make the grief component worthwhile. You must immediately terminate anyone who doesn't deliver to demonstrate that what *matters* is what is delivered. Deliver and you have a job. Don't deliver and you don't. It's the only way to maintain order in the asylum.

547. Brand Bigots

Brand bigots, those blindly loyal to a particular product brand, are nearly worthless to your organization. They will consistently make design, requirement and procurement decisions based solely on their own prejudices, not the best value or capability.

It is tempting to consider brand bigots relatively harmless in the broad scope of business management, but their poor judgment inevitably leads to long-term loss of productivity, capital and competitiveness.

548. Analysis Paralysis

Analysts get paid to analyze. Analytical people have a limited solution set that features and showcases their abilities. It essentially consists of one solution to every problem - analyze everything to death.

It is very easy for analytical business functions, such as information technology, to become mired in analysis paralysis. They quickly lose sight of the overall business needs, goals and mission, and get tightly wound around the axle of analysis.

Be very careful when managing analytical people and functional groups. Continually communicate and reinforce the priorities of the business relative to their favorite pastime - analysis.

549. The Dirty Little Secret of Security

You can spend as many millions of dollars as you want on technical solutions for security but you will never eliminate the number one security risk: your employees.

That doesn't mean you shouldn't invest in security; by all means you should. Just keep in mind that the employee exit is the most likely exit path for your assets.

550. The Grief Factor

When I began my media production career, building the budget for my first big show was a traumatic experience. I worked on it feverishly for two weeks. I reviewed every line item of previous shows. I carefully researched each new and unique element for its costs. I badgered each vendor for their best price. I sweated and I fretted and eventually the budget was ready for management review.

With great trepidation I walked into the large office of my boss and laid it on his desk. He took one quick, cursory glance at it, flipped through the pages and tossed it back to me.

"It's missing the single most important element," he said, I thought rather curtly.

I was dumbstruck. I mentally reviewed all the main budget segments, every item and sub-item. They rattled off in my brain like a machine gun. I couldn't think of anything I'd missed, much less a primary element.

"What, what element is that?" I managed to stammer.

He looked at me over his reading glasses and said, "The Grief Factor."

He pulled the budget back, turned to the last page and pointed to the total, the bottom line.

"It goes right here, under the total," he said, with a tone of voice you'd use with a four-year-old who forgot to put their pants on in the morning.

I was speechless. I'd never even heard of the Grief Factor. I tried to be brave, still playing the role of someone actually qualified for my brand new job. My face betrayed my ignorance.

"Every show, every client, has a Grief Factor," he said, his tone softening almost to mentor level.

"Take your total and add enough Grief Factor markup percentage to make the project worthwhile. These people are a pain to work with, so they are at least eight percent. The rest looks OK."

So ended the management review of my two-week budget building effort: "The rest looks OK," along with a plop of invaluable business life lesson on top, like a Maraschino cherry: the Grief Factor.

From that day forward I never built a project budget, made an estimate or provided a quote without including the Grief Factor. It has served me well throughout my business life.

Don't forget the Grief Factor.

551. Pick a Horse and Ride It

You can't make headway trying to jump from one horse to another as you head down the trail. You can't ride two or three or four or five horses at once. You can't be all things to all people.

Scattering resources across multiple market segments, having incoherent product and service offerings, having little to no integration in your business units and having insufficient resources for the number of initiatives you are simultaneously executing are all hallmarks of a business trying to jump from horse to horse. You cannot make headway down the trail in this manner.

Business is not the Wild Bill trick show filled with harmless thrills. Business is the Lewis and Clark Expedition, fraught with undiscovered country, unexpected challenges, endless trying circumstances and life and death stakes. You cannot overcome that level of challenge by jumping from horse to horse as you struggle down the trail.

Pick a horse and ride it.

552. Fail Fast

It costs a pharmaceutical company between $500 million and one billion dollars to bring the typical drug to the retail market. A drug that fails in its final stage of testing, or even worse, reaches market only to induce negative outcomes in patients, is a $500 million to one billion dollar disaster. For that reason, pharmaceutical companies are highly motivated to discover if a potential new drug is safe and effective as early as possible. Consequently, the operating philosophy of a pharmaceutical company is "Fail Fast."

The same is true of any company's concepts, ideas, prototypes and potential products or services. It is essential that your company discovers as early as possible if the business model or any of its products or services is not viable. A fatally flawed business model, product or service that is sustained in the market is a business disaster that gets worse every minute it survives. Fail fast.

553. Tomorrowland

We once visited the Walker Art Center in Minneapolis to view an exhibit of the engineering drawings, conceptual art and other items associated with the conception, design and building of Disneyland and Disney World.

It was a fascinating exhibit for me, having grown up in Iowa, as far away from the Disney empires as you could possibly get, while simultaneously awakening a flood of memories for my wife, who had the luxury of growing up in Southern California, immersed in the Disney culture.

That culture, unlike the high-G force, thrill centric theme parks of today, included a very large educational component to accompany the family-oriented entertainment. One of the primary manifestations of that educational vision,

Tomorrowland, turned out to be one of the Disney team's greatest ongoing challenges.

Every time they built a futuristic attraction, it was quickly antiquated by the fast moving advancements of everyday life.

Anyone attempting to buy or build business solutions faces the same challenge. By the time you get a solution built, the challenges have all changed.

Consequently, it can be a fatal mistake to position any proposed solution, be it technological, process or cultural, as a complete or final answer.

554. Sales vs. Marketing Wars

If there is one constant in business it is that sales hates marketing and vice versa.

Marketing often considers sales a lower form of life. Marketing considers every single sale ever made to be solely due to perceived need created by the brilliant work of the marketing department. Marketing knows, without a doubt, that if only the bumbling, crude, half-formed efforts of the sales department employees could be eliminated, revenues would triple.

Sales often considers the marketing department the largest single waste of money in the business. They view marketing department employees as their underlings, assistants and errand runners. Sales often views the entire marketing department as dead weight, nothing more than a prima donna laden drag on what otherwise could be a lean, mean selling machine of a company.

The ongoing war of sales versus marketing can usually be managed and maintained at a reasonable level of slow boil, but it has been known to erupt into open corporate warfare.

Finding common ground between the two groups can be challenging, but one additional constant is almost always present. Sales and marketing may hate each other, but they both usually each hate the finance department even more.

555. The Law of Software Development

At some point in your business life, you will be tempted to undertake, or be actively engaged in, a custom software development project. During that time you will learn the immutable law of software development: The project will cost at least twice as much and take at least three times as long as initially forecast.

556. The Gatekeepers

There is a legendary tale of Professor Gale who taught the final course during the final semester of Harvard's Master of Business Administration (MBA) program.

By the time students arrived at his class they were the best of the best. They had passed a one in 10,000 application and acceptance process and survived the duration of one of the world's most rigorous academic tracks.

For the students who performed well during the MBA program, this was a critical time. If they finished out the program with top grades, they could literally write their own ticket for a career and a future. The cachet of a top finishing position in Harvard's MBA program was worth millions in the job market, and made the difference between running and not running one of the world's best companies. The top students were good. In fact, they were the best the world had to offer.

The challenge many of the best students had was that they knew they were the best. All they had to do was ace this last course and the rest of the world would know it too.

The last hurdle was Professor Gale's final exam. This was the last test they would take in the MBA program, the last test they would take before they received their master's degrees. The students filed in, the tests were distributed, and at the stroke of 2 PM the tests were opened and the race began.

For the students already leading their peers in grade point average (GPA), those who performed well on this test would finish in the top positions of their class and be guaranteed the best future the business world had to offer.

The best students, those leading in GPA, became more and more confident as they progressed through the questions and problems. The material was tough, no doubt about it. Old Man Gale was no pushover, he was renowned for his lust for detail and high standards. But, that was why they were there, and their ability to surmount these challenges was why they were the best.

There were about 10 who were in competition for finishing first in the graduating glass, and six of them happened to be in this class. They were well ahead of the rest of the group in completing the test. Their pages turned rapidly as they burned through the questions.

Professor Gale sat stoically at his desk, reading. He knew from the sounds of the turning pages that the leading students, those who knew they were good, who knew they were the best, were nearing the end.

Professor Gale also knew that although these top students had all the academic skills required to test out at the top of their class in Harvard's MBA program, they were all, every one of them, lacking one critical skill required to be an effective business leader.

One by one, the pages stopped turning. Professor Gale peeked out over the top of his reading glasses at the 20 students. Fourteen were still head-down, plowing through the questions. The best six, the Cocky Six, as Professor Gale and the rest of the MBA faculty referred to them, were all looking up at him with a look of abject horror, their faces frozen in fear and the certain knowledge they were doomed.

On the last page of the test they read:

Passing this course is required to receive your MBA. This test will account for 70 percent of your grade in this course. The previous 131 questions account for

20 percent of the grade for this test. The remaining 80 percent of your grade for this test will be determined by question 132.

132. What is the name of the cleaning lady who scrubs the hallway outside this room every Thursday when you arrive for class?

The lesson Professor Gale and his fellow faculty conspired to teach the Cocky Six is that academic knowledge and a weighty degree are not all that is required to be a successful business leader, or to be successful in life. Rubbing shoulders with your fellow superstars will not deliver all that is required to effectively lead a business or a life.

To effectively lead you must also invest in relationships in every level of life and the organization. You must have the communication and human skills required to interact with everyone from the people on the loading dock to the people in the board room.

Of the people most important to know and interact with, the supremely critical relationships to cultivate are the gatekeepers. The gatekeepers are the administrative assistants, the receptionists, the executive assistants, the loading dock workers and, yes, even the cleaning ladies.

Do you know the names and something about the gatekeepers in your life? Can you carry on a meaningful conversation with them?

Remember Professor Gale. Remember question 132. Remember the gatekeepers.

557. The Tin Man

On a cross country flight I found myself engaged in conversation with another businessman who called himself "the Tin Man." We worked through the topics of family, the news of the day and finally to business.

He was a senior executive of an American company that had been around for generations. Just about every American had touched, used or owned one of his products in their lives, but few would ever know it. His company made tin boxes and containers for product packaging and decorative uses in an incredible array of product offerings in a diverse product line.

He was returning from a trip to the Far East. He'd been visiting one of their manufacturing plants in Indonesia and scouting out sites for new plants in Vietnam and China. They previously manufactured in Mexico and Latin America, but moved manufacturing to the Far East in search of lower costs.

He explained that their business had such thin profit margins they were forced to chase low labor costs across the globe. As economies matured and the middle classes grew and wages rose, his company was forced to move to lower cost locations.

His major worry was that he and the other senior managers believed the business model would only be valid for a few more decades at most. Because a fundamental variable of his business depended on macro-economics, his company did long-range planning which extended out 10 to 50 years. They felt that China would be their final source of low cost labor in the Far East. The next place they could turn for light manufacturing would normally be Africa, but that continent was being ravaged by AIDS, and he felt that it may not have a viable base of workers in the time frame in which they would need to utilize that work force.

I found this long-range view extraordinarily rare. In my long career interacting with senior leadership of the world's leading and largest corporations, I couldn't think of a single one that exhibited this type of deep integration of long-range planning with global economic development patterns. For most U.S. corporations, long-range planning meant six to nine months.

Even though almost all large organizations had senior executives tasked with "strategic planning," they were mostly concerned with having a viable "long-range" strategy to trot out for shareholders. I had never seen one actually drive day-to-day operations unless it was tied to survival or a quarterly financial goal, usually in the case of having "global" operations.

In the case of the Tin Man, it was indeed a matter of core survival. As a result of his scouting mission, the board of directors had decided on the ultimate move. The Tin Man was flying back to the East Coast to meet with investment bankers about the sale of the privately-held business.

Because they had clear view of what the global realities related to their business were likely to be 10 to 20 years into the future, the management team knew that the peak value of their business was that very moment. The management team had the vision, forethought and courage to maximize their potential return based primarily on long-range planning and forecasting.

When most people hold a tin box, they don't think of much more than the color or decorative design, and certainly wouldn't think its manufacturer could represent the state-of-the-art in long-range strategic planning for American companies.

As you can see, we may have much to learn from such a humble product. It is critical to your career, team and business that you invest in long-term planning and observation, as well as have the courage to apply those observations, just as the Tin Man and his company did.

558. Houston, We Have a Problem

In the summer of 1969, the United States landed two men on the moon and returned them safely home. The Apollo 11 flight was the culmination of the efforts of over 400,000 workers and the manifestation of an investment that reached a peak of over 50 cents per week for every man, woman and child in the country. Thousands celebrated in Times Square in an impromptu mid-summer celebration of joy, relief and champagne. Millions welcomed the triumphant crew back home with ticker tape parades, parties and civic celebrations. The entire aerospace community, and especially NASA, was at the very peak of success, luxuriant in the praise and adulation of an entire nation and the respect of the entire world.

NASA had a long series of Apollo flights laid out, 18 in all. These were to be quickly followed by the space station and then a manned flight to Mars. The future seemed endlessly bright and infinitely promising for NASA and for every boy who dreamed of growing up to be an astronaut, just as I did lying on our family room floor watching the flickering, ghostly images of Neil Armstrong descend the ladder of the lunar module and hop down to luna firma.

But soon, all too soon for the space enthusiasts and the entire aerospace industry, the bloom came off the rose. Within a few more moon landings, even while the astronauts were jauntily cruising around the moon in their battery powered buggy, Congress was pondering the un-ponder-able: "Just why are we funding this project, anyway?" The Apollo program soon fell victim to the budget ax, well short of achieving the lofty, elegant, scientific goals set out for it. Although there was no technical reason for ending the program (in fact, new discoveries were being made on each flight), the program became politically untenable, and thus, unsustainable.

Fast forward to today, in your business. How many generalist, panacea solutions that do very little for anybody do you see? How many solutions looking for a problem do you see? How many projects and initiatives that do nothing but expand fiefdoms do you see? How many half-way solutions do you see that don't solve anybody's problem completely?

Of those projects and programs, how many do you think will survive the inevitable budget reviews when a new management regime comes on the scene?

Lessons? Don't build Apollos. If you want to have a sustainable project or program, you must build specific solutions to specific business pain.

The initial euphoria in response to a partial solution is not sufficient to sustain ongoing resource requirements for sustenance and maintenance, much less expansion. Just as the attention of the U.S. public and elected officials was quickly diverted by the turmoil of the late 60s and early 70s, your business and its leaders will soon be drawn to battle by the day-to-day challenges of typical business life. Only if you are providing a 100 percent solution to life-threatening pain will your project or program achieve "mission critical" status, and continue to survive and thrive.

How do you achieve this goal? Here are some quick pointers:

- Build to pain. Do not create anything except in response to specific, definable, discrete pain that can be 100 percent solved by your project or program.

- Scope small. Start with very, very small scope and build iteratively from there. Don't try to build the entire solution as your first or even second step. Completely solve a critical and discrete piece of the grand problem first, and then expand in small, measured steps from there.

- Make someone a hero. Identify life-threatening pain, build a 100 percent solution and save someone's life. Sit next to them for as long as it takes to solve the problem and relieve the pain, thus making them a hero to the business.

- Leverage that success across the business. Use the hero's example of how your team, project or program can solve specific problems for the business to build and leverage support for ongoing efforts. Market your team, project or program and your success relentlessly.

- Manage expectations. Do not let the business get on a runaway expectation binge. If you leave them to their own devices, they'll have you curing the common cold long before you even roll out your first test solution. Continually drive home the message of specific relief of specific pain.

- Build measurable solutions. You cannot leverage the success of a solution that is immeasurable. Build only solutions that you can measure the success or failure of with discrete metrics. For instance, don't build a solution to "customer satisfaction" problems if your business doesn't have a widely respected way to measure that metric. Stick to dollars and cents for your first few iterations. You must be able to return to the business with a solid example of success using metrics the business understands.

If your only goal is to deliver a purely technical solution or capability you will quickly find yourself with little left but a Mylar flag hanging over a lifeless lunar landscape. Today's world demands specific solutions to specific problems. Note the deliverables of NASA's current efforts: specific goals for specific research. Make sure you are emulating their approach. Don't build Apollos.

559. Sponsorship

In a corporate environment every project or program must have a sponsor. If you are responsible for the project or program your sponsor can often make or break your initiative.

To maximize your chances for sponsorship success:

- Match your sponsor to your project or program. A small, short-term (less than one budget cycle), low resource requirement project is a good match for a director-level sponsor. A major, long-term (multiple budget cycle), high resource requirement project or program requires CEO-level sponsorship. Having a sponsor mismatch, one with too little organizational stature for your level of project, is a guarantee for failure. By the same token, having a high-level sponsor for a tiny project is equally inappropriate, as the small project will quickly fall off the radar screen of a high-level executive.

- Match your sponsor's level to your project or program scope. If your project or program is cross-functional, one that crosses into multiple corporate fiefdoms, then you must have a sponsor that is above those fiefdoms. Being responsible for a project that requires resources from finance, manufacturing and sales when your sponsor is the Vice President of any of those areas is a recipe for failure. In that scenario, you need CEO- or COO-level sponsorship.

- Match your sponsor's tenure to your project or program's term. Directors and Vice Presidents come and go like the wind. Presidents and C-level executives tend to have longer tenures of at least a few years. Measure where your sponsor is in their expected tenure and make sure your project or program will match their timeline.

- Match your sponsor's area of responsibility to your project or program. This sounds obvious, but it is not uncommon to find project and program sponsors with only distant and tenuous responsibility or reporting relationships with the business area in which the project or program is based.

- Match your project or program's deliverables to your sponsor's overt and covert agenda, and, if possible, compensation plan. Your project or program must advance the agenda(s) of your sponsor or you have no reason to expect their support or resources. The best position is to positively affect their compensation.

- Match your project or program to your sponsor's available bandwidth. If your sponsor candidate is already overworked, overburdened and overtaxed, your project or program is certain to receive minimal, if any, sponsor time and resource commitments. That scenario is simply setting yourself up for failure.

560. The Price of Hubris

Around 3,500 years ago a civilization flourished along the Nile. It had been in existence for over 1,000 years, and had long since determined that it was superior to every other civilization it knew and had cornered the market on the right way to do things. There was one right way: their way. This civilization had the best communication system, the most impressive monuments, a prosperous economy, a tested and triumphant military, international trade, centuries of experience in medicine, vast civic projects, art and culture, a fearsome panoply of gods and a secure and smug ruling class who knew to the core of their beings that nothing could ever change the way things had always been, and always would be: their way.

Until one day, across the trackless deserts to the East that since time began had been an impervious barrier to invasion, came great clouds of dust. A mighty army that swept all before it came raging down upon the people of the Nile. The mighty legions of foot soldiers of the Pharaohs, with their spears and bronze swords were decimated, sliced to pieces by the spinning blades attached to the one thing that the Egyptians had never developed in their long and glorious history: the wheel. Thus, the Egyptians learned the bitter lessons - that to be inwardly focused, to only ask yourselves if you're successful - and to turn your back on the external factors of your environment are marks of fatal hubris.

This sad tale is repeated every day in business by everyone from team leaders to CEOs. It is very tempting to rely only on your own perceptions, your own analysis and your own success criteria at the exclusion of any outside perspectives.

At very high risk are groups and organizations basking in success. They tend to become isolated, resisting any evaluation of their processes, systems and methods that varies from glowing accolades.

In addition, technical teams, groups and functions are susceptible to walling themselves off into an isolated world that rejects any world view but their own and those of their mercenaries, the technology analysts. These groups quickly become self-reinforcing circles of increasing ignorance of the world outside their technical fortresses, and are often blind-sided by business political and cultural fundamentals, such as the maxim that the business makes the rules, not the technologists.

By isolating themselves, they become the functional equivalent of the ancient Egyptians. The technology teams are led astray by surveys that only ask technologists the questions about cost and success (when was the last time the technologist and the business could even agree on the definition of success?). They are also led down the path of destruction by an army of analysts, gurus, theorists and vendors who are completely self-absorbed in the culture of technology.

Just as the ancients were fatally ensconced in the comfort of their "our way is the only way" approach to civilization, technology teams and departments are often sliced apart by the razor sharp knives of the political and cultural realities of the business that they long ignored.

How can you survive?

You must look beyond your isolated world, especially if you are involved in technology. Advice, statistics, analysis and recommendations regarding technology systems that are based solely on technological perspectives, surveys, interviews and input are, at best, skewed and at worst a direct route to dismal failure. You must look outside your technical world to understand the market, business, cultural and political dynamics that will determine your fate.

In business, the more successful you are, the more you must seek out unbiased, objective evaluations of your group, your function and your business. You must resist adopting the view of the successful: ours is the best way, the only way.

561. Surviving the Bulls-Eye Seat

It's always the smiles that get you. Old cars have a way of generating smiles that is magical. On this day, the smiles were accompanied by stumbles, wide eyes, thumbs up and desperate attempts to catch us in traffic for a closer look. We were cruising in the 1966 Lincoln close-coupled convertible sedan owned by my lifelong friend, Mark Kuyrkendall. "Close-coupled convertible sedan" is a car buff's way of saying it's a four-door Lincoln convertible with rear suicide doors, most prominently burned into our collective consciousness as the car that President John F. Kennedy was riding in on that fateful day in Dallas.

As we silently coursed the historic streets filled with Victorian homes, bathed in sunshine and warmed by the reactions of those we encountered, I pondered the position I enjoyed. With Mark at the controls and my wife in the passenger seat, I enjoyed the expanses of the rear seat alone. I instinctively chose the right rear seat, and practiced the "screw in the light bulb" wave taught to every beauty queen, politician and minor celebrity who had ever shared in my experience of the parting seas of smiles and waves, rolling and spreading like a wake on each side of this most extraordinary automobile. This was the very same position that JFK was in. It was the target seat. It was the bulls-eye seat.

I don't suppose we'll ever really know what JFK did to attract those bullets, or who or how many delivered them. All we can do is to try to ensure that we don't make any of the moves sure to attract the fire of the potential assassins that surround us in our efforts to bring access to information, and therefore change, to business organizations.

There are, after all, some sure ways to draw fire.

1. Tell the truth. As any veteran of business can tell you, there's no better way to discover the full impact of the phrase "shoot the messenger" than to deliver an unpleasant truth to an audience that doesn't profit by the telling. In your efforts to deliver clean, unvarnished information to your enterprise, you will almost inevitably discover that the business has been using inaccurate information for years. Many times individuals, management layers or entire organizations may be compensated based on erroneous information. Woe to the unwary person, project team or department that simply delivers the actual truth to an unprepared organization.

    Your first challenge will be that the organization will attack your credibility and label your entire information system as inaccurate and filled with unreliable data. You will find it very challenging to recover from the resulting loss of utilization. Your second challenge will be to stay alive as the people whose economic futures are put in peril come seeking your blood.

To avoid this ugly fate, you must document and communicate any deltas between your new, accurate data and the old, inaccurate data prior to pilot test or rollout of your new system. You must also inform your entire management hierarchy of all such disparities, so they can provide for their own political air cover, and hopefully, yours as well.

2. Change the established order. The immutable rule still holds true: knowledge is power. By creating access to information for everyone in the business you forever change the distribution of power in the enterprise. A second immutable rule also holds true: those in power will seek to retain power. By enabling people with information, you can be viewed as threatening the power and control of those who currently hold it.

Successful, sustainable information access systems forever change the balance of power by allowing anyone to access information, perform analysis and drive decisions. By removing the need for the gatekeepers who historically controlled access to the information, those gatekeepers find they no longer have a reason to exist. Pushing decisions down in the organization can eliminate entire information access departments.

In our society, there always must be someone to blame for anything unpleasant. In this case, you will most likely be the target.

To ensure your long-term health, enlist your management consultant team or internal resources that are tasked with change management. Start out by contacting the teams and people who are responsible for change management issues centered on business process re-engineering.

3. Focusing on "wow." The first three or four times Mark put down the convertible top on his Lincoln, children and adults from the entire neighborhood came running to watch. The synchronized dance of the 11 relays progressively activating four huge hydraulic rams, a top lock motor, two window motors, the deck motor, pump assembly and the twin screw deck lock motor was irresistible to watch as the trunk lid rose open like a giant clam to swallow the top. However, now it is old hat, and few locals turn out to watch the show.

    The same fate will befall your information access system if you don't concentrate on delivering specific business value. The "wow" of "now we finally have access to the data" wears off quickly. You must deliver long-term value to the organization by providing solutions to specific business problems.

    Customer relationship management, churn management, marketing program ROI analysis, uptime optimization, etc. are what are important to the business, not how many petabytes of data you have available, how many queries per hour you run or other technical niceties.

After JFK was shot, American presidents were consigned to armored, bulletproof sedans. No American president since 1963 has known the wonder and charm of a ride in an open car on a warm day. Because the world changed, there was no longer a need for a close-coupled convertible sedan. The engineering triumph of the technical complexity was not enough to save it, and it won't be enough to save you or your system either. To survive the bulls-eye seat, you must build specific business solutions.

Humans hate change. If you bring change to a human organization, you will draw fire. If you do not provide for your own defense and carefully plan and manage the change you initiate, you can fall victim to a career or business assassin.

But, if you maintain awareness and effectively manage the change, there is no view, no experience that compares with a ride on a warm summer's day in the bulls-eye seat.

Enjoy the ride.

Entrepreneurship

562. Business Existence

The only reason for a business to exist is to profitably serve an unmet need in the marketplace.

If an entity does not meet that definition then it is a charity, a hobby, a tax dodge, a research lab or something else, but it is not a business.

563. The Seven Myths of Self-Employment

Just about everyone, sooner or later, fanaticizes about working for themselves. Stuck in a cubicle or in a dead-end job, they dream of the day when they will run their own business.

Along with visions of freedom, the dream almost always contains these outcomes:

1. More money
2. More free time
3. More control
4. Easier success
5. Less hard work
6. Less grief
7. Less hassle

In reality, working for yourself is almost always the exact opposite of these outcomes. If you are thinking about quitting your job and starting a business because you think most, some, or even any of those seven outcomes are likely, you need to think again.

To start with, your first few businesses will probably fail. That is ruinous both financially and psychologically. It often destroys marriages and families.

If you survive that, by the third or fourth iteration you may have finally figured out what it takes to be successful running your own business.

Be sure you are ready for the realities and the struggles of self-employment.

It can be a rewarding and ultimately fulfilling way to live your life, but it is not in any way easy.

564. The Two Types of Businesses

There are two types of small- to medium- sized businesses: a) Lifestyle business or b) Business business.

A Lifestyle business exists to fund a lifestyle.

A business that exists for purposes other than to fund a lifestyle is a real business, a Business business.

A lifestyle business is all about maintaining a lifestyle.

Real business, a Business business, is all about the exit.

It is important to know which type of business you are thinking about starting or are already in. If you've got a steady little business and say things such as, "I don't want us to get any bigger," or, "I like things just the way they are," you have a lifestyle business.

If you compromise your business for your personal interests, you are in a lifestyle business. Conversely, if you sacrifice everything in your life - family, health, relationships, interests, hobbies, etc. - but are not on a defined plan for exit, you are in a lifestyle business, albeit a destructive lifestyle.

There is nothing inherently wrong with a lifestyle business, but there are very real dangers to that model.

First, it is extremely difficult, if not impossible, to successfully exit from a lifestyle business. In order to exit, there must be something, some assets, for a purchaser to acquire. In a lifestyle business, the business is usually the owner and the owner is the business.

Since there is no exit, a lifestyle business owner must work until they die or establish financial independence. And, since the point of a lifestyle business is to fund a particular lifestyle, all the money is usually spent as soon as, or in advance of, earning it. This "direct to lifestyle" economic model means very few lifestyle business owners properly plan for and save early for retirement. Often, lifestyle business owners will come to a financial planner at age 58 and say, "We thought we'd better get started on saving for retirement."

Secondly, a lifestyle business has very poor or non-existent business processes. The business is typically run fast and loose, with no documented processes and with everything of importance stored in the owner's head. This includes business plans, marketing plans, human resources, product / service development plans, etc. With no active business plan, there can be no financial plan or marketing plan, and with no financial or marketing plan there can be no ability to survive the inevitable downturns in the business cycle. Lifestyle businesses can be quite successful in times of economic expansion but often succumb to downturns and recessions.

A real business, a Business business, has a business plan, documented processes, financial processes, marketing processes, human resources processes, supply processes, product / service processes, etc. It has a plan for growth. It has a plan for recruitment and retention. It has a plan to survive and thrive regardless of the business cycle. It has a plan for exit.

Know what type of business you are in. And, be aware of the characteristics and upsides and downsides of each.

565. The Exit

Real business is all about the exit.

There are three common types of exit:

1. Merger and Acquisition (M&A)
2. Initial Public Offerings (IPO)
3. Employee Stock Ownership Plan (ESOP) and other variations of an Employees Ownership Plan (EOP)

A fourth variation is to develop enough personal wealth with the business to achieve financial independence and then to simply wind down or close out business operations. This option is very rare given the materialistic / endless acquisition nature of American society.

To achieve exit:

1. Determine the most likely scenario for your small- to medium-sized business. This is commonly M&A.
2. Define the reasons why another company would buy your company, e.g., proprietary technologies, customer relationships, market share, etc.
3. Define the optimum acquisition partner (OAP).
4. Develop a list of companies that align with your OAP criteria.

5. Develop and implement a plan to develop or expand relationships with the companies on your OAP list.

6. Define the characteristics the OAP is looking for in an acquisition target.

7. Compare the current characteristics of your business with the desired characteristics.

8. Develop and implement a plan to move your business from its current state to the desired state reflecting the OAP's most important acquisition target characteristics.

Caveats and Realities:

1. If your business is you and you are the business, your M&A prospects are dim. You need to construct a real business, with a balance sheet reflecting assets, to qualify for M&A.

2. To qualify for the general M&A market you will need to be at or on a run rate of about $10 million in revenues.

3. You may qualify for a strategic M&A by a competitor or a company wishing to gain your capabilities within your market segment even if you show very little revenue.

4. Acquiring companies may purchase you for your market share or to remove a strong competitor from the market.

5. Acquiring companies do not write a check for the value of your company. In other words, no one is going to write you a lotto check for your company.

6. Acquiring companies will do everything they can to limit the amount of cash in a deal. They will want to pay you in their company's stock.

7. For most small- to medium-sized businesses, the acquiring company will be another small- to medium-sized business with very illiquid stock. In essence, their stock is Monopoly money - there may be a lot of it offered, but it is very, very difficult to turn it into real cash.

8. No one else in the world perceives the value of your company as you do.

9. The acquiring company's M&A team will do everything they can to beat down the price, usually by denigrating and demeaning many aspects of your prized company, its market, employees, processes, products, assets, etc.

10. The acquiring company's M&A team is measured and rewarded based on how much they can get for as little as possible, not by how much wealth they can transfer to you.

11. The negotiation and execution of an M&A deal is usually one of the most emotionally traumatizing and challenging events of a lifetime.

12. The acquiring company will require you to work for them for 24-36 months. This is the "Golden Handcuffs" period.

13. You will have no real power or control during the Golden Handcuffs period.

14. Very often, most of what you worked extremely hard to build will be wasted, ignored or disposed of during or soon after the Golden Handcuffs period.

15. The acquiring company will attempt to impose very, very challenging sales and performance goals that must be met during the Golden Handcuffs period.

16. You must meet the required performance targets to be paid the full M&A purchase price.

17. You will be responsible for meeting the performance targets, but usually have little or none of the power and control required to achieve them.

18. It is common to be parked in a position, such as V.P. of Special Projects, that has no power, no responsibilities, no resources, no budget and no respect. This might sound great right now, but it is psychological torture for most entrepreneurs. It is often designed to drive you to resign and walk away from the final portions of your M&A payments.

19. The after-tax net of an M&A deal is often less than simply growing and operating your company very profitably for a comparable length of time.

20. ESOPs/EOP scenarios usually end very badly, with the company run into the ground and no ongoing annuity stream for the former owner. Everybody has to start over again from ground zero. Employees do not usually make gifted, or even good, entrepreneurs.

21. IPO scenarios are usually limited to high tech in general, and software in particular.

22. If you have an idea that you think could go IPO, the most critical ability is to know when to step aside and let the MBA types take the company from your initial start-up stage through IPO.

23. IPOs require multiple rounds of venture capital, usually three plus a mezzanine round. Each new round dilutes the ownership equity of the shareholders of the previous rounds.

24. As founder, starting with 100 percent equity, you will retain from 2 percent (common) to 10+ percent (very rare) at the time of IPO.

25. The venture capitalists (VCs) sell their stock at the time of IPO. They cash out and realize huge gains, often 50:1 or more. The return ratio for the successes makes up for all the companies that the VCs fund that never make it to IPO.

26. Post IPO, you will be very wealthy on paper. Your real wealth will be minimal.

27. Post IPO, as a founder, board member, executive and insider, you will be very heavily regulated, restricted and monitored regarding the sale of company stock.

28. As an insider, if you sell shares in the company to realize some real wealth versus paper wealth, your trades will be publicized and viewed as evidence that you have no confidence in the future of the company. The company's stock will plunge and you will consequently destroy most of your remaining paper wealth as well as that of every other stockholder.

566. The Heartbeat Model

One of the most popular business models employed by entrepreneurs is the heartbeat model. It is the simplest of models. You find something the market is willing to pay for and you, individually, do it. You must be standing there, with your heart beating, to generate any revenue, thus the name.

The upsides to the heartbeat model include its being very direct and generally easy to manage. The downsides include the brutal fact that no matter how much you charge for your time, whether it is $100 a day or $10,000 a day, you will never, ever get ahead.

With a heartbeat model you are always chasing revenue. If you are working you cannot be marketing to create your next engagement.

The dream engagement, a long-term job paying top rates, is actually your worst possible nightmare. While working you cannot conduct marketing and sales to lay the groundwork for future work, while others are doing so, locking up all the future engagements.

Meanwhile, you adjust your spending to match your large incoming cash flows from your dream project. Eventually, the dream project ends, the incoming revenue dries up, your outflows continue and you are in yet another cash flow crisis.

And that is just the tip of the iceberg of the challenges and dangers of the heartbeat model.

The heartbeat model is seductively simple and also fraught with many challenges directly tied to the core attributes of human nature. Beware the siren song of the heartbeat model.

567. Technology vs. Product

Having a product idea or a product prototype does not mean you have a product.

In addition to the fundamental technology or service offering, a product includes documentation, relevant marketing campaigns, sales training, sales support materials, technical and field support capabilities, order fulfillment processes, ongoing product development resources, business management resources and back office functions - plus the profit margins and capital resources to sustain all of these elements.

It's a long way from the idea drawn on the bar napkin to a real product.

568. Product vs. Company

Having a product, especially one product, does not mean you have a company.

A company includes all of the documented processes, resources and capital required to create demand in the marketplace and meet that demand profitably in a sustainable manner.

There is more implied in that sentence than anyone who has never built a business could ever contemplate, anticipate or understand.

569. The Missing Startup Steps

The most common missing steps for entrepreneurial startup businesses are market sizing and market research. It is almost impossible to succeed long-term without knowing the answers those steps provide.

Market sizing is determining how big the overall opportunity is. How big is this market worldwide? How big is this market nationwide? How big is this market regionally? How big is this market locally? Only by answering these questions can you build a model that determines how much capital is required to fund the required resources over what timeline to meet those opportunities.

Market research is determining if there truly is an unmet need in the marketplace and, if there is, what offering at what price point will fill it. Only by answering these questions can you determine if a sustainable business model is possible.

A business is only possible if there is a sustainable unmet need in the marketplace and if that unmet need, that market opportunity, is large enough to sustain your business and the inevitable competitors who will follow.

570. The Business Lifecycle

Businesses have a natural life cycle. For startups and small- to medium-sized businesses that period is usually five to seven years. By the end of that cycle, the business must be re-invented or re-modeled to adapt to the new environment or it will most likely fail.

The length of time of the cycle can be shortened or extended by internal or external factors. If the external market is changed due to regulation or new technologies or geopolitics, the cycle could be much shorter or extended. If there is internal turnover with key personnel or product innovation, the cycle could be dramatically shortened.

Do not become wedded to your existing business model or ever think that what works today will profitably work forever. The context of business is continuously changing, with internal change and external change conspiring to create an average five- to seven-year business life span.

You must be aware of where your business is in its life span and be ready with a new business model suited for the new challenges of the evolved internal and external world in which it operates.

571. The Two R's

Running a business has many challenges, from finance to technology to regulation to marketing to product development, and the list goes on and on. All of those are valid concerns and can become worries, but the ones that will wake you up and keep you up in the middle of the night are the two R's: Recruitment and Retention.

Recruiting and retaining good people is the single biggest challenge in business success. You can achieve some initial success with a good idea or an innovative product, but you cannot grow or sustain a business without good people.

Keep those priorities in mind as you determine where to invest your personal energy.

572. The Two-Page Plan

Every business requires a business plan. You need a business plan before you start and you need one as you build the business. The business plan is not a static, one-time effort, but a living document that is updated regularly, usually quarterly.

Most first-time entrepreneurs are very intimidated by the concept of a business plan. They are overwhelmed by assuming they need a document the size of the Manhattan phone book. This is an unfortunate and incorrect assumption. A business plan's viability is not measured by page count but by the ideas and plans it contains.

Some of the best business plans I've ever reviewed have been the briefest. In fact, I advocate that initially you don't need more than two pages.

The first page needs to cover, in a sentence or two per topic:

- The market
- The market size
- The market's unmet need which this business will fill
- The product or services of the business
- The competition
- The differentiation versus the competition
- The barriers to entry erected to stave off the competition
- The required resources
- The marketing plan
- The risks

The second page is used for the basic financial projections.

That's it, two pages.

Start there and build upon that foundation.

573. Time is the Enemy

In a startup business there is only one enemy. It is not the competition, the government, the employees, the suppliers or the customers. The only enemy is time.

You can overcome all the other challenges in business, but if you don't do just about everything just about exactly right you will run out of time.

Time is the enemy.

574. Own a Niche

Many entrepreneurs and businesses make the classic mistake of trying to be all things to all people. The only route to survival as a startup business, or a business with limited resources, is to own a niche and expand from there.

Before you can own the market, you must first own a tiny little segment of it.

Identify a market niche with a clearly defined unmet need that you can fill profitably, utilizing a sustainable business model.

Define that niche. Create the marketing terms in that niche. Become the recognized market leader in that niche. Dominate that niche. Own that niche. Then, expand from there.

575. The Better Mousetrap

A common flaw of entrepreneurial thinking is often expressed as "If I build a better mousetrap, the world will beat a path to my door."

In reality, the gutter of the road of life is filled with better mousetraps and the remains of the failed businesses that built them and couldn't sell them. Having a better mousetrap is meaningless if you didn't first discover hard evidence the world was in need of a better mousetrap.

A viable, sustainable business is not contained in your product or service idea, regardless of how innovative it is. A viable, sustainable business can only be built by answering an unmet need of the market.

If you research the market, perform statistically-valid market testing, test market prototypes and conduct pricing sensitivity research and, as a result, determine the market needs a better mousetrap, and you can profitably build and sell them in a sustainable way, then, and only then, is it time to build a better mousetrap.

You must ensure your business exists in response to a market need, not a better mousetrap idea.

576. The Ideal Customer

One of the basic first steps of any business startup is defining the ideal customer.

Before you can build an effective marketing program for your business, you must know who you are talking to and what characteristics they posses. To know those things you must first define your ideal customer.

Your ideal customer is defined by:

- Unmet need
- Market context
- Demographics
- Technical characteristics
- Geography
- Non-financial resources
- Financial resources
- Propensity for innovation
- External drivers (regulation, public policy, etc.)

During the startup phases of your business, you must concentrate your resources on opportunities that have a high correlation to your defined ideal customer. You will have a very limited amount of resources so you must invest them wisely.

By definition, the ideal customer is ready and willing to buy your product or services. Consequently, a prospect that aligns with your ideal customer will be an easy sell, one that uses few resources. It is a waste of precious resources to try to win a prospect who is not a close match with your ideal customer.

This is one of the biggest challenges of the startup phases of a business - walking away from prospects who might buy, but don't correlate well to the definition of an ideal customer. It is very tempting to pour resources into any and all prospects instead of separating the wheat from the chaff, concentrating your resources on the customers most likely to buy from you with the lowest investment of your limited resources. Many startups fail because they run out of resources before they learn this lesson.

Own the ideal customers first.

577. The Lifestyle Dream

First time entrepreneurs are often afflicted with the lifestyle dream. They enjoy scrapbooking or woodworking or photography so they start a business doing just that. They think that having the business will give them a life where they can spend more time doing the activity they enjoy.

Unfortunately, the reality is they will end up having much, much less time to do the thing they used to enjoy. And, even worse, running a business around a favorite activity usually kills any enjoyment they had in the activity in the first place.

Business is not about lifestyle, business is about business. If you want to start a business, make sure you are in it for the business first and the lifestyle second.

578. Chasing Revenue

A common killer of young startups is chasing revenue. Early in the life of the business there will be opportunities for sales if only this or that is changed, modified or added to the product or service offering. Most first-time entrepreneurs will run after this potential revenue regardless of the costs of meeting the potential customer's needs. Only later, after the business runs out of time and money before it was profitable, will they realize they were chasing revenue that was not realizable with their given resources.

Stick to your business plan and your defined ideal customer. Chasing revenue leads to only one destination: failure.

579. Barriers to Entry

When considering a potential business model, pay particular attention to the barriers to entry.

No business model short of monopoly can ever erect and sustain permanent barriers to entry due to the evolving nature of the business, its culture and the market. However, effective barriers to entry during the first business cycle are critical to mid- and long-term success.

Barriers to entry based on innovation are nearly worthless. Others can innovate too. Barriers to entry based on cost are even worse, as there will always be a lower cost supplier sooner or later, most likely sooner.

Seek sustainable and flexible barriers to entry that can be altered as the company grows and the market matures.

580. The Greatest Tragedy

The greatest entrepreneurial tragedy is to have your business fail and realize you expended all of your time and resources chasing the wrong or a non-existent market opportunity.

The way to prevent this tragedy is to conduct market research and match your business model's available products or services to a sustainable, profitable, unmet need in the marketplace.

581. Startup Press Rules

When you are considering a business startup you must monitor the general, business and trade press. If you find mention of your market segment in the general or business press, it has become passé. If you find mention of your business concept in the trade press, then the ship for that business model has left the dock without you.

The goal is to have your company's press release be the first mention of your business offering in the trade, business and general press. Anything less and the viability of your business model is in serious jeopardy.

582. The Unfilled Niche

I was a board member and officer of our homeowner's association in Carlsbad, California. One of our challenges was dealing with residents using the mailbox kiosks to post notices of garage sales, lost pets, etc. The homemade signs inevitably looked ragged as they tattered and were drawing complaints. Much to my amazement, we quickly and easily identified a business that existed solely to clean and maintain mailbox kiosks in Southern California.

Who could have imagined a business could exist that solely cleaned and maintained mailbox kiosks?

The lesson here is there are no unfilled sustainable business niches in a capitalist economy.

When someone can make a viable business out of the tiny niche of mailbox cleaning, you know it doesn't take much of an unfilled niche to make a viable business model. The good news is that a vibrant, evolving, ever-changing economy constantly opens up new unfilled niches. The bad news is, just like our mailbox kiosks, they don't stay unfilled for long.

If you want to be in business, identify and meet an unfilled market niche.

583. "No" Disease

If you are an entrepreneur, especially in a heartbeat model service business, you will likely be terrified of ever telling a prospective or existing customer "no" to any request for your services. You will be convinced if you ever tell someone you are not available or you can't do the job, they will never call again, and for that matter, no one else will ever call again. This condition is "no" disease.

"No" disease leads to loss of social life, broken marriages, lost families, forgotten friends, abandoned hobbies and total burn out. It can be stopped. All you have to do is learn to say "no."

It will be a fearful experience and it takes a lot of courage the first few times.

But take heart; after you say no, they will call again.

584. Long Hours – Entrepreneurs

If an entrepreneur is regularly working more than 50 to 60 hours a week, the fundamental business model is not sustainable.

A business model is only viable and valid if it can be executed within the context of a balanced life. If the business model requires an unbalanced life to execute, then it is not a business - it is an escape path from personal life or is another form of psychological dependency vehicle.

585. The Personality Cult

One viable option for a startup, especially in the high technology space, is the personality cult business model.

The personality cult model builds notoriety and celebrity around a personality, elevates them into a deity and structures the business model underneath and around them.

Once the personality achieves minor celebrity in their small niche of technology, given the state of celebrity worship in the American culture, it quickly follows that a full-blown cult will form around the personality. And because celebrity equals credibility in this culture, the personality takes on the authority of a minor deity, and soon a fully-fledged god. Given a talented vice president (VP) of marketing and support staff, this is remarkably possible to achieve even with very little original source material in the initial personality.

The personality cult strategy works best in a greenfield opportunity, where no existing solution exists to an unmet market need. In this virgin market the business can define the space, create the lexicon, delineate the taxonomy and determine eligibility. In this way, by definition, no one will be qualified to point out that the emperor, the personality at the center of the cult, has no clothes, should they be bereft of factual credibility or original thought.

The advantages of the personality cult model include exponentially massive returns of public relations (PR) investment for a very minor input. Once the pump is primed by the celebrity equals credibility rule, the personality is quoted as the authoritative source in the new market segment. Because the personality is the buzz, they are quoted and covered in a way very difficult to match by traditional models that simply invest in buying media coverage.

Another advantage is primary authority. The only alternative credible voices, the technology analysts, are purchased, co-opted and silenced in the normal way by contracting their coverage of the new segment by the personality's startup, thus ensuring a market landscape devoid of alternative narratives.

The single greatest challenge of the personality cult business model is it is nearly impossible to prevent the personality from believing the business's press releases. The personality inevitably comes to believe they actually are a minor deity, if not a fully-fledged god, who sees all, knows all and is beyond reproach. Because the personality usually start out as a C, or, at best, a B player technology nerd, these delusions of grandeur often become a significant challenge for the management team striving to bring the business to IPO before the personality spirals out of control. The model usually becomes a race to achieve IPO prior to personality implosion.

The personality cult model works best in high-technology plays on a fast track to IPO. The prerequisites for the model are: first, adequate venture capital to prime the PR pump, purchase the loyalty of the technology analysts and fund pre-IPO growth; second, and most critical, the model requires a management team that can overcome the normal challenges to build IPO qualifying revenues while simultaneously managing the marketing, image and delusional psychological aspects of the cult of personality and the sycophants the model attracts.

586. The PR Trap

You will never escape the trap of believing your own Public Relations (PR) messaging. Keep a firm grip on reality and understand clearly the difference between what you are presenting to the media and what you and your organization really are.

587. The Idea is Out There

"If you have an idea that means the idea is out there, and others have it too." – Antje Stant.

Once you've got an idea that means it is in play. Others have had, are having or will soon have the same idea.

You have a very limited amount of time to gather the capital and resources required to make your idea a business reality.

588. Good vs. Bad Business

In every business there is good and bad business. Good business advances your business toward its strategic goals, in parallel with its mission and in alignment with its values and standards.

Bad business diverts your business from achieving its goals, is tangential to its mission and forces it to compromise its values and standards.

Bad business is very tempting, especially when it appears to be lucrative or easy. Bad business is nearly irresistible in a startup, offering quick cash when you need it most.

Bad business is a siren song; it will do nothing but lead your business onto the rocks.

Stay the course, strap yourself to the mast if you need to, but ignore the sweet song of the sirens.

Stick to good business.

589. The Opportunity Space

Your business opportunity lies in the area of intersection between the unmet needs of the marketplace (determined by market research and defined in the business plan) and your strengths (products and services you can deliver and sustain with excellence).

590. Forcing Functions

A customer is motivated by several basic forces, the most helpful of which is a forcing function. A forcing function is a factor that compels a business to change, and due to that change, to procure products or services. It is very advantageous to offer products or services that enable customers to meet the needs and requirements of a forcing function.

Forcing functions include:

- Public policy

- Changing market demands

- Competition

- Technology

- Human resources (HR) context, e.g., staff at retail

- Globalization

- Internal environment

- External environment

- Stasis stagnation

- Success stagnation

- Leadership change

Examine your available or potential product and services offerings. Identify those that can meet the needs of forcing functions of your customers. Review your marketing and positioning of those products to ensure they feature relief from forcing functions.

591. The Sustainable Business Model

A business model must be sustainable, e.g., hours worked, market demand, product and service viability, etc.

From the entrepreneurial perspective, sustainability is primarily about available energy and hours worked.

You cannot sustain 80-hour weeks or your business will suffer the consequences. Heroic bursts of energy and endless strings of all-nighters do nothing but reduce your effectiveness and provide a flawed example for your employees.

If your business model is not sustainable, especially in terms of energy and hours, you must modify it or abandon it. The only other possible outcome is failure.

592. Show Me the Money

A viable business model must be capable of producing sufficient free cash flow to fund:

- Taxes
- Cost of capital and other debt service
- Payroll and benefits
- Marketing, Advertising and Public Relations (PR)
- Cost of sales
- Administration
- Management
- Product and services development
- Research and development
- Infrastructure development and maintenance
- Miscellaneous operations

If the business model does not produce sufficient free cash flow to fund these needs, then the business model is not viable. It must be modified or abandoned.

593. The Headcount Rule

The culture of a business goes through distinct changes as the business grows. Specifically, there are major culture changes that correlate to headcount – meaning the number of employees.

During the initial stages, from one to 10 employees, the atmosphere will be highly charged with energy, the relationships will be intimate, communications will be instantaneously direct and everyone will be completely in line with the strategic and tactical goals of the business.

During the next stage, from 11 to 30 employees, the atmosphere will be one of rapid, almost overwhelming change. The relationships will still be informal, but the first instances of hierarchy and formal reporting relationships will form. Communications will still be fast, but message propagation will begin to be required. Everyone will still be highly engaged with the strategic and tactical goals of the business, but it will come at a price. Outside of the core equity founders, emotional rewards and engagement will no longer be enough of a reward; financial remuneration and shared upside will become requirements.

From 30 to 120 employees there will be a major change of cultural character, with the tipping point usually coming when you employ 60 to 70 people. By the time the business has a headcount of 120, formality of reporting relationships and hierarchies will be deeply entrenched. Fiefdom building, expanding and defending will become an executive priority, often at the expense of the overall strategic and tactical goals of the business. Communication will become challenging, with the employees at the fringes having only distant and fleeting interaction with the company principals. Formal messaging will become muddled and discredited, with informal rumor and speculation ascending to maximum relevance and credibility. Personal agendas will come to dominate the day-to-day operations of the business, again at the expense of the strategic and tactical goals of the business. Financial gain and upside potential become the predominant, if not the only, motivational factor. Skill at successfully managing corporate politics becomes more important than capability in achieving success. Original equity founders, and their founding philosophies, may be forced out by investors and/or the board of directors. The business model may be modified to pursue the earliest return for the venture capital investors. Due to the radical change in culture compared with the early stages, the business will experience high turnover rates among the original employees, often with only the remaining equity founders and a few employees heavily invested emotionally in the original dream remaining.

From 121 to 500 employees the company becomes a standard-issue corporate entity. All the factors that began to surface and dominate on the road from 30 to 120 employees permeate through every aspect of the corporate culture. The company may or may not have exceptional public and private aspects and manifestations of personality, such as major philanthropic initiatives, extemporaneous executive activities, casual corporate events or showy public relations extravaganzas. But, regardless of whether it does or does not have a hot air balloon staked to the front lawn of its headquarters, the fundamental corporate culture cannot escape the laws of corporate cultural change related to headcount.

As an executive of a growing business it is important to recognize these realities. It is impossible to retain the aspects of a one-to-10 headcount corporate culture in a 500-employee business. The core aspects of human psychology and behavior preclude it.

Instead of fighting a futile, and, in the end, false battle to retain the culture and relationships of a small startup, learn to leverage the inherent power and strengths of a large organization to achieve the tactical and strategic goals of the business.

There is no escaping the headcount rule, but a savvy executive learns to use the rule to their advantage.

594. Startup Survival

Surviving a business startup requires three simple things:

1. Move the ball forward every day. Advance the cause every day, in a measurable way.
2. Have a clearly defined, measurable, time-specific goal. The goal must be challenging, but achievable. As you approach your goal, create the next goal.

3. Have an out point. Define a clear, immovable set of quantifiable, measurable circumstances that denote an exit. If you do not achieve a goal, if resources are depleted, if you run out of time, etc., exit the scenario.

595. The 95/5 Rule of Human Relations

The immutable rule of the human relations (HR) component of a business is 5 percent of employees consume up to 95 percent of the HR resources. Due to the basic components of human nature, in a sample set of more than 10 to 20, you will almost always have high-maintenance employees.

One of the more challenging management tasks is balancing the drain of HR resources against the net contribution of an employee. As soon as an employee moves into net negative territory and stays there for any length of time, you need to remove them. Once they become an HR glutton, they very rarely move back into net-positive territory.

596. The Perceived Value of a Business

The immutable law of business valuation is: No one will ever value your business as much as you do.

No one else will ever be capable of perceiving the amount of work you have invested. They will never recognize the uniqueness of what you have created. They will never truly understand the upside potential of your business.

When this happens to you, resist the temptation to be offended. They are not blind and they are not stupid; they are normal and so are you.

There is no one alive capable of valuing your business as much as you do.

597. Startup Operating Capital

The general rule of thumb for startup operating capital requirements is you must have six months of operating capital to survive the startup phase. This is wrong on two counts.

First, you will always, without fail, underestimate the amount of money required to start the business. This means you will eat into your six months of operating capital reserves even before you open the doors.

Second, you will make many, many mistakes in your first six months of operations. Those mistakes will cost money, often significant amounts of money, further reducing your six months of capital reserves.

An entrepreneur who follows the six-month rule usually runs out of money before the end of month three. Before they ever really know if the business can or will be successful they slip into a cash-flow crisis that is almost always fatal.

To give yourself and your business a fighting chance, don't start the business without at least one year of operating capital.

598. Razors and Razor Blades

"Give them the razor, sell them the razor blades." – American business wisdom.

One proven route to business success is to create a recurring revenue model. The classic method is to seed the market with a free component that requires revenue-generating refill components.

You may not be in the business of razors or razor blades, but if you take a fresh look at your segment, it is very likely you can create similar recurring revenue scenarios.

599. The Government, Suppliers and Customers

"If it wasn't for the government, suppliers and customers, business would be great." – Anonymous entrepreneur.

Business is never easy. Fundamental components such as regulations, supply chains and sales ensure that the complexity is always high and the challenges are never ending.

If you don't or can't enjoy the basic, inescapable aspects and characteristics of business, then you don't belong in business.

Be realistic about who and what you are as it relates to business. Business is not going to change. If you don't enjoy it, then you should get out of business.

600. The Startup Phase

The initial startup phases of a business, from drawing it out on a bar napkin to getting it up and running with a few employees, can be one of the most enjoyable, passionate, rewarding and fulfilling chapters of your life.

Enjoy it while it lasts.

601. Business vs. Life

Never confuse your business with your life.

Your life is not your business.

Business facilitates and can enhance life, not the other way around.

Acknowledgements

A work of this type, by definition, is due entirely to the experiences, interactions, lessons and collective wisdom of every friend, enemy, teammate, coach, group leader, teacher, employer, mentor, peer, partner, competitor, cousin, aunt, uncle, grandparent, parent, child and grandchild in my life.

I cannot name one without forgetting many, so I will not endeavor to list all to whom I owe so much.

I cannot, however, omit my grandfather, Clarence Hackney, who for me personified wisdom, and who invested the time and energy to share some of it with me.

In addition, I wish to thank those in my life who I have directly quoted or attributed:

Lee Wochner	Jimmy Sones
Kemal Ertem	Billy Taylor
Earl Watson, Sr.	Esther Zimmerer
Dennis Stajic	Dave Waugh
Avery Innis	Kazim Uzunoglu
John Kretschmer	Bob Gramling
Tim Williams	Gary DuBois
Tim Butler	John DeSalvo
Don Ivener	Neil Raden
Richard Tanler	Fredy Baumann
Glen Heggstad	Steve Willard

My grandparents, Zane and Lois Strickland

My father, Keith Hackney

My brother, Jeff Hackney

My wife's mother, Antje Stant

My wife's father, Jim Stant

I owe special thanks to our children, Chari, Adam, Shaun and Amber, and our granddaughter, Nakeya, for providing me the reason and motivation to produce this work.

And, especially, I wish to thank my wife, Stephanie Hackney, for her contributions to and unwavering support of this effort.

All that is worthy in this work is due to those above. All flaws, errors and omissions are mine alone.

About the Author

Douglas Hackney is a published book author and periodical writer with over 100 articles and columns to his credit.

Beginning as an award-winning writer at age 13, he became a professional commercial photographer at age 16 and continued a media career that included lead acting roles in television commercials; modeling; editor and director of film and video; stage manager; production manager; producer and executive producer.

He subsequently pursued a variety of careers including microcomputer technology, computer graphics, software, enterprise class computing environments, business intelligence and technology, marketing and management consulting.

Mr. Hackney has management, executive, entrepreneur and consultant experience in media production, computer graphics, software development, high technology, marketing and business management.

Mr. Hackney's writing and photography have appeared in a wide and eclectic assortment of books and periodicals including poetry collections, motorsports, public policy, travel, information technology and business management.

As a market segment luminary and leader, Mr. Hackney has often been quoted in trade and general business publications, and has participated in more than a score of judging panels for industry awards.

Mr. Hackney served on corporate for- and non-profit boards of directors. He is an award-winning public speaker and has keynoted and chaired industry conferences worldwide.

In addition, Mr. Hackney has lectured at leading MBA programs.

Mr. Hackney holds no undergraduate or graduate degrees and was self-taught in each of his careers.

Since 2003 Mr. Hackney has been on an extended sabbatical exploring the world with his wife, Stephanie, primarily in developing countries.

Index

9 780982 171912